VOCABULARY WORKSHOP®

ACHIEVE

Jerome Shostak

Senior Series Consultant

Vicki A. Jacobs, Ed.D.
Lecturer on Education
Harvard Graduate School of Education
Cambridge, Massachusetts

Series Consultants

Louis P. De Angelo, Ed.D.
Superintendent of Schools
Diocese of Wilmington
Wilmington, Delaware

John Heath, Ph.D.
Professor of Classics
Santa Clara University
Santa Clara, California

Sarah Ressler Wright, M.A. English Ed, NBCT
Head Librarian
Rutherford B. Hayes High School
Delaware, Ohio

Carolyn E. Waters, J.D., Ed.S.
Georgia Dept. of Education (Ret.)
English Language Arts Consultant
Woodstock, Georgia

Reviewers

The publisher wishes to thank for their comments and suggestions the following teachers and administrators, who read portions of the series prior to publication.

Sr. Maureen Lawrence McDermott, IHM, PhD
Superintendent, Secondary Schools
Archdiocese of Philadelphia Schools
Philadelphia, PA

Aidan T. Brett
Teacher, Language Arts
Springfield High School
Springfield, PA

Kristy L. Raymond
English Teacher, Dept. Chair
Livermore High School
Livermore, CA

Audrey G. Silverman
National Board Certified English Teacher
Dr. Michael Krop Senior High School
Miami, FL

Dawn S. Wolfe
Teacher, English Department
Walnut Hills High School
Cincinnati, OH

Cover: Concept/Art and Design: MK Advertising, Studio Montage and William H. Sadlier, Inc. Cover pencil: Shutterstock.com/VikaSuh.
Photo Credits: age fotostock/Datacraft: 196; Sharon Day: 100; Fotosearch: 176; Fotosearch LBRF/CSP_karapas: 152; ImageSource: 124 *inset*; The Print Collector: 120. Alamy Stock Photo/AF archive: 13 *right*; By Ian Miles-Flashpoint Pictures: 25; D. Hurst: 36 *right*; DIZ München GmbH, Süddeutsche Zeitung Foto: 60; Europe: 172; Everett Collection: 36 *left*; Les. Ladbury: 24 *bottom*; Paul Rapson: 148; Pictorial Press Ltd: 25 *left*; Sandra Baker: 32; BibleLandPictures/Zev Radovan: 84; INTERFOTO: 64; nsf: 16; Visions of America, LLC: 208. Art Resource, NY/Adoc-photos: 81 *left*, 81 *center*; Fitzwilliam Museum, Cambridge: 128; SSPL/ National Railway Museum: 56 *left*. Associated Press/Bill Allen: 220; Efrem Lukatsky: 57 *top*; Eric Gay: 189 *top*. Bridgeman Images/ The Explosion of a Bomb on the Avenue de la Republique, Paris by the Russian anarchists and nihilists, illustration from 'Le Petit Journal', February 1905 (litho), French School, (20th century)/Private Collection/Roger-Viollet, Paris: 80. Cross-Cultural Solutions: 200. Digital Vision: 144-145. Getty Images/ Bettmann: 28, 12 *left*, 37 *top*, 108, 116; Paula Bronstein/Stringer: 56 *right*; Corbis: 88; Hulton Archive/Stringer: 216; Imagno: 44; Wolfgang Kaehler: 169 *bottom right*; MCT: 156-157; PhotoLibrary/Nativestock Pictures: 40; George Rinhart: 213 *top*; Time & Life Pictures: 81 *right*. Granger, NYC : 213 *bottom*. The Image Works/Jim West: 125 *top*; Wesley Bocxe: 125 *bottom*. iStockphoto.com/monkeybusinessimages: 10. Lebrecht Music & Arts: 12 *right*. Library of Congress, Prints & Photographs Division, LC-DIG-ppmsca-31280: 212; New York Herald, LC-USZC4-5624: 69. Mary Evans Picture Library/ Ronald Grant Archive: 68. Masterfile: 101, 112, 201 *left*; Robert Harding Images: 204. National Portrait Gallery/Elliot & Fry: 24 *inset*. NativeStock Pictures/Marilyn Angel Wynn: 169 *bottom left*. Newscom.com/Columbia Pictures: 76; EPA/Mohamed Omar: 57 *bottom*. Photo Researchers, Inc./Chris Butler: 189 *bottom*; Roger Harris: 188. Photodisc: 36 *inset*, 81 *background*. Eric Reed: 20. Reuters/ Dylan Martinez: 72. Shutterstock.com/Sharon Day: 100-101; javarman: 169; miha de: 132; nagib: 12-13; Lisovskaya Natalia: 201 *right*; Nixx Photography: 200-201; Kovalchuk Oleksandr: 192; Phase4Photography: 81 *background*; REX/Paramount: 164; Robbi: 124; Vjom: 112-113; Superstock/age fotostock: 104. Timothy Hughes Rare & Early Newspapers: 37 *inset*. Wikimedia Commons: 69 *inset*; Pete Souza: 156. Wikipedia: 160.

Illustrator Credits: Zina Saunders: 168.

Address inquiries to Permissions Department,
William H. Sadlier, Inc.,
9 Pine Street, New York, New York 10005-4700.

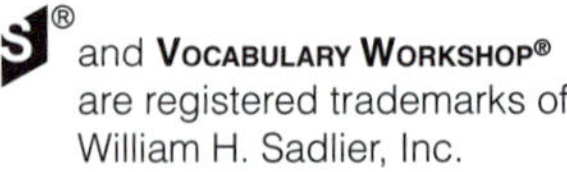
and VOCABULARY WORKSHOP® are registered trademarks of William H. Sadlier, Inc.

Printed in the United States of America.
ISBN: 978-1-4217-8513-4
1 2 3 4 5 6 7 8 9 10 EB 21 20 19 18 17

For additional online resources, go to SadlierConnect.com.

CONTENTS

PROGRAM FEATURES

For more than five decades, **Vocabulary Workshop** has proven to be a highly successful tool for vocabulary growth and the development of vocabulary skills. It has also been shown to help students prepare for standardized tests. **Vocabulary Workshop Achieve** maintains that tradition in a newly designed format.

Each of **Vocabulary Workshop Achieve's** 15 Units introduces 20 words in two 10-word lists—**Set A** and **Set B**. Both Set A and Set B contain exercises to help you develop deeper understanding of the 10 words in each set. Combined Sets A and B then provide practice with all 20 of the words in the Unit. Review and Word Study activities follow Units 3, 6, 9, 12, and 15 and offer practice with the 60 vocabulary words in the preceding three Units.

Each level of **Vocabulary Workshop Achieve** introduces and provides practice with 300 vocabulary words and contains features such as reading passages, writing prompts, vocabulary in context, evidence-based questions, and word study that will help you to master these new vocabulary words and succeed in using skills to comprehend unfamiliar words.

Each Unit in **Vocabulary Workshop Achieve** consists of the following sections for **Set A** and **Set B**: an introductory **Reading Passage** that shows how vocabulary words are used in context, **Definitions** that include sentences that give examples of how to use the words, **Using Context, Choosing the Right Word**, and **Completing the Sentence**—activities that provide practice with the vocabulary words. Each introductory **Reading Passage** is a nonfiction text that includes most of the vocabulary words from the Unit to which it belongs. In addition, **Synonyms**, **Antonyms**, and **Vocabulary in Context** in combined Sets A and B round out each Unit with practice with all 20 Unit words.

The five Review sections cover all 60 words from their corresponding Units. **Vocabulary for Comprehension** is modeled on the reading sections of college entrance exams. It presents reading comprehension questions, including vocabulary-related items and evidence-based items that are based on the reading passages.

Word Study sections that contain activities on **Idioms**, **Denotation and Connotation**, and **Classical Roots** follow the Review. These sections will help you develop your understanding of figurative language and practice skills that will help you to determine the meaning of new and unfamiliar vocabulary.

The Final Mastery Test assesses a selection of words from the year and allows you to see the growth you have made in acquiring new vocabulary words and in mastering the comprehension skills you need to understand unfamiliar words.

ONLINE RESOURCES

SadlierConnect.com

Go to **SadlierConnect.com** to find iWords, an audio program that provides pronunciations, definitions, and examples of usage for all of the vocabulary words presented in this level of **Vocabulary Workshop Achieve**. You can listen to the entire **Reading Passage** and the 20 Unit vocabulary words one word at a time, or download all of the words in any given Unit.

At **SadlierConnect.com** you will also find interactive vocabulary quizzes, flash cards, and interactive games and puzzles that will help reinforce and enrich your understanding of the vocabulary words in this level of **Vocabulary Workshop Achieve**.

VOCABULARY IN CONTEXT

The context of a word is the printed text of which that word is part. By studying a word's context, we may find clues to its meaning. We might find a clue in the immediate or adjoining sentence or phrase in which the word appears; in the topic or subject matter of the passage; or in the physical features—such as photographs, illustrations, charts, graphs, captions, and headings—of a page itself.

The **Reading Passages** as well as the **Using Context**, **Choosing the Right Word**, **Vocabulary in Context**, and **Vocabulary for Comprehension** exercises that appear in the Units, the Reviews, and the Final Mastery Test provide practice in using context to decode and to determine the meaning of unfamiliar words.

Three types of context clues appear in the exercises in this book.

A **restatement clue** consists of a synonym for or a definition of the missing word. For example:

Faithfully reading a weekly newsmagazine not only broadens my knowledge of current events and world or national affairs but also ______________ my vocabulary.

a. decreases **b.** fragments **c.** increases **d.** contains

In this sentence, *broadens* is a synonym of the missing word, *increases*, and acts as a restatement clue for it.

A **contrast clue** consists of an antonym for or a phase that means the opposite of the missing word. For example:

"My view of the situation may be far too rosy," I admitted. "On the other hand, yours may be a bit (**optimistic, bleak**)."

In this sentence, *rosy* is an antonym of the missing word, *bleak*. This is confirmed by the presence of the phrase *on the other hand*, which indicates that the answer must be the opposite of *rosy*.

An **inference clue** implies but does not directly state the meaning of the missing word or words. For example:

"A treat for all ages," the review read, "this wonderful novel combines the ______________ of a scholar with the skill and artistry of an expert ______________."

a. ignorance . . . painter
c. wealth . . . surgeon
b. wisdom . . . beginner
d. knowledge . . . storyteller

In this sentence, there are several inference clues: (a) the word *scholar* suggests knowledge; (b) the words *novel*, *artistry*, and *skill* suggests the word *storyteller*. These words are inference clues because they suggest or imply, but do not directly state, the missing word or words.

VOCABULARY AND READING

There is a strong connection between vocabulary knowledge and reading comprehension. Although comprehension is much more than recognizing words and knowing their meanings, comprehension is nearly impossible if you do not know an adequate number of words in the text you are reading or have the vocabulary skills to figure out their meaning.

The **Reading Passages** in this level provide extra practice with vocabulary words. Vocabulary words are in boldface to draw your attention to their uses and contexts. Context clues embedded in the passages encourage you to figure out the meanings of words before you read the definitions provided on the pages directly following the passages.

Test Prep

Your knowledge of word meanings and your ability to think carefully about what you read will help you succeed in school and on standardized tests, including the SAT® and ACT® exams.

The **Vocabulary for Comprehension** exercises in each Review consist of a reading passage followed by comprehension questions. The passages and questions are similar to those that you are likely to find on standardized tests.

Types of Questions

You are likely to encounter the following types of questions in **Vocabulary Workshop Achieve** and on standardized tests.

Main Idea Questions generally ask what the passage as a whole is about. Often, but not always, the main idea is stated in the first paragraph of the passage. You may also be asked the main idea of a specific paragraph. Questions about the main idea may begin like this:

- The primary or main purpose of the passage is . . .
- The author's primary or main purpose in the passage is to . . .
- Which of the following statements most nearly paraphrases the author's main idea in the ninth paragraph (lines 77–88)?
- The main purpose of the fourth paragraph (lines 16–45) is to . . .

Detail Questions focus on important information that is explicitly stated in the passage. Often, however, the correct answer choices do not use the exact language of the passage. They are instead restatements, or paraphrases, of the text.

Vocabulary in Context Questions check your ability to use context to identify a word's meaning. For example:

- As it is used in paragraph 2, "adherents" most nearly means . . .

Use the word's context in a passage to select the best answer, particularly when the vocabulary word has more than one meaning. The answer choices may contain two (or more) correct meanings of the word in question. Choose the meaning that best fits the context.

Inference Questions ask you to make inferences or draw conclusions from the passage. These questions often begin like this:

- It can be most reasonably inferred from the information in the fifth paragraph (lines 53–69) that . . .
- The passage clearly implies that . . .

The inferences you make and the conclusions you draw must be based on the information in the passage. Using the facts you learn from the passage in addition to the knowledge and reasoning you already have helps you understand what is implied and reach conclusions that are logical.

Evidence-Based Questions ask you to provide evidence from the passage that will support the answer you provided to a previous question. These questions often begin like this:

- Which choice provides the best evidence for the answer to the previous question?
- Which statement is the best evidence for the answer to the previous question?

Questions About Tone show your understanding of the author's attitude toward the topic of the passage. To determine the tone, pay attention to the author's word choice. The author's attitude may be positive (respectful), negative (scornful), or neutral (distant). These are typical questions:

- The author's primary purpose in the passage is to . . .
- Which word best describes the author's tone?

Questions About Author's Technique focus on the way a text is organized and the language the author uses. These questions ask you to think about structure and function. For example:

- In the context of the passage, the primary function of the fourth paragraph (lines 30–37) is to . . .
- The organizational structure of the passage is best described as . . .

To answer the questions, you must demonstrate an understanding of the way the author presents information and develops ideas.

VOCABULARY AND WRITING

The **Writing: Words in Action** prompt provides you with an opportunity to practice using text evidence to respond to a prompt about the introductory **Reading Passage**. You will have the opportunity to demonstrate your understanding of the Unit words by incorporating the new vocabulary you have learned into your own writing.

WORD STUDY

Word Study helps build word knowledge with strategies to help you look closely at words for meanings. Word Study instruction and practice include **Idioms**, **Denotation and Connotation**, and **Classical Roots**.

Idioms

Three Word Study sections feature instruction on and practice with idioms. An idiom is an informal expression whose literal meaning does not help the reader or listener understand what the expression means, such as "raining cats and dogs," "the apple of my eye," or "a dark horse." While every language has its own idioms, English is particularly rich in idioms and idiomatic expressions. Developing a clear understanding of idioms will help you better understand the figurative language that authors use in their writing.

Denotation and Connotation

Instruction in **Denotation and Connotation** and practice with connotations is included in two of the Word Study sections. Understanding a word's connotation will develop your skills as a reader, writer, and speaker.

Understanding the difference between denotation and connotation is important to understanding definitions and how concepts are used, as well as in choosing the right word. In these exercises, practice choosing the correct word by determining the emotional association of the word.

Classical Roots

Each Word Study includes a **Classical Roots** exercise that provides instruction in and practice with Greek and Latin roots. Developing a useful, transferable technique to make sense out of unfamiliar words through Greek and Latin roots will help you unlock the meanings of thousands of words. An example word drawn from the vocabulary words in the previous Units is referenced at the top of the page and serves as a guide to help you complete the exercise.

PRONUNCIATION KEY

The pronunciation is indicated for every basic word in this book. The pronunciation symbols used are similar to those used in most recent standard dictionaries. The author has primarily consulted *Webster's Third New International Dictionary* and *The Random House Dictionary of the English Language* (*Unabridged*). Many English words have multiple accepted pronunciations. The author has given one pronunciation when such words occur in this book except when the pronunciation changes according to the part of speech. For example, the verb *project* is pronounced **prə jekt'**, and the noun form is pronounced **präj' ekt**.

Vowels	ā	l*a*ke	e	str*e*ss	ü	l*oo*t, n*ew*
	a	m*a*t	ī	kn*i*fe	u̇	f*oo*t, p*u*ll
	â	c*a*re	i	s*i*t	ə	j*u*mp, brok*e*n
	ä	b*a*rk, b*o*ttle	ō	fl*ow*	ər	b*ir*d, bett*er*
	au̇	d*ou*bt	ô	*a*ll, c*o*rd		
	ē	b*ea*t, word*y*	oi	*oi*l		

Consonants	ch	*ch*ild, lec*t*ure	s	*c*ellar	wh	*wh*at
	g	*g*ive	sh	*sh*un	y	*y*earn
	j	*g*entle, bri*dg*e	th	*th*ank	z	i*s*
	ŋ	si*ng*	t͟h	*th*ose	zh	mea*s*ure

All other consonants are sounded as in the alphabet.

Stress The accent mark follows the syllable receiving the major stress: en rich'.

Abbreviations	*adj.*	adjective	*n.*	noun	*prep.*	preposition
	adv.	adverb	*part.*	participle	*v.*	verb
	int.	interjection	*pl.*	plural		

Read the following passage, taking note of the ***boldface*** *words and their contexts. These words are among those you will be studying in Unit 1. It may help you to complete the exercises in this Unit if you refer to the way the words are used below.*

Fascinating Rhythm: The Life of George Gershwin

<Biographical Sketch>

It is no exaggeration to say George Gershwin (1898–1937) composed some of the most exciting, original, and popular music of all time: Songs that have become standards, like "I Got Rhythm," "Embraceable You," and "Someone to Watch Over Me," plus more than two dozen Broadway shows and film scores—including *Funny Face, Shall We Dance?,* and *Of Thee I Sing*—and dazzling orchestral pieces and jazz compositions. Not bad for a poor Brooklyn kid who dropped out of high school.

Gershwin, born Jacob Gershvin in New York to Russian-Jewish immigrants, displayed a precocious talent for piano playing and studied with a master teacher who gave him a classical foundation. At age 15, he resisted the **hidebound** restrictions that school placed on his time and talents and left it for good. His parents, perhaps realizing George's remarkable musical potential, had a **laissez-faire** attitude: Maybe their son was destined for greater things?

Young George got a job as a song plugger on Tin Pan Alley for the princely sum of $15 a week. (A song plugger demonstrated new songs to promote the sale of sheet music. Tin Pan Alley was the name given a New York street where Manhattan-based music publishers and songwriters congregated.) His rise was swift. His first hit was the somewhat **ribald** "When You Want 'Em, You Can't Get 'Em, When You've Got 'Em, You Don't Want 'Em." But then he and lyricist Irving Caeser wrote "Swanee," which was recorded by popular entertainer Al Jolson and took the country by storm, selling more than two million records. After that, success seemed a done deal, a **fait accompli**. It allowed him to

Piano music from *Porgy and Bess*, 1935

George Gershwin, 1937

escape the **hierarchy** of the music business and forge his own career path, on his own terms.

In the productive 1920s and 1930s, Gershwin wrote countless pieces, including the jazz-influenced "Rhapsody in Blue" and music for the groundbreaking folk opera *Porgy and Bess*. His music became a **bellwether** for the dramatic changes in American popular music. To create an **adjunct** to his Broadway work, he started writing for the movies. In light of his classical and theatrical background, some in Hollywood thought Gershwin too highbrow or too **oblivious** to the realities of scoring a movie. But he was quickly able to win skeptical moviemakers over, and many became not just fans but **proselytes** of his music.

Gershwin's main musical collaborator was his lyricist brother, Ira, but he also had fruitful **quasi**-partnerships with several others, including Kay Swift, a trailblazing American woman composer. But such luck was not to last. In 1937, after complaining of headaches and other symptoms that left him feeling **effete**, Gershwin was diagnosed with a brain tumor. He collapsed during a concert and lay **supine** on the floor. Doctors operated, but he died in July of that year at just 38 years of age. Ira, grief-stricken, floundered in a **morass** of self-pity. How could he go on writing without his beloved brother and partner? But Ira eventually teamed up with other composers, including Jerome Kern.

George Gershwin's stellar reputation has only grown since his death. Singers from Frank Sinatra to Sting have recorded his songs; and films, TV shows, and commercials utilize his music. In the early 1950s, the Oscar-winning musical-comedy film *An American in Paris* featured many Gershwin songs and musical **vignettes** plus an elaborate, **chimerical** dance sequence created around Gershwin's symphonic tone poem, which remains one of his best-known works.

Audio

For iWords and audio passages, go to **SadlierConnect.com**.

Gene Kelly and Leslie Caron, *An American in Paris*, 1951

Definitions

Note the spelling, pronunciation, part(s) of speech, and definition(s) of each of the following words. Then write the appropriate form of the word in the blank space in the illustrative sentence(s) following.

1. adjunct
(aj′ ənkt)

(*n.*) something added to something else as helpful or useful but not essential; an assistant or helper; a valuable quality or characteristic; (*adj.*) added or connected in a subordinate capacity; attached to a faculty or staff in an auxiliary capacity

The ____________________ was given free with purchase.

An ____________________ art professor will be hired.

2. caterwaul
(kat′ ər wôl)

(*v.*) to howl or screech like a cat; to quarrel; (*n.*) a harsh or noisy cry; a racket

The couple ____________________ about their problems.

The ____________________ in the alley kept us awake.

3. effete
(i fēt′)

(*adj.*) lacking in wholesome vigor or energy; worn-out or exhausted; sterile or unable to produce; out-of-date

The ____________________ club used to be popular.

4. hierarchy
(hi′ ə rär kē)

(*n.*) any system of things or people arranged or graded one above another in order of rank, wealth, class, etc.

Maslow developed a ____________________ of needs.

5. laissez-faire
(lesā fe(ə)r′; lezā)

(*adj.*) a philosophy or practice characterized by a usually deliberate abstention from direction or interference, especially with individual freedom of choice and action

She is ____________________ in her role as a director.

6. morass
(mə ras′)

(*n.*) a patch of low, soft, wet ground; a swamp; a confusing situation in which one is entrapped, as in quicksand

He wallowed in a ____________________ of self doubt.

7. oblivious
(ə bliv′ ē əs)

(*adj.*) forgetful; unaware

The hikers were ____________________ of danger ahead.

8. proselyte
(pros′ ə līt)

(*n.*) a convert; a disciple

The zealous ____________________ rallied in the square.

9. ribald (rib′ əld) — (*adj.*) irreverently mocking; coarse, vulgar, or indecent in language

The actor tells ____________________ stories about life in the theater world.

10. vignette (vin yet′) — (*n.*) a short description or sketch; a picture or illustration with edges that gradually shade off; a decorative design on the title page of a book or at the beginning or end of a chapter

All enjoyed the writer's ____________________ of country life.

Using Context

*For each item, determine whether the **boldface** word from pages 14–15 makes sense in the context of the sentence. Circle the item numbers next to the six sentences in which the words are used correctly.*

1. It is difficult to compare the two works, since one is a complex novel that explores several different levels of society, and the other is a mere **vignette**.

2. The business owners chose to settle the lawsuit, fearing that otherwise they would be drawn into a legal **morass** that would drag on for years.

3. Despite his humble background, the ambitious young soldier was determined to reach the top of the military **hierarchy**.

4. It is neither safe nor practical to adopt a **laissez-faire** attitude when babysitting a group of restless, unruly children.

5. An **adjunct** team of engineers will be recruited to ensure that the project is completed in a timely manner.

6. Tens of thousands of **oblivious** fans lined the streets during the parade celebrating their team's victory in the world championship.

7. Everyone in the kingdom bowed to the authority of the **proselyte**.

8. The troops defending the harbor could not withstand the **caterwaul** of the invading ships and were forced to surrender.

9. Some of the folk songs in this anthology are sweet and poignant, whereas others, by contrast, are quite **ribald**.

10. The high school senior's **effete** biochemistry project won first prize in the competition and earned her a full scholarship to a prestigious state university.

Choosing the Right Word

*Select the **boldface** word that better completes each sentence. You might refer to the passage on pages 12–13 to see how most of these words are used in context. Note that the choices might be related forms of the Unit words.*

1. A lauded short story writer and novelist, Ernest Hemingway was far from (**effete, ribald**), as he also thrived in such endeavors as bullfighting, hunting, and skiing.

2. I am willing to listen to any reasonable grievances you may have, but this constant (**caterwauling, hierarchy**) about trivia has exhausted my patience.

3. Hiking in the woods, we came upon an expansive and impassable (**caterwaul, morass**).

4. The great historian Edward Gibbon sought to explain how and why the (**proselytizing, ribald**) efforts of the early Christian church met with such extraordinary success.

5. The lyrics of the song, presented as though they were devastating wit, were in my opinion no more than a coarse and (**effete, ribald**) jest.

6. As the family set up their tent, a distant (**caterwauling, proselytizing**) of an unseen and mysterious creature sent the children running for the comfort of their parents' arms.

7. With penetrating insight and a marvelous ear for dialogue, the author gave us in a few words an unforgettable (**adjunct, vignette**) of a confused but hopeful adolescent.

8. How can you expect a prompt response from an agency that is bogged down in a veritable (**morass, vignette**) of unnecessary red tape?

9. A superintendent is at the head of the (**hierarchy, vignette**) of educators responsible for the schooling of our children and young people.

10. Her unfailing courtesy to others is not a mere (**adjunct, morass**) of her personality; it reflects the essential values and standards by which she lives.

11. After a brief period of popularity, their cheap and vulgar novels lost their appeal and sank into well-deserved (**proselyte, oblivion**).

12. A policy of (**oblivious, laissez-faire**) economics makes sense in a textbook, but certain governmental regulations and oversight are necessary in a mixed economy.

Completing the Sentence

Choose the word from the word bank that best completes each of the following sentences. Write the correct word or form of the word in the space provided.

adjunct	**effete**	**laissez-faire**	**oblivious**	**ribald**
caterwaul	**hierarchy**	**morass**	**proselyte**	**vignette**

1. As a rule, I am not a particularly proud or combative person, but I cannot be ____________________ to the fact that you have deliberately insulted me.

2. She used talent, charm, energy, and determination to fight her way up the corporate ____________________ until she attained the highest position in the company.

3. Taking advantage of the young man's naïve idealism, they sought to make him a(n) ____________________ to serve in their revolutionary plots.

4. The baby-sitter had a(n) ____________________ manner about him, so the children got to stay up late when he was in charge.

5. If you think that the literature of earlier ages was always staid and proper, take a look at some of the ____________________ stories in the *Decameron*, written more than 600 years ago.

6. The newspaper published my Aunt Alice's series of charming ____________________ —brief sketches of the town in which she grew up.

7. Ever since she learned of the failure of her project, she has been mired in a(n) ____________________ of disappointment and self-recrimination.

8. Their youthful enthusiasm for literature degenerated over the years into a(n) ____________________ preoccupation with quibbling criticism and minor details.

9. I think that the critic was a little harsh when he observed that the band's lead vocalist did not sing so much as ____________________.

10. The local Parents' Association has on many occasions served as a willing ____________________ to the administration and staff of our school.

End Set A

Note the spelling, pronunciation, part(s) of speech, and definition(s) of each of the following words. Then write the appropriate form of the word in the blank space in the illustrative sentence(s) following.

1. **bellwether** (bel′ weth ər) — (*n.*) the male sheep that leads the flock to the slaughterhouse; a leader, as in a desperate or violent undertaking; an indicator of trends

   When their ____________________ was captured, the mob disbanded.

2. **chimerical** (ki mer′ i kəl) — (*adj.*) absurd; wildly fantastic; impossible

   They proposed yet another ____________________ get-rich-quick scheme.

3. **fait accompli** (fe ta kôm plē′) — (*n.*) an accomplished and presumably irreversible deed, fact, or action

   The proud generals confidently declared the fall of the rebel stronghold a ____________________.

4. **hidebound** (hīd′ baůnd) — (*adj.*) narrow-minded and rigid, especially in opinions or prejudices; stubbornly and unthinkingly conservative

   The ____________________ administrator stood by the outdated ways of previous administrations.

5. **liturgy** (lit′ ər jē) — (*n.*) a religious service or rite; the form of a ritual or other act of public worship

   The ____________________ has been modernized.

6. **noisome** (noi′ səm) — (*adj.*) offensive or disgusting; foul-smelling; harmful or injurious

   The ____________________ atmosphere of the slaughterhouse overwhelmed the visitors.

7. **poltroon** (pol trün′) — (*n.*) a base coward

   The ____________________ was caught deserting.

8. **quasi** (kwā′ zī) *or* (kwä′ zē) — (*adj.*) resembling but not actually being; seemingly but not actually or completely

   They formed a ____________________ partnership.

9. raillery
(rā′ lər ē)

(*n.*) good-humored ridicule; teasing

The good-natured ____________________ in the locker room pleased the coach.

10. supine
(sü pīn′)

(*adj.*) lying flat on one's back; listless or lethargic; apathetic or passive

The hiker relaxed in a ____________________ position.

Using Context

*For each item, determine whether the **boldface** word from pages 18–19 makes sense in the context of the sentence. Circle the item numbers next to the six sentences in which the words are used correctly.*

1. The athlete was discouraged to learn that she would have to recover from her injury by remaining mostly in a **supine** position for the next several weeks.

2. The **raillery** that my colleague unleashed at me for borrowing a pen without asking was so severe that I assumed something else was wrong.

3. Although I do not have a degree in world literature, I have read enough of the classics and done so much research that I consider myself a **quasi** expert.

4. The author's description of the **noisome** setting of a quiet field on a sunny day transported me to a serene place.

5. He studied the **liturgy** closely in the hopes that one day he would be able to lead people in its rituals.

6. My sister is so **hidebound** that I sometimes wish I could find a way to read her thoughts and feelings, since she would never willingly share them with me.

7. As she watched the younger kids get picked on, she decided that she would take action by defending them instead of standing by as a **bellwether**.

8. We were disappointed to learn that the acquisition of our company was not in negotiations, but rather a **fait accompli** that would almost certainly result in some layoffs.

9. Everyone who had dismissed his dream of becoming a famous actor as **chimerical** was humbled when he got the leading role in the summer's biggest action film.

10. Although he bragged incessantly about his strength and bravery, he was proven to be a **poltroon** when faced with an actual challenge.

Set B

*Select the **boldface** word that better completes each sentence. You might refer to the passage on pages 12–13 to see how most of these words are used in context. Note that the choices might be related forms of the Unit words.*

1. Martin Luther King, Jr. appealed to his countrymen to abandon the (**noisome, hidebound**) stereotypes of racism and rise to a new level of understanding.

2. As I listened to the talk of those unlettered people, suffused with love and reverence, I felt that their simple words were a (**raillery, liturgy**) worthy of respect.

3. He is so (**supine, hidebound**) in his political views that he won't even listen to opinions that differ from his own.

4. Overly sensitive to any suggestion of ridicule, young Rogers seemed to be hurt even by a friend's good-natured (**raillery, fait accompli**).

5. The (**chimerical, supine**) form of the sculpted figure suggests that the artist is interested in revealing—and drawing attention to—life's peaceful moments.

6. They have confronted us not with a theoretical possibility but with a (**bellwether, fait accompli**); now we must decide what we can do about it.

7. Failure to stand up for your rights is not being "prudent" or "moderate"; it is the behavior of a (**poltroon, bellwether**).

8. (**Supine, Noisome**) vapors from the manufacturing plant contributed to the overwhelming public outrage concerning disposal of waste in the community.

9. Although the old senator no longer holds any public office, her fame and prestige are so great that she is still regarded as a (**quasi, hidebound**) public figure.

10. Financial analysts carefully watch the performance of certain stocks, which they regard as (**bellwethers, poltroons**) for indications of economic trends.

11. We have lived to see the acceptance and enactment of reform programs that, when first proposed, were dismissed as absolutely (**chimerical, noisome**).

12. Almost incredibly, a formidable resistance movement had been organized by people whom we had always associated with (**supine, noisome**) submission to authority.

Choose the word from the word bank that best completes each of the following sentences. Write the correct word or form of the word in the space provided.

bellwether	fait accompli	liturgy	poltroon	raillery
chimerical	hidebound	noisome	quasi	supine

1. Advocates of equal rights maintain that we must reject the ____________ prejudices that bar the physically impaired from many occupations.

2. As late as the seventeenth century, researchers known as alchemists devoted their lives to the pursuit of ____________ schemes for turning iron into gold.

3. I detected an undertone of hostility and ridicule in the remarks, which were ostensibly no more than good-natured ____________.

4. Polluted by the spill from a nearby chemical plant, the once beautiful lake had become a foul pool, ____________ and hideous.

5. As the Smithsonian Institution is only partly under the control of the United States government, it is considered a(n) ____________ governmental institution.

6. I regret Jackie's resignation as much as anyone, but I think that we must regard it as a(n) ____________ and find someone to take her place.

7. A handful of self-appointed "leaders" served as the ____________ who induced the mob to surge through the barriers.

8. Failure in itself is no disgrace, but the ____________ acceptance of failure certainly is.

9. The use of English rather than traditional languages in religious ceremonies is evidence of efforts to modernize and revitalize the ____________ of various denominations.

10. The rigid king dismissed as a mere ____________ anyone who refused to join in his crusade against the forces of evil.

End Set B

Synonyms

*Choose the word or form of the word from this Unit that is the same or most nearly the same in meaning as the **boldface** word or expression in the phrase. Write that word on the line. Use a dictionary if necessary.*

1. startled by the sudden **wail** ______________
2. a steady stream of **banter** ______________
3. has a **fanciful** notion of what the future holds ______________
4. at the pinnacle of the **pecking order** ______________
5. a **supplement** to the main textbook ______________
6. achieved **nominal** fame ______________
7. unfamiliar with the **ceremony** ______________
8. embarrassed by the **bawdy** prose ______________
9. remained **inflexible** in his beliefs ______________
10. recognized the **irreversible situation** ______________
11. felt **enfeebled** by a bout of pneumonia ______________
12. a **nonrestrictive** management style ______________
13. **unobservant** about what's going on ______________
14. a congregation full of **neophytes** ______________
15. the **quagmire** of red tape ______________

Antonyms

*Choose the word or form of the word from this Unit that is most nearly opposite in meaning to the **boldface** word or expression in the phrase. Write that word on the line. Use a dictionary if necessary.*

1. soothed by the **pleasant** odor ______________
2. a **follower** of the crowd ______________
3. enjoyed a deserved reputation as a **hero** ______________
4. a charming **epic** of Victorian life ______________
5. told to assume an **upright** posture ______________

Writing: Words in Action

George Gershwin had both great talent and great fortune. Is it fortune or talent that is more consequential in a person's life? In a brief essay, support your opinion with specific examples from your studies, reading (pages 12–13), and experience. Use three or more words from this Unit.

Vocabulary in Context

Some of the words you have studied in this Unit appear in **boldface** *type. Read the passage below, and then circle the letter of the correct answer for each word as it is used in context.*

A symphonic poem, or tone poem, is an orchestral piece, usually composed in a single, continuous movement, which illustrates or evokes the content of a poem, painting, or landscape. The Hungarian composer Franz Liszt is often credited with the invention of this form, which peaked in popularity between 1850 and 1930. No **poltroon** when it came to taking on such giant predecessors as Liszt, Claude Debussy, and Richard Strauss, the American composer George Gershwin produced two classics of the form: *Rhapsody in Blue* (1924) and *An American in Paris* (1928). The purpose of the latter, Gershwin stated, was "to portray the impressions of an American visitor in Paris as he strolls about the city, listens to various street noises, and absorbs the French atmosphere." Gershwin's symphonic poem was to be an evocative **vignette** of the City of Light.

Never bound by any conventional **liturgy** of classical forms, Gershwin infused *An American in Paris* with jazz rhythms and harmonic structures borrowed from the blues. His orchestration of the piece was also unconventional: for example, he included the **caterwaul** of genuine Parisian taxi horns. On a visit to Paris in 1928, Gershwin himself procured about twenty such klaxons from local auto shops. Stacked on top of a grand piano in his hotel room, the horns occasioned some good-natured **raillery** from Gershwin's visitors. At the New York premiere, the unusual instruments did not impart a **noisome** sound to the piece. On the contrary, as the program notes suggested, the horns were an authentic stroke that helped to establish the French atmosphere as "triumphant."

---

1. What is the meaning of **poltroon** as it is used in paragraph 1?

a. complainer
b. enthusiast
c. coward
d. simpleton

2. What is the meaning of **vignette** in the context of the passage?

a. sketch
b. reverie
c. prediction
d. prelude

3. In paragraph 2, what does **liturgy** suggest about classical music forms?

a. They are flexible.
b. They are ritual.
c. They are outmoded.
d. They are disorganized.

4. In paragraph 2, what does **caterwaul** suggest about the horns' sound?

a. hostility
b. glamor
c. stridency
d. congeniality

5. What does **raillery** most likely mean as it is used in paragraph 2?

a. condescension
b. rebuttal
c. zealotry
d. teasing

6. What characteristic is suggested by **noisome** in paragraph 2?

a. offensiveness
b. pervasiveness
c. pretentiousness
d. hilarity

UNIT 2

*Read the following passage, taking note of the **boldface** words and their contexts. These words are among those you will be studying in Unit 2. It may help you to complete the exercises in this Unit if you refer to the way the words are used below.*

The Code-breakers of Bletchley Park

<Historical Nonfiction>

"They were my geese that laid the golden eggs and never cackled." Thus did British Prime Minister Winston Churchill, with a touch of **paternalism**, describe the code-breakers who worked at Bletchley Park during World War II. Churchill's geese were indeed crucial to the war effort. Maintaining rigorous secrecy about their work, they produced high-level intelligence that had a profound impact on Allied strategy and success.

A tranquil estate tucked into the countryside some fifty miles northwest of London, Bletchley Park stood far from the **melee** and devastation of the war, and remained, with one minor exception, beyond the **purview** of Nazi air raids. The property had been acquired for the British government in 1938, not long before the war's outbreak, under the **aegis** of Admiral Sir Hugh Sinclair, chief of the British intelligence service. To maintain secrecy, the first government visitors to the site **obfuscated** the true nature of Sinclair's interest in the property, claiming to be members of a hunting party. No doubt the rural setting lent a certain **verisimilitude** to their pretense.

Code-breakers and support staff moved into the Bletchley Park mansion in August 1939. Analysts immediately set to work deciphering German communications, with special focus on codes produced by the German's Enigma cipher machines, which were notoriously difficult to break. British intelligence officials were **sanguine** about their prospects, however,

Bletchley Park's main decryption establishment, Buckinghamshire, England; Alan Turing, the most successful code breaker, 1951

Engima Machine in use by German Soldiers during World War II

Far from **polarizing** the place, American personnel worked comfortably alongside the **indigenous** Britishers who constituted the effort's nucleus. Perhaps the most famous and successful cryptanalyst at the site was Alan Turing, now widely regarded as the father of computer science.

Ultra—the code-name given to intelligence produced at Bletchley Park—made significant contributions to Allied victories at sea and on land, providing information about enemy troop positions, movements, and plans. Ultra informed the Allies of the exact location of all but two of the 58 German divisions on the Western front on D-Day on June 6, 1944.

having been lately **apprised** of Polish cryptologists' success in the task.

The Enigma ciphers were electro-mechanical rotor machines, superficially resembling old-fashioned typewriters, that encrypted messages by scrambling alphabetical letters in complex sequences. Used correctly, Enigma codes were practically impossible to break. But seemingly **minuscule** departures from correct procedure could make transmissions vulnerable to analysis by expert cryptologists. Ultimately, it was human error on the part of the German operators of the Enigma machines that let British analysts break the codes.

Bletchley Park analysts, many of whom were academics **deracinated** from British universities, waged war against the Enigma machines, armed with expertise in mathematics and linguistics. Some were selected for extraordinary skill at solving crossword puzzles. Others were polyglots familiar with the **lexicons** of various languages. After the United States entered the war in 1941, Americans began to join the staff.

With the war over, Churchill remarked to King George VI, "It was thanks to Ultra that we won the war." But the strict secrecy maintained about the program, even decades after the war's end, prevented the full story of the contribution made at Bletchley Park from becoming public knowledge. The men and women who served there, those geese that never cackled, had vowed to remain silent about their work. No **lachrymose** farewells saw these staffers off to duty, no **claques** of admirers cheered them as they returned home. It was only in the late twentieth century that the extent of their contribution to the Allied victory was publicly acknowledged.

Audio

For iWords and audio passages, go to **SadlierConnect.com**.

Definitions

Note the spelling, pronunciation, part(s) of speech, and definition(s) of each of the following words. Then write the appropriate form of the word in the blank space in the illustrative sentence(s) following.

1. apprise (ə prīz′)
(*v.*) to inform of; to make aware of by giving oral or written notice
The spokesperson will ____________ us of the latest developments.

2. bibulous (bib′ yə ləs)
(*adj.*) fond of or inclined to drink; absorbent
The retired sailor was a ____________ old codger.

3. claque (klak)
(*n.*) a group of people hired to applaud a performer or performance; enthusiastic or fawning admirers; an opera hat
The soprano's ____________ was in attendance, as usual.

4. lachrymose (lak′ rə mōs)
(*adj.*) given to tears or weeping; causing to shed tears; mournful, lugubrious
It was a ____________ tale of poverty and woe.

5. lexicon (lek′ sə kən)
(*n.*) a dictionary of a language; the special vocabulary of a person, group, or subject; a compendium
The ____________ of computer technology is large and growing.

6. microcosm (mī′ krə kos əm)
(*n.*) a miniature world or universe; a group or system viewed as the model of a larger group or system
The ocean liner is a ____________ of society in the novel *Ship of Fools*.

7. obfuscate (ob′ fə skāt)
(*v.*) to darken or obscure; to confuse or bewilder
The pedantic lecturer's long-winded explanation served only to ____________ the meaning of the thesis.

8. purview (pər′ vyü)
(*n.*) the range, extent, or scope of something; in law, the scope or limit of what is provided in a statute
The subject was outside the ____________ of the mayor's authority.

9. sanguine (saŋ′ gwin)

(*adj.*) having a ruddy complexion; of a naturally cheerful, confident, or optimistic outlook

Scientists remain ____________________ about the chances of finding a cure for the deadly disease.

10. vassal (vas′ el)

(*n.*) a person under the protection of a feudal lord to whom he or she owes allegiance; a subordinate or dependent; a servant; (*adj.*) subservient

The duke's ____________________ was forced to fight for the king, to whom the duke owed allegiance.

As a ____________________ nation, India provided troops for British armies.

Using Context

*For each item, determine whether the **boldface** word from pages 26–27 makes sense in the context of the sentence. Circle the item numbers next to the six sentences in which the words are used correctly.*

1. Is it true that it is within the **purview** of a sea captain to perform a marriage ceremony?

2. Now that the patient's condition has been diagnosed, the doctor will **apprise** her of her options for treatment.

3. In the tale called "The Emperor's New Clothes," the **claque** that surrounds the monarch cannot be relied on to tell him the truth—namely, that he, in fact, is not wearing any clothes at all.

4. Only one of the math students was able to quickly solve the **lachrymose** problem.

5. The **bibulous** puppy became the center of attention, and everyone asked to hold her.

6. If you wish to understand a sport such as football or basketball, you must not only learn its rules, but also its **lexicon**.

7. The **vassal** lord was forced to choose between his sworn allegiance to the king and his heartfelt sympathy for the rebels.

8. The delay in the issuing of construction permits will **obfuscate** the cost of the project.

9. The company's stock value dropped dramatically after a famous financial guru remarked in an interview that she was quite **sanguine** about its future.

10. Just about every block in this bustling, vital neighborhood is a **microcosm** of the entire city.

Set A

Choosing the Right Word

*Select the **boldface** word that better completes each sentence. You might refer to the passage on pages 24–25 to see how most of these words are used in context. Note that the choices might be related forms of the Unit words.*

1. In the tragedy that overtakes the pathetic Lennie in *Of Mice and Men*, we see in (**microcosm, purview**) the cruelty and injustice that pervade our society.

2. The grandmother was impressed by the child's (**sanguine, obfuscated**) complexion and generally healthy appearance.

3. Morality is not a criterion that can be used to judge whether or not a word belongs in a (**microcosm, lexicon**) of the language in which it is used.

4. Under the American system of personal liberty, there are many aspects of daily life that are not within the (**claque, purview**) of any governmental authority.

5. The movie started off well, but the later scenes, with the young heroine slowly dying of a mystery disease, became overwrought and (**bibulous, lachrymose**).

6. Is it any wonder that the young quarterback is getting a swelled head when he seems always to be surrounded by a (**claque, lexicon**) of fawning admirers?

7. Even the public opinion polls, which showed a strong trend toward our candidate, did not make us overly (**bibulous, sanguine**) about our chances of winning.

8. Thankfully, the beach towels are extremely (**lachrymose, bibulous**), and they were able to control the spread of water from the bucket that tipped over in the back of the van.

9. Compared to today's free agents, the ballplayers of yesteryear were practically the (**lexicon, vassals**) of the team owners.

10. Please do not try to (**apprise, obfuscate**) your responsibility in this matter by irrelevant criticisms of other people's behavior.

11. Falstaff, as conceived by Shakespeare, is not just a (**lachrymose, bibulous**) old braggart, but an archetype of human appetites and joy in living.

12. I think it was very inconsiderate of her to wait until this late date before she (**apprised, obfuscated**) us of her intention to quit the class show.

Completing the Sentence

Choose the word from the word bank that best completes each of the following sentences. Write the correct word or form of the word in the space provided.

apprise	claque	lexicon	obfuscate	sanguine
bibulous	lachrymose	microcosm	purview	vassal

1. "The rash and ____________________ behavior of that young hothead almost cost us the battle, to say nothing of the war," the general remarked sourly.

2. A case of that type, which does not involve a federal law or constitutional issue, does not come within the ____________________ of the Supreme Court.

3. The issue is basically a simple one, and your efforts to ____________________ it by raising endless technical objections will have no effect on us.

4. She defended her policy of hiring a(n) ____________________ by noting that even with a supportive audience, someone is needed to get the applause started.

5. If you are ever to get out of this tangled mess, now is the time for action, not indulgence in ____________________ self-pity.

6. At the outset of World War II, Lithuania lost its sovereignty and became an unwilling ____________________ of the Soviet Union.

7. He came to realize that the inner city in which he had been raised was a(n) ____________________ of the sufferings of impoverished people all over the world.

8. Without expressing opinions, simply ____________________ us as promptly as possible of the results of the conference.

9. My classics professor was compiling a complete ____________________ of the Latin language.

10. I am not given to undue optimism, but the preliminary results of the polls make me ____________________ about the outcome of the election.

End Set A

Definitions

Note the spelling, pronunciation, part(s) of speech, and definition(s) of each of the following words. Then write the appropriate form of the word in the blank space in the illustrative sentence(s) following.

1. aegis (ē′ jis)
(*n.*) protection; patronage; sponsorship
The arts and education programs of the United Nations are under the ________________ of UNESCO.

2. deracinate (di ras′ ə nāt)
(*v.*) to pull up by the roots; to root out, uproot, or dislocate; to eliminate all traces of
One way to ________________ prejudice from our society is to heighten public awareness.

3. exegesis (ek si′ jē sis)
(*n.*) an explanation or critical interpretation (especially of a text)
The newest ________________ of Abraham Lincoln's presidency purports to be the final word on the subject.

4. indigenous (in dij′ ə nəs)
(*adj.*) originating in the country or region where found, native; inborn; inherent
Grizzly bears and mountain lions are two examples of wildlife ________________ to the Rocky Mountains.

5. melee (mā′ lā)
(*n.*) a confused struggle; a violent free-for-all; a tumultuous mingling
Many fans were hurt in the ________________ that followed the soccer match.

6. minuscule (min′ əs kyül)
(*adj.*) very small, tiny; (*n.*) a lowercase letter
I ate only a ________________ portion of the dessert.
In the typeface that the poet chose, every letter used in the poem is a ________________.

7. paternalism (pə tûr′ nə liz əm)
(*n.*) the policy or practice of treating or governing people in the manner of a father dealing with his children
The President won over the worried populace with his attitude of kind ________________.

8. polarize (pō′ lə rīz)
(*v.*) to cause to concentrate around two conflicting or contrasting positions; to cause light to vibrate in a pattern
The debate served to ________________ public opinion on the issue.

9. solecism (sol′ ə siz əm)
(*n.*) a substandard or ungrammatical usage; a breach of etiquette; any impropriety or mistake
One common ____________________ is "irregardless."

10. verisimilitude (ver ə si mil′ ə tüd)
(*n.*) the quality of appearing to be true, real, likely, or probable
The play's ____________________ won praise from critics.

Using Context

*For each item, determine whether the **boldface** word from pages 30–31 makes sense in the context of the sentence. Circle the item numbers next to the six sentences in which the words are used correctly.*

1. His appearance on the television show could be described as **minuscule** because of his minimal on-screen time and lack of a speaking part, but he was happy to have a role to put on his résumé.
2. Your speech would have been more effective if you had not repeated the **solecism** "between you and I" so many times.
3. Self-assured responses and a positive attitude during a job interview will help to **deracinate** a feeling of confidence in the employer about your abilities.
4. The hostess of the dinner party had a change of subject prepared if anyone brought up a topic that was likely to **polarize** the guests.
5. The author's latest beautifully illustrated and appealing children's book stands out as the **aegis** of his body of work.
6. The two directors displayed very different management styles: one assumed an attitude of **paternalism** toward employees; the other, detachment and indifference.
7. The best salespeople are able to present their goods or services as top-of-the-line with **verisimilitude**, so retain some skepticism when hearing a sales pitch.
8. I was excited for my favorite store's annual sale, but I did not foresee having to fight through the **melee** of other shoppers just to get in the door.
9. When I stepped outside after studying in the library for most of the day, the sunlight was so **indigenous** to my eyes that I felt momentarily blinded.
10. The lack of evidence at the scene added to the **exegesis** surrounding the crime.

Set B

Choosing the Right Word

*Select the **boldface** word that better completes each sentence. You might refer to the passage on pages 24–25 to see how most of these words are used in context. Note that the choices might be related forms of the Unit words.*

1. From the observatory atop the Empire State Building, the pedestrians on the streets below look as (**indigenous, minuscule**) as ants.

2. A basketball team will be sent to the Far East under the (**solecism, aegis**) of the State Department to play native teams in various countries.

3. At rush hour, I always have a hard time fighting my way through the (**melee, aegis**) of tired commuters scurrying through the station.

4. When light from the sun hits the surface of the pond, the light is (**indigenous, polarized**), and then we see mysterious reflections on the placid water.

5. Those later scenes, in the opinion of many critics, had so much self-conscious pathos that they lacked conviction and (**verisimilitude, paternalism**).

6. If we disregard the emotions and desires of other groups in our area, we are simply going to increase partisanship and (**deracinate, polarize**) the whole community.

7. I came to resent the company's (**solecism, paternalism**) because it assumed that employees lacked the self-reliance to take care of themselves.

8. Some call our city a cosmopolitan melting pot of cultures, but my grandparents from Eastern Europe felt (**minuscule, deracinated**) and even apprehensive at times.

9. Their standards are so rigid and so devoid of a sense of proportion that they elevate every minor (**exegesis, solecism**) to the level of a major crime.

10. A(n) (**verisimilitude, exegesis**) of Virginia Woolf's work reveals that she is an exceptionally modern writer concerned with the psychology and emotion of her subjects.

11. For many years, Americans and Europeans tended to ignore the highly developed (**deracinated, indigenous**) cultures of the peoples of Africa.

12. It is not enough merely to push aside our prejudices and pretend they don't exist; we must (**deracinate, polarize**) these evils from our minds and personalities.

Completing the Sentence

Choose the word from the word bank that best completes each of the following sentences. Write the correct word or form of the word in the space provided.

aegis	exegesis	melee	paternalism	solecism
deracinate	indigenous	minuscule	polarize	verisimilitude

1. Is the expression "It is me" to be regarded as a(n) ____________________ or as an acceptable idiomatic form?

2. Both sides let on that the negotiators were still miles apart, when in fact the distance that separated their opinions was ____________________.

3. When South Korea was invaded, the United States organized a collective defense effort under the ____________________ of the United Nations.

4. Surprisingly, the white potato, which I have always associated with Ireland, is ____________________ to the Americas.

5. ____________________ from their Old World environments, European immigrants had difficult adjustments to make.

6. No matter how fantastic and far-fetched the themes of Ray Bradbury's stories may be, he seems able to achieve an extraordinary effect of ____________________.

7. A hardline speech may gain the congressperson the applause of her followers, but overall it will ____________________ sentiments throughout the country and impair national unity.

8. The third period was marred by a bench-clearing ____________________ that left the hockey rink littered with discarded gloves and sticks.

9. The people of this underserved area need a program that will "help them to help themselves"—not a form of ____________________ that will make them completely dependent on outside aid.

10. The goal of this course in world history is ____________________; therefore, we will carefully examine primary texts from the time periods we study.

End Set B

Synonyms

*Choose the word or form of the word from this Unit that is the same or most nearly the same in meaning as the **boldface** word or expression in the phrase. Write that word on the line. Use a dictionary if necessary.*

1. a **model** of the entire park ____________
2. an **interpretation** of Joyce's *Ulysses* ____________
3. a **menial** in the royal family's service ____________
4. the **tearful** mourners ____________
5. to **divide** voters' sympathies ____________
6. **confuse** the answer with half-truths ____________
7. a species **endemic** to the Amazon rainforest ____________
8. unable to read the **microscopic** letters ____________
9. under the **auspices** of the state government ____________
10. neglected to **notify** the townspeople ____________
11. ruled with **benevolence** ____________
12. the **hangers-on** waiting by the stage door ____________
13. **eradicate** all traces of polio ____________
14. using the programmers' **special vocabulary** ____________
15. within the **jurisdiction** of the sheriff ____________

Antonyms

*Choose the word or form of the word from this Unit that is most nearly opposite in meaning to the **boldface** word or expression in the phrase. Write that word on the line. Use a dictionary if necessary.*

1. invited all their **teetotaling** relatives ____________
2. encouraged to join the **friendly chat** ____________
3. had the appearance of **inauthenticity** ____________
4. **pessimistic** about our chance of winning ____________
5. **correct usage** essential in a cover letter ____________

Writing: Words in Action

Suppose that you are a member of the British government during World War II, and you need to convince other officials to increase funding to the code-breakers at Bletchley Park. Write a persuasive essay, using examples from your reading (pages 24–25) and three or more words from this Unit.

*Some of the words you have studied in this Unit appear in **boldface** type. Read the passage below, and then circle the letter of the correct answer for each word as it is used in context.*

Cryptography is as ancient as the written word, and every cryptogram is a **microcosm** of human history. The need to share information has always been qualified by the need to conceal from everyone but the intended recipient. As early as the third millennium BC, Egyptian scribes were adapting conventional written forms—changing front-facing pictograms into profiles, adding or subtracting elements from the more abstract glyphs, and committing other apparent **solecisms**—in order to conceal meanings from those who did not know the secret principles that governed the construction of these new characters.

The *skytale* (pronounced like "Italy") was a particular favorite of the Spartans—who valued simplicity, and regarded other Greeks as decadent and **bibulous**. All cryptology of this form comprised two wooden batons of uniform and identical diameter, and a long, narrow strip of tape, or leather. The sender would wrap the tape around the baton and write the message across the tape. A messenger (often a loyal slave or **vassal**) would deliver the tape to the recipient—who possessed the other baton, and used it to turn the apparently senseless mass of letters on the tape back into a coherent message, with no need of any further **exegesis** or reference to any **lexicon** or code-book.

Until modern times, cryptography involved some form of *encryption*—the conversion of ordinary information (*plaintext*) into gibberish (*ciphertext*). *Decryption* refers to the translation of ciphertext back into plaintext.

---

1. What is the meaning of **microcosm** as it is used in paragraph 1?

a. exaggeration
b. full statement
c. unified vision
d. miniaturized version

2. What is the meaning of **solecisms** in the context of the passage?

a. suggestions
b. errors
c. changes
d. corrections

3. In paragraph 2, what does the word **bibulous** suggest about other Greeks?

a. They are inclined to drink.
b. They are frivolous.
c. They laugh for no reason.
d. They eat too much.

4. In paragraph 2, what does the word **vassal** suggest about messengers?

a. They are heroic.
b. They understand codes.
c. They are lowly.
d. They are essential.

5. What does **exegesis** most likely mean as it is used in paragraph 2?

a. planning
b. cryptogram
c. addition
d. explanation

6. What does **lexicon** most likely mean as it is used in paragraph 2?

a. library
b. dictionary
c. journal
d. examination

Read the following passage, taking note of the ***boldface*** *words and their contexts. These words are among those you will be studying in Unit 3. It may help you to complete the exercises in this Unit if you refer to the way the words are used below.*

Charles Ponzi and His Scheme

<Informational Essay>

Charles Ponzi was not the first **mountebank** who used a "Ponzi scheme" to swindle investors out of money, and he wasn't the last. But his success, though fleeting, was so great, that it is only natural that schemes of his sort have come to bear his name.

Ponzi emigrated from Italy in 1902 to start a new life in Boston, at first working odd jobs separated by **interstices** of unemployment. Before long he'd landed a job as a restaurant dishwasher and quickly worked his way up to become a waiter—only to be fired for shortchanging customers and stealing. That sad anecdote epitomizes the **macrocosm** of Ponzi's life: He may have been willing to work hard, but he wouldn't **condescend** to work honestly. He snatched at any chance for an easy fortune, his **rapacity** leading him from one half-baked scam to another, from one **enclave** of rogues to another, and from one prison to another. Along the way, the inveterate two-bit hustler somehow managed to **cozen** thousands of unwary investors out of millions of dollars. But even his greatest success as a scam-artist quickly wound up in failure.

Charles Ponzi

It was postage stamps that made Ponzi an **icon** and immortalized his name. In 1919, he began telling people that he'd found a way to pay for United States postage stamps overseas and sell them for a profit in the U.S., taking advantage of currency fluctuations after World War I. Ponzi's trade in postage may have sounded good in theory, but **pragmatic** considerations made it impossible for the plan to yield big profits. If Ponzi knew that his story was full of holes, he didn't show it. Instead, he played the role of a **virtuoso** investor. Relying on his true **forte**, the con man made the most of his charisma, his knack for small-talk, flattery, and **persiflage**, and his flair for stretching the truth. He convinced thousands of people to invest their money with him and promised he could double their money in 90 days. Ponzi wasn't the only person in America who wanted to make a quick buck, and a **plethora** of investment money came pouring in.

What attracted so many investors to Ponzi's scam is that it seemed to be paying off, because when early investors wanted to cash out, Ponzi would simply give them money he had received from new investors. In truth, there was no underlying investment, no genuine return. Ponzi didn't bother to put his investors' money into postage stamps or anything else that might actually yield a substantial profit—he was just

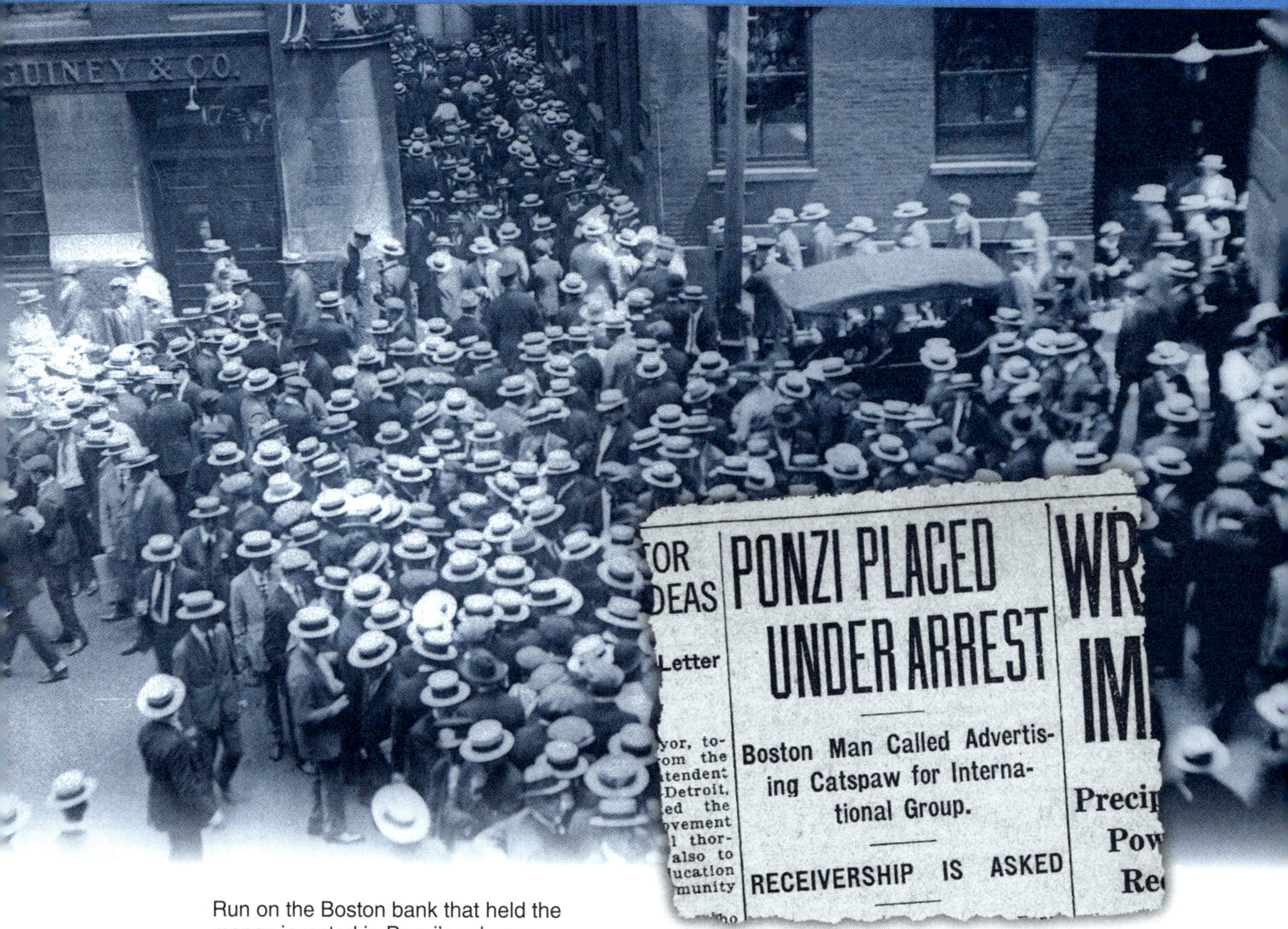

Run on the Boston bank that held the money invested in Ponzi's scheme

robbing Peter to pay Paul, while skimming a tidy sum for himself. When people saw the incredible rate of return that investors with Ponzi seemed to achieve, more investors came running. Monkey see, monkey do.

As Ponzi's reputation grew, the authorities became increasingly **quizzical** about his apparent success. The *Boston Post* began to investigate, and when the newspaper spilled the beans, Ponzi's operation was shut down and its mastermind was brought up on charges. It may have been **therapeutic** for his former investors to hear that he'd landed penniless in jail, but to most of them, Ponzi's fate must have been an **ancillary** concern: Those who stayed with Ponzi till the end lost more than 70 cents on the dollar when the scam collapsed.

As punishment for his crimes, Ponzi spent over ten years in prison. He was deported in 1934 and died a lonely and destitute man. Few people today remember Charles Ponzi or the crimes that he committed a century ago, but his name lives on. At least that's something, Mr. Ponzi.

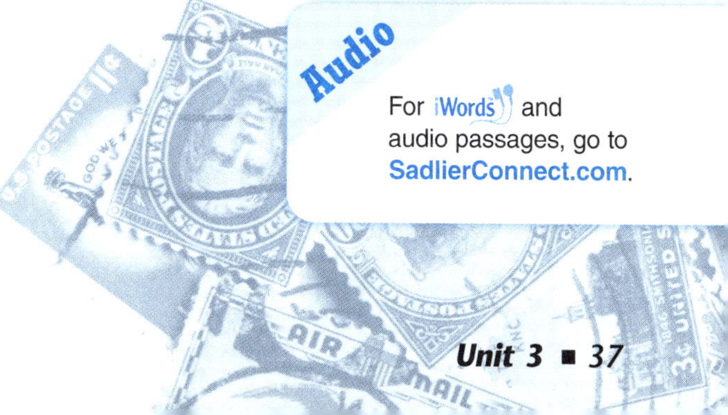

Note the spelling, pronunciation, part(s) of speech, and definition(s) of each of the following words. Then write the appropriate form of the word in the blank space in the illustrative sentence(s) following.

1. bowdlerize (bōd′ lə rīz)

(*v.*) to remove material considered offensive (from a book, play, film, etc.)

The writers refused to ____________________ the book when they turned it into a screenplay.

2. condescend (kon di send′)

(*v.*) to come down or stoop voluntarily to a lower level; to deal with people in a patronizing manner

The fashion designer ____________________ to speak to reporters.

3. cozen (kəz′ ən)

(*v.*) to trick; to cheat or swindle

Some taxi drivers ____________________ unsuspecting tourists.

4. enclave (en′ klāv)

(*n.*) an enclosed district, region, or area inhabited by a particular group of people or having a special character

The mountains afforded the displaced townspeople and the local militia an ____________________ of resistance.

5. icon (ī′ kän)

(*n.*) a representation or image of a sacred personage, often considered sacred itself; an image or picture; a symbol; a graphic symbol on a computer monitor display; an object of blind devotion

The museum's exhibit of ____________________ included several from czarist Russia.

6. macrocosm (mak′ rō koz əm)

(*n.*) the universe considered as a whole; the entire complex structure of something

During the course of their college educations, many students study the economic ____________________.

7. persiflage (pər′ sə fläzh)

(*n.*) lighthearted joking, talk, or writing

The friends engaged in ____________________ from the moment their reunion began until the last of them left.

8. pragmatic (prag mat′ ik)

(*adj.*) concerned with practical considerations or values; dealing with actions and results rather than with abstract theory; stiff in one's opinions

The mayor takes a ____________________ approach to the city's problems.

9. quizzical (kwiz′ i kəl)
(*adj.*) puzzled; mocking; odd; equivocal
The politician's unexpected comment left all who heard it with ____________________ expressions on their faces.

10. rapacity (rə pas′ ə tē)
(*n.*) inordinate greed; the disposition to obtain one's desires by force, extortion, or plunder
With the ____________________ of a shark, the ruthless new company went after its competitors' clients.

Using Context

*For each item, determine whether the **boldface** word from pages 38–39 makes sense in the context of the sentence. Circle the item numbers next to the six sentences in which the words are used correctly.*

1. Scientists believe that a rare but pestilent **macrocosm** has caused the decline in the lake's fish population.
2. In this game, which tests your skills of deception, you score points when you **cozen** your fellow players into believing facts that are not really true.
3. The president valued **pragmatic** advice over abstract and theoretical solutions.
4. I chose the emoticon with the raised eyebrow to express my **quizzical** response to the text message.
5. The skillful attorney was able to completely **bowdlerize** the testimony of the eyewitness and win the case for her client.
6. During the summer months, the beautiful but rugged island was an **enclave** for artists, but during the rest of the year it was largely uninhabited.
7. The Eiffel Tower is an **icon** of the city of Paris as well as French culture.
8. Since both parties in the dispute still refuse to **condescend**, a judge will have to decide the matter.
9. The spy agency employed hundreds of individuals who excelled in the arts of duplicity and **persiflage**.
10. "Robber barons" were industrialists in the late nineteenth century who were infamous for their **rapacity**.

*Select the **boldface** word that better completes each sentence. You might refer to the passage on pages 36–37 to see how most of these words are used in context. Note that the choices might be related forms of the Unit words.*

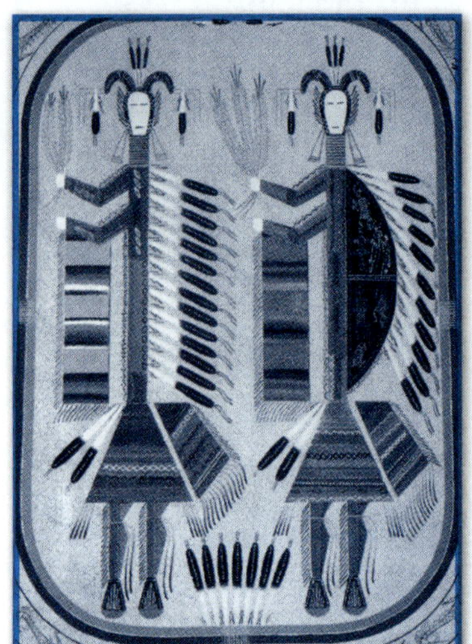

1. In sandpainting, an art still practiced by the Navajos and Pueblos of the American Southwest, designs are created of (**icons, enclaves**) representing animals, deities, and natural phenomena.

2. A theory that seems valid in the confines of a small family group may be proved useless when applied in the (**macrocosm, persiflage**) of society at large.

3. A truly great leader must possess both the inspiration of a visionary and the (**quizzical, pragmatic**) skills of an experienced politician.

4. They can't force you to do anything, but it is quite possible that they will be able to (**condescend, cozen**) you into actions against your best interests.

5. We exchanged agitated and (**quizzical, pragmatic**) looks after the customs agent instructed us to carry our luggage to a special table for a thorough investigation.

6. Our little group of would-be writers, painters, and musicians formed a(n) (**enclave, macrocosm**) of culture in what we considered a hostile world.

7. Because he sees life as a pattern of ambiguities and contradictions, he likes to express himself in the form of (**quizzical, pragmatic**) witticisms.

8. A(n) (**macrocosm, icon**) of urban Australia, the Sydney Opera House is a building of unique and masterful construction.

9. If you find those people so unpleasant, why do you (**cozen, condescend**) to associate with them?

10. It is a common mistake to assume that shrewdness in business affairs must be accompanied by extreme (**rapacity, enclave**).

11. We did drop a few objectionable words from the dialogue, but this does not justify the critic's claim that we (**cozened, bowdlerized**) the play.

12. The clash of wits between those two brilliant columnists was no mere (**persiflage, rapacity**), but an exchange of clever insults.

Completing the Sentence

Choose the word from the word bank that best completes each of the following sentences. Write the correct word or form of the word in the space provided.

bowdlerize	**cozen**	**icon**	**persiflage**	**quizzical**
condescend	**enclave**	**macrocosm**	**pragmatic**	**rapacity**

1. The stubborn old-timers who refused to sell their homes came to form a(n) ________________ of "natives" surrounded by "city people."

2. In attempting to make the novel acceptable to the general public, the editor so ________________ it that it lost its quality of stark realism.

3. Although we pride ourselves on the advance of civilization, the sad fact is that the ________________ of modern humanity has resulted in more destruction and suffering than ever before in history.

4. Playing on his vanity and his desire to be known as a "good guy," I tried to ________________ him into lending me his car.

5. What point is there in dwelling on unproven theories when the problem we are facing demands that we be as ________________ as possible?

6. He considers himself such a marvelous chess player that I'm surprised he would ________________ to sit down at the board with a beginner like me.

7. At the height of Beatlemania in the mid-1960s the Fab Four assumed the stature of pop ________________.

8. She thought of herself as a combination of Mark Twain and H. L. Mencken, but her attempts at "devastating ________________" were not very funny.

9. I would have welcomed any firm answer, no matter how unfavorable, but all that I got from her was a(n) ________________ smile.

10. His self-importance stems from his inability to appreciate the very minor part he plays in the ________________ of human affairs.

End Set A

Definitions

Note the spelling, pronunciation, part(s) of speech, and definition(s) of each of the following words. Then write the appropriate form of the word in the blank space in the illustrative sentence(s) following.

1. ancillary
(an′ sə ler ē)
(*adj.*) subordinate or supplementary
The aide serves in an ________________ position.

2. forte
(fôrt) *or* (fôr′ tā)
(*n.*) a person's strong point; what a person does best
Although I love listening to piano music, playing the instrument is not my ________________.

3. gratis
(gra′ tis)
(*adj.*) free; (*adv.*) without charge
The food provided was ________________.
During the filming, a local restaurant provided meals to the crew ________________.

4. interstice
(in tər′ stis)
(*n.*) a small, narrow space between things or parts of things
Once it slipped through the ________________ in the fence, the rabbit headed straight for the vegetables.

5. mountebank
(mau̇n′ tə baŋk)
(*n.*) a trickster or swindler; a charlatan
The ________________ who sold surefire remedies for every imaginable ailment was finally exposed.

6. paean
(pē′ ən)
(*n.*) a song of praise, joy, or triumph
The audience responded with a ________________ of exultation when the ceremony ended.

7. plethora
(pleth′ ə rə)
(*n.*) overfullness; superabundance; superfluity
The inquisitive journalists besieged the harried celebrity with a ________________ of personal questions.

8. schism
(siz′ əm) *or* (skiz′ əm)
(*n.*) a formal split within a religious organization; any division or separation of a group or organization into hostile factions
What began as a disagreement over a minor issue led to a bitter ________________ within the party.

9. therapeutic (ther ə pyü′ tik)
(*adj.*) having the power to heal or cure; beneficial
Many believe in the ________________ effects attributed to the waters of natural hot springs.

10. virtuoso (vər chü ō′ sō)
(*n.*) a brilliant performer; a person with masterly skill or technique; (*adj.*) masterly or brilliant
Franz Liszt was a piano ________________.
I was treated to a ________________ performance.

Using Context

*For each item, determine whether the **boldface** word from pages 42–43 makes sense in the context of the sentence. Circle the item numbers next to the six sentences in which the words are used correctly.*

1. There is nothing more **therapeutic** after a tough day than relaxing with a good book.

2. The crowd erupted in a **paean** of unbridled joy when the home team scored the winning goal right before the clock ran out.

3. The teacher asked us to write a summary of the **ancillary** plot—the one that was central to all the subplots in the drama.

4. The planets, moons, stars, suns, and galaxies all make up the vast **interstice** that we call the universe.

5. The **schism** that the two sides reached after weeks of negotiations was a relief to everyone involved.

6. It was apparent after only a few perfectly pitched notes from the singer that we were in the presence of a **virtuoso**.

7. She is known throughout our organization as a **mountebank**, a leader who is honest and forthright in all her dealings.

8. After I told the waiter that it was my mother's birthday, he brought over a cake and waved off the money I offered, saying the dessert was **gratis** on this special occasion.

9. The new parents were bombarded with a **plethora** of unsolicited advice when their baby was born.

10. "Cooking is not exactly my **forte**," I said as my friend noticed the pile of takeout menus on the kitchen counter.

Set B

*Select the **boldface** word that better completes each sentence. You might refer to the passage on pages 36–37 to see how most of these words are used in context. Note that the choices might be related forms of the Unit words.*

1. Many of the celebrated composers of classical pieces, including Mozart, were (**interstices, virtuosos**) long before they were even teenagers.

2. A political candidate who promises to solve all our social problems without ever mentioning higher taxes would certainly be dismissed as a (**mountebank, schism**).

3. After the great victory, his quiet and modest statements were far more impressive than the most effusive (**paean, interstice**) could have been.

4. In the great crises of life, you must depend basically on yourself; the help you get from others can only be (**therapeutic, ancillary**).

5. Her easygoing attitude and resilience, far from being weaknesses, proved to be her (**mountebank, forte**) in surviving during that trying period.

6. The sun left its mottled imprint on the wall as the rays filtered through the (**paeans, interstices**) of the iron grating.

7. The first (**schism, forte**) in the Communist world of the postwar era occurred in 1948, when Yugoslavia began in earnest to distance itself from the Soviet Union.

8. The introductory membership letter stated that the monthly magazine was delivered (**ancillary, gratis**); however, the membership fees were exorbitant.

9. Your (**virtuosity, mountebank**) as an orator may earn you votes, but it cannot make up for your lack of experience in and knowledge of public affairs.

10. In this situation, when I desperately needed material help, I was deluged with a(n) (**plethora, interstice**) of glib and gratuitous advice.

11. Though acupuncture has been practiced in Eastern medicine for centuries, its (**therapeutic, ancillary**) value has only recently been acknowledged in the West.

12. The dictum "There's no such thing as a free lunch" means that nothing worthwhile in life comes to us (**forte, gratis**).

Completing the Sentence

Choose the word from the word bank that best completes each of the following sentences. Write the correct word or form of the word in the space provided.

ancillary	**gratis**	**mountebank**	**plethora**	**therapeutic**
forte	**interstice**	**paean**	**schism**	**virtuoso**

1. My classmates selected me to address the community affairs committee because public speaking is a(n) ____________________ of mine.

2. The "minor difference of opinion" developed into a(n) ____________________ that split the political party into two opposing factions.

3. A good laugh invariably makes me feel better; I honestly believe that it has a(n) ____________________ effect on my disposition.

4. To know if the promises are those of a(n) ____________________ consider whether they seem too good to be true.

5. To promote circulation, the publisher offered to throw in home delivery ____________________ for new subscribers to the Sunday edition.

6. The coach used diagrams to show our receivers how to slip through the ____________________ in our opponent's zone pass coverage.

7. When the soldiers realized that they had defeated the far more numerous enemy, their cheers rose in a great ____________________ of jubilation and victory.

8. Once the advance and royalties were settled, the publisher and agent negotiated ____________________ rights to be covered in the author's contract.

9. When she neatly faked out the guard, pivoted, and drove in for a layup, I realized that I was seeing a true ____________________ on the basketball court.

10. The situation is growing worse because there is a(n) ____________________ of good intentions but a dearth of common sense and willingness to work hard.

End Set B

Choose the word or form of the word from this Unit that is the same or most nearly the same in meaning as the ***boldface*** *word or expression in the phrase. Write that word on the line. Use a dictionary if necessary.*

1. urges writers to **censor** their screenplays ______________
2. participated in the witty **repartee** ______________
3. belonging to a **subsidiary** organization ______________
4. to **dupe** out of a fortune ______________
5. **deign** to respond to the question ______________
6. a writers' **retreat** in the woods ______________
7. a widely known **symbol** of freedom ______________
8. offered a **hymn** of praise ______________
9. an outgrowth of weeds in the **gap** in the walls ______________
10. a **logical** way of thinking ______________
11. received a **surfeit** of gifts ______________
12. confused by the **peculiar** remark ______________
13. conned by an **impostor** ______________
14. awed by the gifts of the young **master** ______________
15. the **curative** benefits of mineral water ______________

Antonyms

Choose the word or form of the word from this Unit that is most nearly opposite in meaning to the ***boldface*** *word or expression in the phrase. Write that word on the line. Use a dictionary if necessary.*

1. with a **generosity** heretofore unseen ______________
2. the workers formed a **united front** ______________
3. acquired the stroller **for a price** ______________
4. a **microcosm** of the universe ______________
5. an **ineptness** for learning new languages ______________

Writing: Words in Action

Research a recent, infamous Ponzi scheme. Compare how the more modern scheme is similar to and different from the original Ponzi scheme. Write an essay in which you categorize your findings. Use at least three details from the passage (pages 36–37) and three or more words from this Unit.

Vocabulary in Context

Some of the words you have studied in this Unit appear in ***boldface*** *type. Read the passage below, and then circle the letter of the correct answer for each word as it is used in context.*

Serge Alexandre "Sasha" Stavisky (1886–1934) was the son of Ukrainian immigrants who settled in Paris in 1890. His father was a dentist. His mother, like her son, was a dreamer. Stavisky was twelve years old when he caused an irreparable **schism** between his parents by stealing the gold from which his father made fillings and crowns. "If Sasha steals," said his mother, "it's only because he needs money." It is better to omit his father's reply than to **bowdlerize** it. Stavisky would always need money, and he always stole more than he needed.

Stavisky's career was a **paean** to criminal invention. When he discovered a theatre on the Champs d'Élysées that was only open in winter, he found investors for an imaginary summer season, and he invented a soup factory around an imaginary soup so exquisite that investors would make a fortune.

With his charisma, good looks, and **rapacity**, things that other people had to pay for came to Stavisky **gratis**. Inevitably, he found his way into the Paris social elite. Government ministers and grand financiers became discreetly aware of an irresistible opportunity: the lost Crown Jewels of the Empress of Prussia had somehow turned up in a municipal pawnshop in Bayonne, in southwest France, and the enterprising pawnshop manager was putting them up as collateral in an irresistible bond offering. It was a **virtuoso** fraud. Many unsuspecting investors took the bait, and Stavisky raised hundreds of millions of francs. He believed that by implicating such powerful people, he had made himself immune to prosecution. He was not, however, bulletproof.

---

1. What is the meaning of **schism** as it is used in paragraph 1?
a. disagreement
b. accord
c. split
d. obstacle

2. What is the meaning of **bowdlerize** in the context of the passage?
a. ignore
b. emphasize
c. censor
d. praise

3. In paragraph 2, what does **paean** suggest about Stavisky's career?
a. It was triumphant.
b. It was tragic.
c. It was committed.
d. It was heroic.

4. In paragraph 3, what does the word **rapacity** suggest about Stavisky?
a. He was plausible.
b. He was insatiable.
c. He was audacious.
d. He was unbelievable.

5. What does **gratis** most likely mean as it is used in paragraph 3?
a. cheap
b. honorably
c. free of charge
d. out of nowhere

6. What characteristic is suggested by **virtuoso** in paragraph 3?
a. dishonesty
b. persistence
c. candor
d. expert

Vocabulary for Comprehension

Part 1

*Read this passage, which contains words in **boldface** that appear in Units 1–3. Then choose the best answer to each question based on what is stated or implied in the passage. You may refer to the passage as often as necessary.*

Questions 1–10 are based on the following passage.

In the seventeenth century, many of the settlers in New England had attended the British universities of Cambridge and Oxford and considered education to be indispensable. Their belief in university education, and the Puritans' belief in educated clergy and civil leaders, led to the establishment in Massachusetts of Harvard College in 1636. Harvard's initial curriculum prepared men to become ministers, which did not appeal to **pragmatic** men training for secular jobs. Between 1636 and 1775, religion was the basis for eight other colleges, including Columbia in New York and the College of William and Mary in Virginia. These other institutions focused on proper conduct, character development, and civic virtue. Prior to 1776, these colonial colleges with their limited scope were accessible only to the top of the socioeconomic **hierarchy**.

In 1789, there was a movement toward specialized curriculum, even as college enrollments expanded and universities moved west. Small liberal arts schools were more **laissez-faire** in their approach to curriculum; although modeled on the original nine colonial schools, they were less sectarian and developed new courses. For example, Oberlin College in Ohio was the first school in the U.S. to establish a Conservatory of Music to prepare future **virtuosos** to perform **paeans** that they had composed. College became accessible for the middle class.

Colleges for women soon followed to prepare young women for their societally acceptable **purview** of career fields. New England schools like Mount Holyoke, Vassar, Wesleyan, Smith, and Wellesley based their curriculum on the men's colleges, but also taught social work, home economics, music, art, childcare, and elementary education. In 1870, women's colleges had a **minuscule** effect on society as less than one percent of women attended college. By 1890, this number increased to 2.5 percent.

The Morrill Act of 1862 established a land-grant program whereby states received the profits from the sale of western land if it was used to establish agricultural, mechanical, and military science institutions. Later, one provision of the "Second Morrill Act" of 1890 helped formerly Confederate states either remove race as a criterion for admissions or establish separate land-grant institutions for African American students. Seventy colleges were formed from this act, including many of today's historically black colleges and universities. Prominent African American college leaders were **polarized** over the curriculum the schools would offer. Booker T. Washington, who founded Tuskegee in 1881, advocated for practical education in business trades, while W.E.B. DuBois of Atlanta University supported a more traditional education.

No longer just a **chimerical** aspiration, 20.4 million students attended U.S. colleges and universities in 2016. American higher education was originally designed to prepare students for the workforce and to have an educated population, and that is still the mission in the 4,140 institutions of higher education In the U.S. today.

1. What is the main idea of the first paragraph?
   A) The first university was founded to educate men for all career fields.
   B) Harvard College was established in 1636 by educated New Englanders.
   C) Religion was a guiding factor in establishing the first colonial schools.
   D) Men planning to work in secular fields could choose any colonial college.

2. According to the passage, liberal arts schools were designed in order to
   A) respond to students who wanted a more specialized curriculum.
   B) enroll students who could not afford to attend the colonial colleges.
   C) make music a required course of study for all students.
   D) offer a traditional colonial college curriculum to more students.

3. As it is used in line 26, the word "laissez-faire" means
   A) a philosophy of nonintervention.
   B) a philosophy of religious instruction.
   C) a philosophy of adherence to tradition.
   D) a philosophy of discipline and rules.

4. As it is used in line 33, the word "virtuosos" means
   A) competent beginners.
   B) inquisitive participants.
   C) brilliant performers.
   D) experimental dilettantes.

5. According to the passage, what was one direct result of the Morrill Act of 1862?
   A) Women's colleges were founded.
   B) The land-grant program established agricultural, mechanical, and military science institutions.
   C) The number of women attending college jumped to 2.5 percent in 1890.
   D) Seventy land-grant colleges were created, including several historically black colleges and universities.

6. The purpose of the third and fourth paragraphs (lines 36–69) is to
   A) debate the benefits of the Morrill Acts of 1862 and 1890.
   B) explore the creation of colleges for women and African Americans.
   C) explain the ideological divide between Booker T. Washington and W.E.B. DuBois.
   D) list the available courses in women's colleges and historically black colleges.

7. As it is used in line 64, the word "polarized" means
   A) concentrated about opposing positions.
   B) settled a debate between two groups.
   C) provided information from two sources.
   D) explored two differing opinions.

8. It can reasonably be inferred that the author would agree with which statement?
   A) The original colonial colleges did not prepare men to serve in the clergy.
   B) The initial mission of college education has changed.
   C) Modern colleges and universities no longer prepare students for the workforce.
   D) More students have a college education now than in the seventeenth century.

9. Which choice provides the best evidence for the answer to the previous question?
   A) Lines 9–12 ("Harvard's … secular jobs")
   B) Lines 36–38 ("Colleges … fields")
   C) Lines 70–73 ("No longer … in 2016")
   D) Lines 73–78 ("American … today")

10. What is the main idea of the passage?
   A) The model of the colonial colleges paved the way for modern higher education in the United States.
   B) Women's colleges and historically black colleges and universities are important parts of U.S. higher education.
   C) Liberal arts schools and land-grant institutions enabled many students to attain a college degree.
   D) The Morrill Acts were the most important pieces of legislation affecting U. S. colleges and universities.

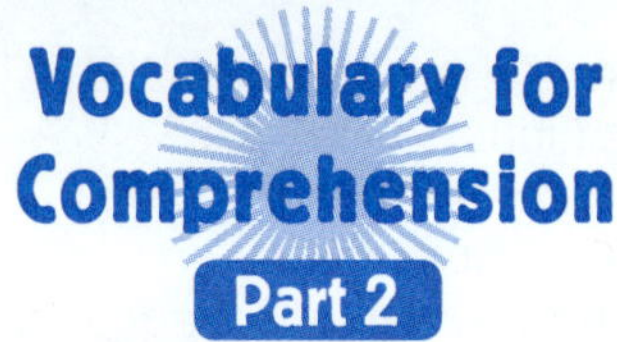

Vocabulary for Comprehension Part 2

*Read this passage, which contains words in **boldface** that appear in Units 1–3. Then choose the best answer to each question based on what is stated or implied in the passage. You may refer to the passage as often as necessary.*

Questions 1–10 are based on the following passage.

On August 14, 1935, in the middle of the Great Depression, Franklin D. Roosevelt signed the Social Security Act of 1935 into law. Roosevelt was **sanguine** that certain provisions of this act would help the United States during the most catastrophic economic collapse in world history. Roosevelt was no **poltroon** in this situation; he confronted the Great Depression with solutions rather than fear. Roosevelt convened a cabinet-level group called the Committee on Economic Security, and this committee labored for one year on the act. Although many debate the context for the Social Security Act of 1935, Frances Perkins, the secretary of labor during the Roosevelt administration and chair of the Committee on Economic Security, claimed that "the real roots of the Social Security Act were in the Great Depression of 1929. Nothing else would have bumped the American people into a social security system except something so shocking, so terrifying, as that depression."

The Social Security Act of 1935 provided income security in the forms of old-age insurance and unemployment insurance programs as well as the Aid to Families with Dependent Children program; all of these programs were under the **aegis** of the federal government. In addition, the act provided federal assistance for means-tested old-age programs run by individual states. The Great Depression was the catalyst for many significant parts of the Social Security Act of 1935; namely, unemployment insurance and means-tested welfare programs to benefit those in immediate need of assistance.

There have been various amendments and **quasi** changes to the Social Security Act of 1935; many of which have expanded coverage and brought more workers into the Social Security system. In 1939, an amendment created dependent benefits and survivor benefits, which were added to the retirement benefits in the original legislation. One of the most significant developments to Social Security was the creation of the Medicare program in 1965. Medicare provides health care coverage and **therapeutic** treatment to people in need who are 65 or older. Some low-income recipients of Medicare may receive healthcare **gratis**.

Scholars consider Social Security to be the most successful government social insurance program in U.S. history. Statistics are available that provide some **verisimilitude** for this statement. By 2008, the Social Security program has paid out more than $11 trillion to almost 213 million people. In addition, Social Security has reduced poverty among the elderly from 35 percent in 1959 to less than 10 percent in 2008. A **plethora** of senior citizens depends on Medicare: one-third of seniors depend on Social Security for 90 percent or more of their retirement income, and two-thirds depend on it for the majority of their income. Moreover, an estimated 49,435,610 people received health coverage through a Medicare program in 2014. Though it may seem like the provisions of the original act are now **effete**, many underlying principles of

Roosevelt's act are reflected in current Social Security programs. This fact is proof that an act that was signed into law during the Great Depression has had widespread benefits for countless Americans for decades.

1. The purpose of the first paragraph is
- **A)** to explain the incidents that led to the Great Depression.
- **B)** to describe the composition of the Committee on Economic Security.
- **C)** to give Frances Perkins's background.
- **D)** to outline the events that precipitated the Social Security Act of 1935.

2. As it is used in line 4, "sanguine" most nearly means
- **A)** having a naturally optimistic outlook.
- **B)** feigning confidence in front of others.
- **C)** strategizing in difficult situations.
- **D)** presenting claims without evidence.

3. The author quotes Frances Perkins in lines 19–25 in order to
- **A)** prove why Roosevelt chose her to chair the Committee on Economic Security.
- **B)** support the claim that the Depression caused the Social Security Act of 1935.
- **C)** explain why the Committee on Economic Security worked for a year on the act.
- **D)** state facts about why Perkins advocated for the Social Security Act of 1935.

4. What is the main idea of the second paragraph (lines 26–41)?
- **A)** The Social Security Act of 1935 provided income security and means-tested old-age and welfare programs.
- **B)** The Social Security Act of 1935 only provided benefits that immediately helped people during the Great Depression.
- **C)** The federal government sponsored old-age insurance and Aid to Families with Dependent Children programs.
- **D)** Individual states managed old-age programs with federal assistance.

5. According to the passages, the most significant amendment to the Social Security Act of 1935 is the
- **A)** expansion of coverage to bring more workers into the system.
- **B)** extension of retirement benefits to dependents and survivors.
- **C)** formation of the Medicare program.
- **D)** establishment of old-age and unemployment insurance programs.

6. Which choice provides the best evidence for the answer to the previous question?
- **A)** Lines 26–31("The Social … program")
- **B)** Lines 42–46 ("There have … system")
- **C)** Lines 46–50 ("In 1939 … legislation")
- **D)** Lines 50–53 ("One of … in 1965")

7. As it is used in line 57, "gratis" most nearly means
- **A)** without risk.
- **B)** without charge.
- **C)** without forms.
- **D)** without precedent.

8. According to the passage, the Social Security Act of 1935 has
- **A)** many outdated provisions.
- **B)** positively affected many American lives.
- **C)** been entirely overhauled in recent times.
- **D)** not kept up with modern advancements.

9. As it is used in line 78, "effete" most nearly means
- **A)** ineffective.
- **B)** important.
- **C)** out-of-date.
- **D)** insignificant.

10. The main idea of the passage is
- **A)** the Depression spawned the Social Security Act, which still provides aid.
- **B)** the Social Security Act was Roosevelt's most significant legislation.
- **C)** despite the flaws in Social Security, it has helped people since 1935.
- **D)** even though Social Security helps people, it comes at a staggering cost.

From the word bank below, choose the word that has the same or nearly the same meaning as the ***boldface*** *word in each sentence and write it on the line. You will not use all of the words.*

adjunct	**condescend**	**gratis**	**morass**
aegis	**effete**	**indigenous**	**quasi**
ancillary	**exegesis**	**laissez-faire**	**paternalism**
claque	**forte**	**lachrymose**	**verisimilitude**

1. Thanks to a generous donation from local businesses, tickets for the dance performance were **free** for all students. ____________

2. Had we known that we would have to wade through a **bog**, we would have worn rubber boots instead of our leather hiking boots. ____________

3. Someone who is constantly surrounded by a **fan club** is unlikely to know the real truth about what others think of him or her. ____________

4. A good teacher knows how to explain a difficult concept in a way that does not **talk down** to introductory-level students. ____________

5. Because we are such big baseball fans, the opening day of the season has become a **kind of** holiday in our home. ____________

6. This **auxiliary** set of exercises offers extra practice for each chapter of the chemistry textbook. ____________

7. In *Alice in Wonderland*, the Mock Turtle is a **tearful** character who wipes his eyes before sadly singing a very odd song. ____________

8. If writing short, catchy songs is your **specialty**, you might want to consider a career in radio and television advertising. ____________

9. The university's administration made an effort to show concern for student welfare while at the same time trying not to project an attitude of overprotectiveness and **fatherliness**. ____________

10. The scholar spent many years traveling around the country in order to collect and record examples of **homegrown** songs. ____________

11. The 17th-century village was restored with such **authenticity** that visitors felt as though they were stepping back in time. ____________

12. Rich and complex works such as *Hamlet* and *Moby-Dick* offer limitless opportunities for **analysis**. ____________

Two-Word Completions

Select the pair of words that best completes the meaning of each of the following sentences.

1. The company's CEO was ______________ of the dire economic outlook and understood, at once, that he would soon be faced with ______________ decisions that would either affect executive payrolls or the benefits currently enjoyed by all employees.

a. caterwauled … oblivious
b. bowdlerized … bibulous
c. apprised … noisome
d. obfuscated … minuscule

2. Your composition is so full of ______________, malapropisms, and general gobbledygook that I suggest you study a grammar book, a ______________, and a style manual before you ever again put pen to paper.

a. persiflage … plethora
b. solecisms … lexicon
c. raillery … microcosm
d. interstices … liturgy

3. The social structure of the South before the Civil War was rigidly ______________, with the gentleman planter at the summit of the edifice and the enslaved at its base. ______________ notions of caste discouraged whites from moving freely within the system, and the "peculiar institution" denied blacks any mobility whatsoever.

a. hierarchical … Hidebound
b. pragmatic … Polarized
c. chimerical … Obfuscated
d. therapeutic … Cozened

4. At the park, the small child's ______________, and yet exuberant, facial expressions revealed that the boy was intrigued and thrilled by the playground equipment. He was positively ______________ to his mother's entreaties to climb into his stroller and return home.

a. quizzical … oblivious
b. iconic … rapacious
c. supine … chimerical
d. noisome … ribald

5. During the Middle Ages, controversy about some point of doctrine ______________ ecclesiastical opinion and produced a temporary ______________ in the church.

a. bowdlerized … fait accompli
b. obfuscated … enclave
c. deracinated … macrocosm
d. polarized … schism

6. As the detachment of knights galloped over the crest of the hill, it collided with a column of enemy foot soldiers moving up the other side. In the brief but bloody ______________ that ensued, two of the king's most prominent ______________ lost their lives.

a. purview … mountebanks
b. melee … vassals
c. vignette … bellwethers
d. schism … proselytes

7. The television series was about two federal agents whose job was to ______________ government information about contact with aliens and other ______________ forms of life.

a. cozen … quizzical
b. apprise… lachrymose
c. caterwaul … noisome
d. obfuscate … chimerical

WORD STUDY

In the biographical sketch “Fascinating Rhythm: The Life of George Gershwin” (see pages 12–13), the writer notes that one of Gershwin’s first hits, performed by Al Jolson, “took the country by storm” and sold more than two million records.

“Take by storm” is an idiom. An **idiom** is a group of words with a meaning different from the literal meanings of each word. For example, “took the country by storm” in the unit opener means that the recorded song was suddenly very successful in the United States. Because the meanings of idioms are sometimes subtle or unexpected, it is important to learn them or look them up in a dictionary.

Choosing the Right Idiom

*Read each sentence. Use context clues to figure out the meaning of each idiom in **boldface** print. Then write the letter of the definition for the idiom in the sentence.*

1. This summer she planted her new garden **by fits and starts**; thus, she will have no yield. ______
2. As full-time college students, they **live from hand to mouth** and have very few possessions. ______
3. Edwyn **hails from** Wales, but he has been living in the United States for many years now. ______
4. The investigation had **gotten nowhere fast** and so the police chief decided to hire new detectives. ______
5. The municipality will **come into line** with state and federal governments and will raise taxes. ______
6. Mr. Perez has been entirely **out of commission** since he fractured a bone in his ankle. ______
7. I suspect my father is **in a stew** about the grass that isn’t mowed and recycling that isn’t sorted. ______
8. If our costs are **cut to the bone**, we should have enough reserves for an emergency. ______
9. Isn’t he a bit too **long in the tooth** to participate in a triathlon? ______
10. Give Liz **a wide berth** today—she slept only two hours last night and then lost her cell phone. ______

a. unable to function normally
b. not made progress
c. irregularly
d. upset
e. old
f. stay far away from
g. live on little money
h. comes from originally
i. conform
j. reduced severely

Classical Roots

sem, simil, simul—like; together; at the same time

This root appears in **verisimilitude** (page 31), which means "the appearance of being true." Some other words based on the same root are listed below.

assemblage	**disassemble**	**simile**	**simulation**
assimilation	**resemblance**	**simulacrum**	**simulcast**

From the list of words above, choose the one that corresponds to each of the brief definitions below. Write the word in the blank space in the illustrative sentence below the definition. Use an online or print dictionary if necessary.

1. the act or process of taking in or absorbing; the state of being absorbed
The brain is uniquely designed for constant ____________________ of knowledge.

2. to broadcast over radio and television at the same time
She had some friends over to enjoy the ____________________ of the rock concert.

3. a comparison, introduced by *like* or *as*; an analogy
A nonfiction essay on a dreary topic can be enlivened by poetic use of ____________________.

4. a collection of people or things; a gathering
The most experienced journalists were sent to cover the annual ____________________ of notables in the field of medical research.

5. to take apart
After the science fair, it took the exhibitors and maintenance crew several hours to fully ____________________ the many displays and booths.

6. a similarity in form or appearance; a likeness
Grandma glows over the strong family ____________________ she already sees in her newborn grandson.

7. an image or representation of something; an unreal or superficial semblance
The first 1950s television sitcoms presented a cheery ____________________ of family happiness.

8. the act or process of taking on the appearance or form of something; a feigning or pretending
Although the children were unable to keep the secret from their mother, she put on a convincing ____________________ of surprise at the presentation of their gift.

*Read the following passage, taking note of the **boldface** words and their contexts. These words are among those you will be studying in Unit 4. It may help you to complete the exercises in this Unit if you refer to the way the words are used below.*

Putting Social Media in Perspective

<Speech>

Rhiannon Marsh, Washington, DC, November 1, 2012

Distinguished guests and fellow media enthusiasts, I am honored to speak with you today at this first-ever Modern Media Forum.

When the Philippine Congress voted to ignore evidence that threatened to secure the impeachment of the Philippine president in 2001, angry Filipinos poured into the streets to protest. That protest was arranged, in part, by text messages exchanged among ordinary citizens, perhaps a million of whom gathered in the capital. In response to the demonstration, the Congress immediately performed a **volte-face**, deciding to put the crucial evidence in play, and the president was forced to resign.

When Ukrainian elections were tainted by suspicions of fraud in 2004, pro-democracy activists in that country went online. The **obloquies** they posted on Internet forums publicized their leaders' **bilious** corruption, helping to spread the word and rouse the **hoi polloi**. With the movement gathering steam, activists and angry citizens used Internet forums and text messages to coordinate mass protests. As a result of these protests, a revote was called and a new president was elected.

Above: Filipinos celebrate their new president after street protests led to the ouster of Joseph Estrada.

Left: Benjamin Franklin operates a printing press.

Increasingly, protesters around the world employ the whole **gamut** of social media tools, including microblogging, social networking, and video-sharing sites, to spread news and organize action. Political **pundits**, excited by the trend, have rushed to declare that social media tools are ushering in a new era of revolution against oppressive regimes. What

Above: Ukrainians celebrate the first anniversary of the Orange Revolution street protests that led to a change of president.

Below: A protest in Tahrir Square, Cairo

commentators' obsession with the role of social media in the popular movements of our new century would be **risible**, were it not for the fact that the noise they make distracts our public discourse from more important themes. In recent months, as millions throughout the Arab world have taken to the streets to shout down their oppressors and demand democracy, too much American ink has been spilled commenting on the protesters' use of cell phones and social networking utilities.

To be fair, not every remark on the subject deserves to be treated as **folderol.** Social media's greatest impact is that they enable ordinary citizens to reach wide audiences instantly. These tools are democratizing communication, putting the power of publication in the hands of the many. But while this welcome trend is noteworthy, we should not let it distract us from the subject that most deserves our attention: the spread of democracy itself.

should we make of these pundits' **divinations**? Do social media really give the world's masses an unprecedented potential to effect political change, or is the excitement about social media's role in twenty-first-century protests merely a **corollary** of the **pundits' affinity** for exaggeration?

No great **lucubration** is required to answer the question. While the technology employed by protesters today is **symptomatic** of our times, the basic **parameters** that cause mass protests, and that determine their success or failure, remain unchanged. The printing press was employed by activists of the American Revolution. Fax machines helped direct the revolutions in Eastern Europe in 1989. Where there's a will, there's a way. When corruption, oppression, and a dearth of economic opportunity combine to wake the **ineffable** spirit of protest in a nation, the people use whatever means are available to express their discontent. When a people rise up to demand democracy, it is the fact of their courage in the face of oppression that deserves our attention, their feats of **derring-do** both great and small, the purpose of their movement, its causes and its course. What tools they use is an inessential matter, an accident of history. Political

Audio

For iWords and audio passages, go to SadlierConnect.com.

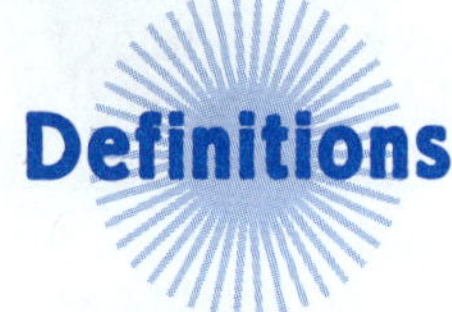

Definitions

Note the spelling, pronunciation, part(s) of speech, and definition(s) of each of the following words. Then write the appropriate form of the word in the blank space in the illustrative sentence(s) following.

1. bilious (bil' yəs)
(*adj.*) peevish or irritable; sickeningly unpleasant
The room was painted a ____________________ shade of green.

2. cognate (kog' nāt)
(*adj.*) closely related in origin, essential nature, or function; (*n.*) such a person or thing
____________________ languages, such as Spanish, Italian, and French, share a common root.
When I studied Latin, I learned that the words *pater* and *father* are ____________________.

3. cul-de-sac (kəl' də sak)
(*n.*) a blind alley or dead-end street; any situation in which further progress is impossible; an impasse
Much to their dismay, the once-optimistic negotiators found themselves in a hopeless ____________________.

4. divination (div ə nā' shən)
(*n.*) the art or act of predicting the future or discovering hidden knowledge
Claiming skill in ____________________, the fortune teller took my money and then told me what my future held.

5. folderol (fol' də rol)
(*n.*) foolish talk, ideas, or procedures; nonsense; a trifle
Right from the outset, the sergeant informed her troops that she would not tolerate any ____________________.

6. hoi polloi (hoi pə loi')
(*n.*) the common people, the masses
By catering to the ____________________, the studio was able to make one very successful movie after another.

7. mnemonic (ni mon' ik)
(*adj.*) relating to or designed to assist the memory; (*n.*) a device to aid the memory
"Please Excuse My Dear Aunt Sally" is a ____________________ device used to remember the order of mathematical operations.
The ____________________ HOMES can help people to recall the names of the Great Lakes.

8. obloquy (ob' lə kwē)
(*n.*) public abuse indicating strong disapproval or censure; the disgrace resulting from such treatment
The press heaped ____________________ on the head of the offending official.

9. pundit (pən′ dit) — (*n.*) a learned person; one who gives authoritative opinions

A renowned ________________ of the theater, the critic had the power to affect a show's success.

10. symptomatic (simp tə mat′ ik) — (*adj.*) typical or characteristic; being or concerned with a symptom of a disease

According to certain sociologists, vulgarity and indulgence are ________________ of a nation's decline.

Using Context

*For each item, determine whether the **boldface** word from pages 58–59 makes sense in the context of the sentence. Circle the item numbers next to the six sentences in which the words are used correctly.*

1. It is generally safe for children to play in this **cul-de-sac** because there is very little traffic here.
2. I should have known that a weekend trip with you was going to be unpleasant after spending one day in your **bilious** presence!
3. "Leaflets three—let it be" is a **mnemonic** that helps people avoid poison ivy plants, which always have clusters of three leaves.
4. Many dog owners feel that their pets are remarkably **symptomatic;** they simply seem to have an innate understanding of human emotions.
5. The English word *blue* and the French word *bleu* are **cognates**, and so are the English word *clear* and the Spanish word *claro*.
6. The information and **folderol** that we gathered from our two-year research program were extremely useful.
7. In the satirical comedy, a snobbish aristocrat loses all of his money and property and suddenly finds himself having to earn a living among the **hoi polloi**.
8. The mayor delivered a moving **obloquy** at the funeral of her longtime aide.
9. The ability to make good decisions and plan well for the future requires no **divination**; rather, it develops when we learn from our experience.
10. The hikers found themselves in a **pundit** and agreed that they had no choice but to turn around and return to camp.

Set A

*Select the **boldface** word that better completes each sentence. You might refer to the passage on pages 56–57 to see how most of these words are used in context. Note that the choices might be related forms of the Unit words.*

1. The devastating stock market crash of 1929 surprised not only laymen, but Wall Street (**cognates, pundits**) as well.

2. We found it more difficult to master the (**mnemonic, obloquy**) than it would have been to memorize the material to which it was keyed.

3. I knew that if I ran for public office, I would be exposed to severe criticism, but I never expected such a flood of (**obloquy, divination**).

4. Your irresponsible behavior has finally caught up with you; you are in a (**cul-de-sac, hoi polloi**) from which it will be all but impossible to extricate yourself.

5. Somehow the athlete prevailed over the (**obloquy, folderol**) resulting from the highly publicized—and emotionally charged—trial of her family member.

6. No student of anthropology can fail to recognize the (**cognate, bilious**) elements in the cultures of societies which seem to be vastly different from one another.

7. Those remarkably accurate predictions were based not on (**folderol, divination**) but on insight into human nature and the objective elements in the situation.

8. The advice that they offered us with such pretentious solemnity turned out to be nothing more than platitudes and (**folderol, hoi polloi**).

9. You have had many difficulties in life, but you are helping no one by behaving in such a (**bilious, cognate**) manner.

10. Is your repeated use of the expression (**cul-de-sac, hoi polloi**) supposed to convey the idea that you are not one of the people?

11. Many sociologists believe that the high divorce rate in the United States is (**symptomatic, cognate**) of basic strains and flaws in our social structure.

12. The study of (**obloquies, cognates**) helped me perform well in the vocabulary portion of the standardized test because many English words are related to Greek and Latin words.

Completing the Sentence

Choose the word from the word bank that best completes each of the following sentences. Write the correct word or form of the word in the space provided.

bilious	**cul-de-sac**	**folderol**	**mnemonic**	**pundit**
cognate	**divination**	**hoi polloi**	**obloquy**	**symptomatic**

1. This short sentence will serve as a(n) ____________________ to help you remember the names of the first eight Presidents: "*W*ill *A J*olly *M*an *M*ake *A J*olly *V*isitor?"

2. In reading a passage in French, I can often guess the meanings of words I have never seen before because they are recognizable ____________________ of familiar English words.

3. Is our blind faith in computerized analysis any different in its essentials from the belief of so-called primitive peoples in ____________________?

4. Foreign visitors sometimes dismiss our national political conventions as mere ____________________ because of all the surface pageantry.

5. The ____________________ tenor of the remarks that they offered to us as "constructive criticism" betrayed just how sorely they envied our success.

6. No sooner did the press conference end than the network correspondent turned to a group of political ____________________ for an instant analysis.

7. The lecturer said that the soaring crime statistics are ____________________ of a society in which traditional values and standards are breaking down.

8. I know that they deserve to be condemned, but I can't bring myself to heap ____________________ on them when they are in such a state of disgrace.

9. Having been maneuvered into a(n) ____________________, the retreating troops could do nothing but turn and fight a battle for survival against superior forces.

10. In a truly democratic society, there are no sharp differences in status and privilege between self-styled aristocrats and the ____________________.

End Set A

Definitions

Note the spelling, pronunciation, part(s) of speech, and definition(s) of each of the following words. Then write the appropriate form of the word in the blank space in the illustrative sentence(s) following.

1. affinity
(ə fin′ ə te)
(*n.*) a natural attraction to a person, thing, or activity; a relationship, connection

The mysterious ________________ between the two leaders could not be explained.

2. corollary
(kôr′ ə ler ē)
(*n.*) a proposition that follows from one already proven; a natural consequence or result; (*adj.*) resultant or consequent

Learning the axiom and its ________________ was no simple matter.

The ________________ effects of today's findings remain to be seen.

3. derring-do
(der′ iŋ dü)
(*n.*) valor or heroism; daring deeds or exploits (often used to poke fun at false heroics)

Breathtaking feats of ________________ are all in a day's work for a Hollywood stuntperson.

4. elixir
(i lik′ sər)
(*n.*) a potion once thought capable of curing all ills and maintaining life indefinitely; a panacea; a sweet liquid used as a vehicle in medicines

Allegedly, the explorer Ponce de León spent years searching for the ________________ of eternal life.

5. gamut
(gam′ ət)
(*n.*) an entire range or series

The reviews of the newest Broadway musical extravaganza ran the ________________ from praise to scorn.

6. ineffable
(in ef′ ə bəl)
(*adj.*) not expressible in words; too great or too sacred to be uttered

The ________________ joy of parenthood is the subject of a psychologist's new bestseller.

7. lucubration
(lü ky brā′ shən)
(*n.*) laborious study or thought, especially at night; the result of such work

The scientist's ________________ took place after midnight, secretly, in the quiet of the laboratory.

8. parameter
(pə ram′ ə tər)
(*n.*) a determining or characteristic element; a factor that shapes the total outcome; a limit, boundary

The committee analyzed the ________________ of the nation's military potential.

9. risible
(riz′ ə bəl)

(*adj.*) pertaining to laughter; able or inclined to laugh; laughable

All in the crowd, not just the children, were delighted by the ________________ antics of the clowns.

10. volte-face
(volt fäs′)

(*n.*) an about-face; a complete reversal

The prosecution's witness's testimony amounted to a completely unexpected ________________.

For each item, determine whether the ***boldface*** *word from pages 62–63 makes sense in the context of the sentence. Circle the item numbers next to the six sentences in which the words are used correctly.*

1. His **affinity** for talking to people and helping them to make decisions led to a career as a high school guidance counselor.
2. The Department of Transportation announced the construction of an interstate highway that will serve as the primary **corollary** through this region of the country.
3. Everyone praised the firefighters for their **derring-do** after they managed to rescue all the people and animals from the burning building and extinguish the last of the flames.
4. She is a person of integrity and stability who approaches every challenging situation with a complete **volte-face**.
5. My grandmother's soup never fails to make me feel better when I'm sick, leading me to believe that it must be some sort of **elixir**.
6. The reporter's **lucubration** during his investigation of the corporation paid off; he uncovered fraud and corruption that became front-page news.
7. In speech class, our next assignment is to give a descriptive, **ineffable** account of what we did over winter break.
8. Must every meeting of our group become so **risible** and fraught with conflict?
9. Lack of sleep usually causes me to experience the full **gamut** of emotions in a single day, and my changing moods baffle my friends.
10. Entry-level employees may find themselves doing tasks outside the **parameter** of their job description to gain experience.

Set B

Choosing the Right Word

*Select the **boldface** word that better completes each sentence. You might refer to the passage on pages 56–57 to see how most of these words are used in context. Note that the choices might be related forms of the Unit words.*

1. Only a supreme actor could express so eloquently the (**risible, ineffable**) quality of the "thoughts that do often lie too deep for tears."

2. We expect to see politicians modify their points of view from time to time, but a sudden, unexpected (**lucubration, volte-face**) by a candidate is more than we can tolerate.

3. In the *Inferno*, Dante introduces personages from history and mythology to portray the full (**gamut, elixir**) of human folly and wickedness.

4. The pithy comments of that brilliant and delightful woman were a(n) (**elixir, parameter**) that we found extraordinarily exhilarating.

5. Henry had an excellent chance to make an honorable career for himself, but he seemed to have a fatal (**affinity, corollary**) for easy money and shady deals.

6. The (**risible, corollary**) effect of the oil spill was a decline in fish population.

7. It is little short of incredible that all their copious (**lucubrations, corollaries**) have brought forth that tiny mouse of an idea.

8. It may seem to be a paradox, but I believe it is true that only a basically serious person can fully appreciate the (**risible, ineffable**) factors in life.

9. The first thing we must do is establish the (**parameters, lucubrations**) of the problem, so that we can begin to think in terms of a practical solution.

10. I have listened to them state that the present situation is hopeless, but I am unwilling to accept the (**gamut, corollary**) that the only course open to us is surrender.

11. It was a test of endurance, to be polite, to pour through the scholar's (**derring-do, lucubrations**) on the origin of the maypole.

12. In an age of genocide, atomic weapons, and threats of ecological disaster, do you really expect a sensible person to be fascinated by such romantic tales of (**parameters, derring-do**)?

Completing the Sentence

Choose the word from the word bank that best completes each of the following sentences. Write the correct word or form of the word in the space provided.

affinity	**derring-do**	**gamut**	**lucubration**	**risible**
corollary	**elixir**	**ineffable**	**parameter**	**volte-face**

1. The relief we felt when we realized they were safe was so profound and overwhelming as to be utterly ________________.

2. All kittens display a natural ________________ for mischief, but I have never known one so bent on monkey business as our Mickie.

3. In estimating the relative military strength of the two powers, we must concentrate on the ________________ by which ability to carry on modern warfare may be judged.

4. It is true that capital punishment has not been proved to be a deterrent to murder, but it would be invalid to draw from this the ________________ that it has been proved *not* to be a deterrent.

5. Your ponderous ________________ seemed to me intended much more to emphasize your own importance than to shed any real light on the subject.

6. The situation calls for courage, in the sense of a sustained, resolute, and patient effort—not occasional feats of ________________.

7. The intensive merchandising and tremendous sale of patent medicines show that mankind has never really ceased its search for an all-purpose ________________.

8. After having strongly supported the teaching of foreign languages, they made a complete ________________ and advocated that this part of the curriculum be dropped or limited to a small minority.

9. The suggestion was so ________________ that I couldn't help laughing out loud as soon as I heard it.

10. The role calls for an actor who can express a(n) ________________ of emotions, from speechless rage to utter bliss.

End Set B

Synonyms

*Choose the word or form of the word from this Unit that is the same or most nearly the same in meaning as the **boldface** word or expression in the phrase. Write that word on the line. Use a dictionary if necessary.*

1. suffered a torrent of **ignominy** ________
2. a **memory aid** for recalling the rainbow's colors ________
3. led the despondent explorers to a **dead end** ________
4. the **scope** of the case before the judge ________
5. spent the late hours in **deep thought** ________
6. had a **penchant** for finding trouble ________
7. the **indescribable** beauty of the canyons ________
8. the critic's **splenetic** newspaper columns ________
9. a volume of data **indicative** of a strengthening economy ________
10. the **augury** of the oracle ________
11. the comedian's **ludicrous** tales ________
12. discouraged by the **turnabout** by the candidate ________
13. establish the **guidelines** before the big game ________
14. wondered what all the **hoopla** was about ________
15. among the **related** procedures ________

Antonyms

*Choose the word or form of the word from this Unit that is most nearly opposite in meaning to the **boldface** word or expression in the phrase. Write that word on the line. Use a dictionary if necessary.*

1. the power of the **aristocracy** ________
2. downplayed the opinion of the **dilettante** ________
3. was not the time for **timidity** ________
4. sought to prove his **postulate** ________
5. the powder was a **poison** to the rats ________

Writing: Words in Action

Consider the causes and effects of some of the great social and political revolutions of the twentieth and twenty-first centuries. Write an essay that describes some causes of these major uprisings. Use details from the passage (pages 56–57), personal experience, and three or more words from this Unit.

Vocabulary in Context

*Some of the words you have studied in this Unit appear in **boldface** type. Read the passage below, and then circle the letter of the correct answer for each word as it is used in context*

Before the advent of paper and pencil, people relied on word of mouth to circulate news. This process forced people to use their memories as well as other **mnemonic** devices to keep track of important events. The invention of the printing press in 1440 made printed materials more accessible to a wider population. In 1721, James Franklin produced the first independent American newspaper. Soon thereafter, daily and weekly newspapers, delivered around the United States to the front doors of apartments and to streets of all kinds, including **cul-de-sacs,** became the main mode of disseminating the news.

Now, there are multiple ways to access the news digitally, including on tablets, smart phones, and computers. Even though some people still have an **affinity** for seeing the news in print, newspaper circulation has steadily decreased since 2007. The fact that digital media has become the new way of accessing news information is **symptomatic** of the extant digital age. Even as digital access to news media is growing, the ways in which people access this news is evolving. Initially, people navigated directly to a destination news outlet to access news stories, but in 2015, 63 percent of people used a social media site to access news.

To address the changing role of technology in presenting the news, communications students today are encouraged to take **cognate** coursework in digital media or new media. There is no **elixir** that will satisfy everyone's news interests, but there are multiple outlets, print and digital, to help people stay connected to world events.

---

1. What is the meaning of **mnemonic** in the context of the passage?

a. designed to aid memory
b. designed to write well
c. designed to find people
d. designed to be printed

2. What is the meaning of **cul-de-sac** as it is used in paragraph 1?

a. an interstate highway
b. a steep incline
c. a dead-end street
d. a traffic circle

3. What is the meaning of **affinity** in the context of the passage?

a. an aversion
b. an inclination
c. a request
d. a reason

4. What does **symptomatic** most likely mean as it is used in paragraph 2?

a. unclear
b. favorable
c. different
d. characteristic

5. What does **cognate** most likely mean as it is used in paragraph 3?

a. affiliated
b. mandatory
c. inessential
d. important

6. What does **elixir** most likely mean as it is used in paragraph 3?

a. formula
b. treatment
c. ritual
d. panacea

UNIT 5

Read the following passage, taking note of the ***boldface*** *words and their contexts. These words are among those you will be studying in Unit 5. It may help you to complete the exercises in this Unit if you refer to the way the words are used below.*

The Comics and Cartoons of Winsor McCay

<Informational Essay>

A century ago, it was not uncommon for Americans, young and old, to spend Sunday afternoons with the comic strips spread out before them in a newspaper. For a nickel, the **insouciant** reader could relax and enjoy the antics of cartoon heroes like the Katzenjammer Kids, Mr. Jack, Happy Hooligan, and Buster Brown. Some early comic strips expressed **tendentious** political opinions; some were, like **homilies**, aimed at shaping the character of their audiences; but almost all of them aimed to get a guffaw out of their readers by means of simple, slapstick humor. One comic strip, however, stood out from the turn-of-the-century **matrix** of high jinks and monkeyshines. *Little Nemo in Slumberland,* by Winsor McCay, was subtle, surreal, and sometimes downright creepy.

Winsor McCay creating storyboards

As a teenager, McCay's parents **browbeat** him into attending business school in Michigan, but the young man felt **immured** by the school, and refused to be corralled into the way of life it represented. What he really wanted to do was draw—he'd been drawing since childhood, and over time his art had become something **sacrosanct** to him. It started to help him earn a living, too. He found work at a dime museum in Detroit, drawing portraits of visitors, for which he received an **emolument** of 25¢ apiece—fair compensation at a time when the average American worker earned about $400 per year.

In 1903, McCay landed a job creating cartoon strips for the *New York Herald.* His masterpiece, *Little Nemo in Slumberland*, debuted two years later. The hero of the strip, a boy named Nemo, had a new dream adventure each week, often barely avoiding disaster in his ongoing attempt to get to Slumberland, the domain of King Morpheus. McCay used inspired graphic experimentation and brilliant colors to present these fantasy sequences with unprecedented **panache**, and in so doing, he revolutionized the comic strip **genre** and influenced generations of cartoonists to come.

McCay made a brilliant **foray** into animated cartoons and in 1914, created the beautiful short film *Gertie the Dinosaur.* Gertie is widely considered to be the first cartoon character created especially for film that had a developed **persona**. While *Little Nemo* had been celebrated among **aficionados** more than it was adored by the average comic strip reader, *Gertie's* popular success was **commensurate** with the critical acclaim it received. By today's standards the film is short and remarkably simple. But in its day, *Gertie* was another landmark achievement for its creator, captivating audiences and cementing McCay's reputation as a pioneering master of his craft who stood head and shoulders above the other cartoonists of his day.

Comics and animated cartoons have evolved in the decades since McCay created his most memorable works, and they continue to evolve today. Artistic techniques keep pace with **systemic** changes in the technologies of print and film; content, styles, and themes vary along with the **vicissitudes** of modern culture. But McCay's influence—acknowledged by subsequent legends from Walt Disney to Chuck Jones, from Walter Lantz to Maurice Sendak—is one of the enduring features of the art.

Audio

For iWords and audio passages, go to **SadlierConnect.com**.

Above: Advertising poster from 1914 for the film *Gertie the Dinosaur*

Left: *Little Nemo in Slumberland*, 1908

Definitions

Note the spelling, pronunciation, part(s) of speech, and definition(s) of each of the following words. Then write the appropriate form of the word in the blank space in the illustrative sentence(s) following.

1. aficionado
(ə fish yə nä′ dō)

(*n.*) an enthusiastic and usually expert follower or fan

I have been an ____________________ of football since my youth.

2. browbeat
(braủ′ bēt)

(*v.*) to intimidate by a stern or overbearing manner; to bully

The dissatisfied customer had to ____________________ the store manager into refunding his money.

3. diaphanous
(dī af′ ə nəs)

(*adj.*) very sheer and light; almost completely transparent

We were asked to use a ____________________ material like gauze to make the costumes.

4. foray
(fôr′ ā)

(*n.*) a quick raid, especially for plunder; a venture into some field of endeavor; (*v.*) to make such a raid

The cavalry's ____________________ behind enemy lines was a great success.

Counting on the element of surprise, the general ordered the troops to begin to ____________________ before dawn.

5. homily
(hom′ ə lē)

(*n.*) a sermon stressing moral principles; a tedious moralizing lecture or discourse

The topic of this week's ____________________ is respect for diversity.

6. immure
(i myủr′)

(*v.*) to enclose or confine within walls; to imprison; to seclude or isolate

The criminal was ____________________ for life in a narrow cell.

7. obsequies
(ob′ sə kwēz)

(*n.*) funeral rites or ceremonies

The nation held somber ____________________ for its beloved leader.

8. persona
(pər sō′ nə)

(*n.*) a character in a novel or play; the outward character or role that a person assumes

The comic ____________________ of Charlie Chaplin is recognizable the world over.

9. prurient (průr′ ē ənt) (*adj.*) having lustful desires or interests; tending to arouse sexual desires

Considered a ________________ novel by some, *Ulysses* was once banned from sale in the United States.

10. systemic (sis tem′ ik) (*adj.*) of or pertaining to the entire body; relating to a system or systems

The singer suffered a ________________ breakdown after the long and demanding season.

Using Context

*For each item, determine whether the **boldface** word from pages 70–71 makes sense in the context of the sentence. Circle the item numbers next to the six sentences in which the words are used correctly.*

1. The friendly, down-to-earth nature of the radio host is not just on-air **persona**—that's how he is in real life.
2. The phrase "sweet sorrow" is a contradiction in terms and therefore can be called a **homily**.
3. It something of a convention in movies and videos to depict ghosts as recognizable but **diaphanous** beings.
4. As a true **aficionado** of science fiction, I look forward to attending the annual nationwide convention for writers and fans of the genre.
5. After her **foray** into television cooking shows, the cookbook author became an international celebrity.
6. Will a flu shot completely **immure** a person from the illness, or does it simply decrease his or her chances of contracting it?
7. On April 20, 1865, *The New York Times* described the **obsequies** of President Abraham Lincoln as "the greatest pageant ever tendered to the honored dead of this continent."
8. It is never acceptable for a player who disagrees with a call to **browbeat** the referee or umpire who made it.
9. Even a **prurient** amount of exercise on a daily basis can make a big difference in a person's health.
10. The doctor assured the patient that the wound was merely **systemic** and that it required nothing more than a bit of antiseptic ointment and a small bandage.

Set A

*Select the **boldface** word that better completes each sentence. You might refer to the passage on pages 68–69 to see how most of these words are used in context. Note that the choices might be related forms of the Unit words.*

1. It is often said that in Russia there are as many (**homilies, aficionados**) of chess as there are of baseball or golf in the United States.

2. The writing instructor requested that we not (**immure, foray**) into poetry until we learn how to master the art of prose.

3. The (**obsequies, persona**) that a public figure displays to the world is often quite different from the personality that he or she exhibits in private.

4. The prosecutor denied that the police had used scare tactics to (**browbeat, foray**) the defendant into a confession.

5. The commission found that police corruption was not confined to one or two isolated precincts but was (**systemic, prurient**) in nature.

6. What we owe to our fallen leader is not mournful (**forays, obsequies**) but a joyful assertion of life and a pledge to continue her work.

7. People involved in drug abuse need practical help in overcoming their addiction—not (**homilies, obsequies**) exhorting them to higher standards of behavior.

8. What gourmet feast can compare with the luscious delicacies that we consumed during our midnight (**forays, homilies**) on the well-stocked refrigerator?

9. Corot painted poetic and (**diaphanous, prurient**) landscapes, in which even solid objects seemed to be suffused with light and movement.

10. How can young people hope to become mature, self-reliant adults if they (**immure, foray**) themselves in a home environment that is overly comfortable and protective?

11. After a hurricane completely ravaged their city, the minister's (**homily, aficionado**) seemed pedantic and heartless.

12. It seems incredible that a few generations ago a novel of such quality could be widely condemned as designed to appeal to (**diaphanous, prurient**) interests.

Completing the Sentence

Choose the word from the word bank that best completes each of the following sentences. Write the correct word or form of the word in the space provided.

aficionado	diaphanous	homily	obsequies	prurient
browbeat	foray	immure	persona	systemic

1. The omniscient narrator is probably the most common ____________________ assumed by novel writers.

2. You should not approach a class in sex education with such a lustful and ____________________ attitude.

3. We found overwhelming beauty in the most common manifestations of nature, such as the colors of sunset, the delicate shape of a flower, or the ____________________ wings of an insect.

4. At first she showed only a mild interest in checkers, but as she played more and developed skill, she became a real ____________________ of the game.

5. When doctors discovered the disease to be ____________________, they held out little hope for the patient's recovery.

6. Our troops returned from their successful ____________________ against the enemy's base in a jubilant mood.

7. What good does it do to regale the prisoners with ____________________ about going straight if they have no chance to make an honest living when they are released?

8. When we reflected on his long and happy life and his unmatched record of public service, we found the ____________________ comforting and even inspiring.

9. She cannot relate to other people in a constructive way because she is ____________________ in her own prejudices and hostilities.

10. The overbearing maître d' ____________________ the diners into meekly accepting the least desirable table in the restaurant.

End Set A

Definitions

Note the spelling, pronunciation, part(s) of speech, and definition(s) of each of the following words. Then write the appropriate form of the word in the blank space in the illustrative sentence(s) following.

1. **commensurate** (kə men′ sə rit) — (*adj.*) equal in size, extent, duration, or importance; proportionate; measurable by the same standards

   All employees got raises ____________ with their efforts.

2. **emolument** (i mol′ yə mənt) — (*n.*) profit derived from an office or position or from employment; a fee or salary

   Choosing an equitable ____________ for the mayor was the latest of the city council's acts.

3. **genre** (zhän′ rə) — (*n.*) a type, class, or variety, especially a distinctive category of literary composition; a style of painting in which everyday scenes are realistically depicted

   The science fiction ____________ has produced several classics.

4. **insouciant** (in sü′ sē ənt) — (*adj.*) blithely indifferent or unconcerned; carefree; happy-go-lucky

   After months of worrying about the fate of his new project, the man was determined to lead a more ____________ life thereafter.

5. **matrix** (mā′ triks) — (*n.*) a mold; the surrounding situation or environment

   Scientists discovered a tiny prehistoric creature fossilized in a ____________ of amber.

6. **panache** (pə nash′) — (*n.*) a confident and stylish manner, dash; a strikingly elaborate or colorful display

   In the film *The Adventures of Robin Hood*, the actor Errol Flynn captures the ____________ of the bandit.

7. **philippic** (fi lip′ ik) — (*n.*) a bitter verbal attack

   The senator delivered a ____________ against the proposed law and those who supported it.

8. **sacrosanct** (sak′ rō saŋkt) — (*adj.*) very sacred or holy; inviolable; set apart or immune from questioning or attack

   Members of the clergy felt privileged to be entrusted with guarding the ____________ relic.

9. tendentious
(ten den′ shəs)

(*adj.*) intended to promote a particular point of view, doctrine, or cause; biased or partisan

The candidate's supporters heartily applauded her ______________ arguments.

10. vicissitude
(vi sis′ ə tüd)

(*n.*) a change, variation, or alteration; (*pl.*) successive or changing phases or conditions

The inevitable ______________ of life affect us all.

Using Context

*For each item, determine whether the **boldface** word from pages 74–75 makes sense in the context of the sentence. Circle the item numbers next to the six sentences in which the words are used correctly.*

1. The arrest of a well-respected figure in our community reminded us that no one is **sacrosanct** in matters of the law.
2. I recommend reading this **tendentious** account of the politician's career because of its unbiased, balanced point of view.
3. When the hiring manager explained that the salary would be "**commensurate** with experience," I wondered what that meant for a person like me with no formal experience.
4. The host introduced the guest of honor with a brief **philippic**, citing all of her generous contributions to the community over the years.
5. We have remained friends throughout the **vicissitudes** of life, supporting each other during various trials and tribulations.
6. I tried to convince my friend who only watches comedy films to branch out and try a different **genre**, but to no avail.
7. Diamonds may be found in a **matrix** of rock called kimberlite.
8. They are looking for a babysitter with an **insouciant** attitude who will be vigilant about keeping the children safe.
9. Although he plays a villain, the actor delivers his lines with such **panache** that it's difficult not to find him charming.
10. The lawyer demonstrated her **emolument** when she performed her services for free.

Set B

*Select the **boldface** word that better completes each sentence. You might refer to the passage on pages 68–69 to see how most of these words are used in context. Note that the choices might be related forms of the Unit words.*

1. James Bond seems to dispose of the villains he faces with all the (**genre, panache**) of the legendary paladins of medieval romance.

2. I admit that you have some grounds for complaint, but those shrieks of outrage are simply not (**tendentious, commensurate**) with having been overcharged five cents.

3. I had hoped to hear a balanced, dispassionate discussion of this problem, but I found their approach to be distressingly one-sided and (**tendentious, sacrosanct**).

4. Certainly your judgment, if not your motives, must be questioned when you choose to associate yourself with an organization of that (**matrix, genre**).

5. The purpose of our policies is to develop bold forms of international understanding and practical cooperation that can serve as the (**philippic, matrix**) for peace.

6. The Flemish painter Pieter Brueghel the Elder is known for his magnificent (**genre, panache**) scenes in which peasants are portrayed in their quotidian activities.

7. When the results of the scholarship competition were announced, we could sense the deep disappointment beneath your (**insouciant, tendentious**) manner.

8. There is no doubt of your oratorical talents, but this is a time for quiet words of reconciliation—not for thundering (**emoluments, philippics**).

9. If the woman thinks her status as a public official renders her (**insouciant, sacrosanct**), she is in for a rude awakening.

10. The fact that they referred to my salary as a(n) (**panache, emolument**) did not disguise the fact that I was being woefully underpaid.

11. Common sense reminds us that even in moments of great joy we should retain some awareness of the (**panache, vicissitudes**) and heartbreaks of life.

12. The dean of students was caught off guard by the protestors' (**philippics, emoluments**).

Completing the Sentence

Choose the word from the word bank that best completes each of the following sentences. Write the correct word or form of the word in the space provided.

commensurate	genre	matrix	philippic	tendentious
emolument	insouciant	panache	sacrosanct	vicissitude

1. It was a cat-and-mouse play about a patient detective and an aristocratic jewel thief who stole with elegance and ____________________.

2. The constitution provides that the ____________________ received by the President is to be neither increased nor decreased during his term of office.

3. In her speech to the entering freshman class, the dean emphasized that the benefits they derived from any course would be ____________________ with the effort that they devoted to it.

4. Time after time, he rose on the floor of the Senate and delivered bitter ____________________ against the lack of effective measures against environmental pollution.

5. Their reverence for all creation was so great that even the most common manifestation of nature was ____________________.

6. Having been conditioned to take wealth and luxury for granted, they tended to take a(n) ____________________ attitude toward money, even when they had only a modest income.

7. She claimed to be an unbiased witness, but I found her testimony to be opinionated and ____________________.

8. My Classics professor said that the epic poem represents the most noble and inspiring of all literary ____________________.

9. One of my fondest hopes is to visit Jerusalem, the city that has had a unique role in history as the ____________________ of three world religions.

10. The true test of her character will be how she is able to deal with the ____________________ of life.

End Set B

SadlierConnect.com:  Interactive Word Games

Synonyms

*Choose the word or form of the word from this Unit that is the same or most nearly the same in meaning as the **boldface** word or expression in the phrase. Write that word on the line. Use a dictionary if necessary.*

1. the **see-through** curtain glowed as night fell ________________
2. **incarcerated** in a dungeon ________________
3. considered to be a **sacred** duty ________________
4. popular among Italian food **devotees** ________________
5. divided the books by **category** ________________
6. the **model** of the modern library system ________________
7. a public **image** of a virtuous, honest leader ________________
8. envied their **nonchalant** approach ________________
9. possessed a certain **flamboyance** ________________
10. **system-wide** reform made in school districts ________________
11. the **fluctuations** of the family's fortune ________________
12. pay **proportionate** to the task ________________
13. delivered a **lecture** on forgiveness ________________
14. was seen as **salacious** behavior ________________
15. **compensation** for the job ________________

Antonyms

*Choose the word or form of the word from this Unit that is most nearly opposite in meaning to the **boldface** word or expression in the phrase. Write that word on the line. Use a dictionary if necessary.*

1. **birth celebrations** in honor of the new prince ________________
2. a **tribute** delivered to memorialize fallen soldiers ________________
3. sweetly **cajoled** into participating ________________
4. a **retreat** through enemy territory ________________
5. stunned by their **impartial** response ________________

Writing: Words in Action

Write a brief essay in which you compare and contrast the political and artistic impact of both print comic strips and animated cartoons. Use details from the passage (pages 68–69), personal observations, and three or more words from the Unit to help a reader understand how the two art forms are similar and different.

*Some of the words you have studied in this Unit appear in **boldface** type. Read the passage below, and then circle the letter of the correct answer for each word as it is used in context.*

During Charles M. Schulz's youth in Minneapolis, he and his father perused the Sunday newspaper comics; this ritual piqued Schulz's interest in becoming a cartoonist. At age 15, he submitted a sketch of his dog Spike that was ultimately published in a nationally syndicated newspaper feature. To capitalize on his artistic proclivities, Schulz enrolled in a correspondence cartoon course with the Federal School of Applied Cartooning.

In 1943, Schulz's mother succumbed to cancer. Schultz subsequently enlisted in the army and served in World War II. In 1945, Schulz returned to Minnesota, thus formally actuating his desire to become a professional cartoonist. His first cartoon, *Li'l Folks*, featured drawings of children with oversized heads whose maturity exceeded their age: in myriad ways, these characters were precursors for Charlie Brown and his *Peanuts* compatriots.

On October 2, 1950, *Peanuts* debuted in seven newspapers nationwide. *Peanuts* exhibited Schulz's **panache** for executing detailed figures and capturing each character's personality. Charlie Brown was the affable underdog, Snoopy was imaginative, Lucy delivered frequent **philippics**, Peppermint Patty had innate leadership abilities, and Linus's **diaphanous** blue blanket was ubiquitous. In an epoch when **prurient** forms of entertainment were popular, the nostalgic, wry, and melancholic humor in *Peanuts* was refreshing for all ages.

Schulz passed away on February 12, 2000, hours before the final *Peanuts* strip appeared in papers. Before Schulz's formal **obsequies**, *Peanuts* **aficionados** worldwide mourned the cartoonist who catalogued the fears and anxieties inherent in children.

---

1. What is the meaning of **panache** as it is used in paragraph 3?

a. humble
b. blasé
c. meticulous
d. confident

2. In paragraph 3, what does the word **philippics** suggest about Lucy?

a. She harangues.
b. She complains.
c. She is generous.
d. She is defensive.

3. What is the meaning of **diaphanous** in the context of the passage?

a. opaque
b. bulky
c. sheer
d. ornate

4. What does **prurient** most likely mean as it is used in paragraph 3?

a. practical
b. lewd
c. conservative
d. expensive

5. In paragraph 4, what does the word **obsequies** suggest about Schulz?

a. He wrote a will.
b. He had a long illness.
c. He had a funeral.
d. He wrote his obituary.

6. What characteristic is suggested by **aficionados** in paragraph 4?

a. enthusiasm
b. rebellion
c. intelligence
d. modesty

UNIT 6

*Read the following passage, taking note of the **boldface** words and their contexts. These words are among those you will be studying in Unit 6. It may help you to complete the exercises in this Unit if you refer to the way the words are used below.*

Origins of Anarchism

<Magazine Article>

by Sonja L. Brinkan

Anarchism is an **iconoclastic** philosophy aimed at abolishing the state. Its rhetoric often takes a **contumelious** tone, and some anarchists advocate violent revolution. But the ideal society envisioned by anarchists is neither a **saturnalian** chaos nor a muddle of masses in perpetual conflict. Essentially, anarchism is motivated by a rosy, even **maudlin** vision of humanity's potential for peace, harmony, and freedom without government control. Though anarchism's goals seem unrealistic, its ideals merit attention, providing a **touchstone** by which scholars might measure social reform.

A lithograph from "Le Petit Journal" depicts an explosion in Paris, 1905.

Roots of Anarchy

Many anthropologists maintain that early human society was anarchic, without government, political institutions, or strict hierarchies of power. Others counter that meaningful hierarchies existed in primitive societies, and even among chimpanzees. Anthropologists may argue, **quid pro quo**, about the prehistoric origins of anarchy. Though it picks up **in medias res**, the record of history is somewhat clearer.

With the emergence of states, strains of anarchism arose among ancient philosophers. Lao Tzu's principle of nonrule, nonaction, or nonintervention is interpreted by many as an example of anarchist thinking in ancient China because it urged nonintervention of governments. Bao Jingyan's **portentous** treatise on the evils of social hierarchy and the futility of government rule clearly displays anarchical tendencies. In Greece, Zeno of Citium argued that the ideal society is a community of free, rational individuals living without regulation by a state. Historians cite countless examples of anarchist tendencies in communal societies of the West, from Europe's Middle Ages through the American colonial period.

Modern Anarchists

William Godwin's *Enquiry Concerning Human Justice,* published in 1793, was among the first modern anarchist treatises. A man of the Enlightenment, Godwin held an optimistic view of human nature and blamed government for corrupting it. Godwin argued that government **vitiates** human character, that our vices result from social conditions imposed by government. He sought progress toward a more **salubrious** and stateless form of society, in which people's rational self-interest would lead them to act in harmony.

Anarchism's heyday dawned in the mid-nineteenth century; Europe was racked with

traumatic revolutions as the continent's governments **modulated** from aristocratic monarchies to more egalitarian social orders. In 1840, Pierre-Joseph Proudhon summarized his anarchist philosophy in the **dictum** "Liberty is the mother, not the daughter, of order." He believed the best society would arise spontaneously from the action of free, rational individuals. Mikhail Bakunin argued, against Proudhon's disciples, that all productive property should be owned collectively. However, Bakunin opposed other Marxist notions that social revolutions must be led by enlightened elites in positions of authority. Instead, he believed in the power of the masses. Decades later, following the Russian Revolution, the **prescience** of Bakunin's anti-elitism was affirmed by anarchists like Emma Goldman, a Lithuanian Jewish immigrant to New York City, who criticized the Bolsheviks' authoritarian, repressive approach to social control, and loathed its rigid centralization and anti-Semitism.

Dissent and Dreams in the Sidelines of History

Anarchists played an important role in the reform of Western society for nearly a century, particularly in the labor movements of the nineteenth and early twentieth centuries. But anarchism was declining by the start of World War II. The movement's effectiveness was hampered by **internecine** disputes and by its essential paradox: How can people who passionately object to imposed social organization come together to act as a coherent political force?

The paradox reflects deeper problems with the very idea of anarchy. Hope is a waking dream, and anarchism's dream of a free society without government is unlikely to be realized. But its nobler yearnings toward social and economic equality continue to inspire reformers.

Sonja L. Brinkan is a professor of economic history at Sutton College in Arborville. Her last article for The Final Word *was "A Maverick Abroad," Vol. xxv, April 2011.*

Audio

For iWords and audio passages, go to **SadlierConnect.com**.

Definitions

Note the spelling, pronunciation, part(s) of speech, and definition(s) of each of the following words. Then write the appropriate form of the word in the blank space in the illustrative sentence(s) following.

1. bruit (brüt)
(*v.*) to spread news, reports, or unsubstantiated rumors
News of the company's closing and the impending job losses was immediately ____________ about the office.

2. contumelious (kon tü mē′ lē əs)
(*adj.*) insolent or rude in speech or behavior; insultingly abusive; humiliating
The ambassador's ____________ reply was completely unexpected.

3. dictum (dik′ təm)
(*n.*) a short saying; an authoritative statement
According to the ____________ of the critics, the play is not worth the price of admission.

4. in medias res (in med′ ē əs rās′)
(*adv.*) in or into the middle of a plot; into the middle of things
Since this episode begins ____________, we need to record it and watch the earlier installments first.

5. internecine (int ər nes′ ēn)
(*adj.*) mutually destructive; characterized by great slaughter and bloodshed
An ____________ feud has existed between the clans for generations.

6. maudlin (môd′ lin)
(*adj.*) excessively or effusively sentimental
The tenor sang a ____________ ballad and then a humorous ditty.

7. modulate (mod′ yə lāt)
(*v.*) to change or vary the intensity or pitch; to temper or soften; to regulate, adjust
Asked to ____________ their voices, the choir responded adroitly.

8. quid pro quo (kwid′ prō kwō′)
(*n.*) something given in exchange or return for something else
Before agreeing to give their support, the representatives insisted on some ____________.

9. salubrious (sə lüʹ brē əs) — (*adj.*) conducive to health or well-being; wholesome

Seeking the ____________ effects of sea air, the family headed for a shore vacation.

10. waggish (wagʹ ish) — (*adj.*) fond of making jokes; characteristic of a joker; playfully humorous or droll

The innkeeper's ____________ stories lifted the flagging spirits of the weary travelers.

Using Context

*For each item, determine whether the **boldface** word from pages 82–83 makes sense in the context of the sentence. Circle the item numbers next to the six sentences in which the words are used correctly.*

1. "There are no gains without pains" is one **dictum** that appears in Benjamin Franklin's famous work titled *Poor Richard's Almanack*.
2. The writer of a nonfiction narrative might begin **in medias res** in order to pique the interest of readers.
3. In the age of social media, anyone can **bruit** news or opinions to a large number of people in a matter of seconds.
4. We must write a note to thank them for the gracious and **contumelious** hospitality they showed us while we were guests in their home.
5. Homer's epic *The Iliad* recounts the story of the **internecine** war between the Greeks and the Trojans.
6. Eight days of gray, gloomy weather left us feeling glum and **waggish**.
7. You can use the remote control to **modulate** the sound of the television set.
8. In Aesop's fable "The Lion and the Mouse," the mouse saves the lion's life as a **quid pro quo**; at an earlier point, the lion had generously spared the little creature's life.
9. Almost universally, critics praised the poems for their startlingly fresh and **maudlin** imagery.
10. I immediately apologized for my **salubrious** remarks and promised to be more careful with my words in the future.

Choosing the Right Word

*Select the **boldface** word that better completes each sentence. You might refer to the passage on pages 80–81 to see how most of these words are used in context. Note that the choices might be related forms of the Unit words.*

1. Homer's *Iliad* begins (**quid pro quo, in medias res**) with a dramatic argument between Agamemnon and Achilles during the Trojan War.

2. My mother passed on her greatest wisdom with the following (**quid pro quo, dictum**): Treat others as you wish to be treated.

3. While the organization's goal is ultimately free trade, each state must have the freedom to (**modulate, bruit**) trade based on its interests.

4. The concessions that we are making are manifest, but I do not perceive a reasonable (**dictum, quid pro quo**) from the other side.

5. Willy-nilly, parents often enter (**in medias res, waggishly**) into a quarrel between siblings, especially when lasting damage seems about to occur.

6. Although those supposedly (**maudlin, waggish**) remarks were dressed in the guise of humor, they betrayed a strong undertone of resentment.

7. In spite of my extreme nervousness, I made every effort to (**modulate, bruit**) my voice and speak the first lines in a calm, controlled manner.

8. In that situation, I don't know which was more distressing—the callous indifference of some of my "friends" or the (**maudlin, salubrious**) sympathy of others.

9. Their cool and detached skepticism now struck me as a(n) (**internecine, salubrious**) factor in that highly emotionalized situation.

10. The decline in the value of the company's stock was attributed to the fact that rumors of a contract cancellation had been widely (**bruited, modulated**).

11. The candidate seemed oblivious to the (**quid pro quo, contumelious**) statements of those in the audience.

12. Warfare has become too (**internecine, waggish**) to risk.

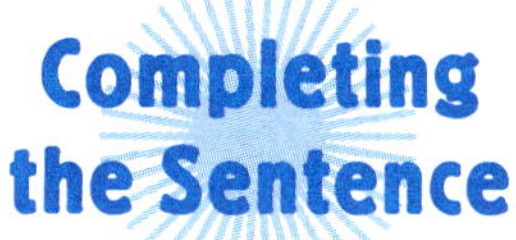

Completing the Sentence

Choose the word from the word bank that best completes each of the following sentences. Write the correct word or form of the word in the space provided.

bruit	dictum	internecine	modulate	salubrious
contumelious	in medias res	maudlin	quid pro quo	waggish

1. The deathbed scene might have been effective if it had been played with restraint, but their woefully ham-handed acting turned it into a(n) ____________________ tearjerker.

2. I certainly have no intention of turning my back on them simply because it has been ____________________ about town that they are involved in some sort of scandal.

3. The speaker paid no attention to the ____________________ remarks of a few hecklers in the crowd but went right on with her speech.

4. Though the critic still has nothing good to say about modern art, age and experience have somewhat ____________________ the intensity of his disapproval.

5. It is one thing to offer a personal opinion; it is quite another to issue a(n) ____________________ as though you are the only one with any knowledge of the subject.

6. To gain the immediate attention of the reader, the short-story writer sometimes begins a narrative ____________________, rather than at the very beginning of events.

7. How can you expect them to cooperate with us unless they receive some reasonable ____________________ for their efforts?

8. In our bored and depressed mood, her buoyant personality had a most ____________________ effect.

9. If he would only devote more time in school to serious study and less to ____________________ pranks, his grades would probably improve.

10. What we are facing in this organization is not healthy competition among the executives but a(n) ____________________ struggle that will destroy the company.

End Set A

Definitions

Note the spelling, pronunciation, part(s) of speech, and definition(s) of each of the following words. Then write the appropriate form of the word in the blank space in the illustrative sentence(s) following.

1. abortive (ə bôr′ tiv)
(*adj.*) failing to accomplish an intended aim or purpose; only partially or imperfectly developed
An ____________ attempt to seize the throne ended badly for the participants.

2. ensconce (en skons′)
(*v.*) to settle comfortably and firmly in position; to put or hide in a safe place
After a very long, difficult day at work, I gratefully ____________ myself in my snug, warm bed.

3. iconoclastic (ī kon ə klas′ tik)
(*adj.*) attacking or seeking to overthrow popular or traditional beliefs, ideas, or institutions
The writer's ____________ opinions always seem to stir controversy.

4. maladroit (mal ə droit′)
(*adj.*) lacking skill or dexterity; lacking tact, perception, or judgment
The supervisor's ____________ interference revealed a lack of experience.

5. portentous (pôr ten′ təs)
(*adj.*) foreshadowing an event to come; causing wonder or awe; self-consciously weighty, pompous
No one realized just how ____________ the strange events of last week would turn out to be.

6. prescience (presh′ əns)
(*n.*) knowledge of events or actions before they happen; foresight
The detectives were skeptical about the psychic's ____________ of the suspect's next crime.

7. saturnalian (sat ər nā′ lyan)
(*adj.*) characterized by riotous or unrestrained revelry or licentiousness
The boisterously ____________ spectacle was truly something to behold, even from a distance.

8. touchstone (təch′ stōn)
(*n.*) a means of testing worth or genuineness
A work's popularity among succeeding generations is thought to be a ____________ of its merit.

9. traumatic (traủ mat′ ik)
(*adj.*) so shocking to the emotions as to cause lasting and substantial psychological damage

People may feel the effects of a ____________ experience for years afterward.

10. vitiate (vish′ ē āt)
(*v.*) to weaken, debase, or corrupt; to impair the quality or value of

____________ by its lack of managerial skill, the company's fortunes went straight downhill.

Using Context

For each item, determine whether the ***boldface*** *word from pages 86–87 makes sense in the context of the sentence. Circle the item numbers next to the six sentences in which the words are used correctly.*

1. Don't you think you would have more fun at social gatherings if you relaxed your **saturnalian** ways every so often?
2. The **maladroit** waiter spilled a drink on a customer, broke several plates, and tripped over a chair within the first hour of his shift.
3. With its ominous visuals and **portentous** music that warned of the villain's presence, the film was criticized for being overly dramatic.
4. The smell of the ocean is enough to **vitiate** memories of my childhood summers spent by the beach.
5. The impending storm and rough seas resulted in an **abortive** exploratory mission to the uninhabited island.
6. I refuse to let any fear of failure **ensconce** me from trying to achieve my goals.
7. This program aims to help participants recover from **traumatic** experiences by allowing them to spend time with calming "therapy pets."
8. Her revolutionary stance on political issues is so different from the **iconoclastic** viewpoints of her parents!
9. The extent of a book's popularity with the masses is often a **touchstone** of whether its movie adaptation will do well at the box office.
10. His success with financial investments is so uncanny that many believe he must have **prescience** of what will happen in the market.

*Select the **boldface** word that better completes each sentence. You might refer to the passage on pages 80–81 to see how most of these words are used in context. Note that the choices might be related forms of the Unit words.*

1. Prior to the Wright brothers' first successful airplane flight in 1903, all of mankind's efforts to fly had been (**iconoclastic, abortive**).
2. A strict sense of honesty, marked by a refusal to take refuge in clever ambiguities, has been the (**touchstone, prescience**) of my career in politics.
3. The cat (**ensconced, vitiated**) herself in safety behind the coats.
4. Historians believe that the Civil War had a collective (**traumatic, abortive**) impact, which was not healed until a new generation had grown to maturity.
5. With her elegance and remarkable feel for style, is it any wonder that she soon became (**vitiated, ensconced**) as the arbiter of fashion?
6. I felt that I had stated my case with sincerity and conviction, but my heart sank when they reacted with a (**maladroit, portentous**) silence.
7. Her (**abortive, saturnalian**) attempt to ruin our plans was malicious but unsuccessful.
8. Some people seem to be natural nonconformists; for them (**prescience, iconoclasm**) is not just a mood or an affectation but a way of life.
9. All the snide rumors that have been spread about them do not (**vitiate, ensconce**) their solid reputation for authentic kindness and decency.
10. When the miners arrived with all of their back pay and intent upon "having fun," our town soon took on the aspect of a frontier (**saturnalia, touchstone**).
11. They survived the critical years due to their uncanny (**prescience, touchstone**) that enabled them to anticipate the moves of their enemies.
12. Their efforts to settle the differences between the two factions were so (**portentous, maladroit**) that what had begun as a rift became a chasm.

Completing the Sentence

Choose the word from the word bank that best completes each of the following sentences. Write the correct word or form of the word in the space provided.

abortive	**iconoclastic**	**portentous**	**saturnalian**	**traumatic**
ensconce	**maladroit**	**prescience**	**touchstone**	**vitiate**

1. As she thoroughly enjoys taking potshots at sacred cows, I'd describe her attitude as definitely ____________________.

2. A group of elderly people sitting about sipping tea and discussing the weather is scarcely my idea of ____________________ revelry.

3. The coach devised a clever strategy, but it proved ____________________ when our team failed to execute it properly.

4. If you are so ____________________ in handling your own personal affairs, how can you presume to advise others on how to manage their lives?

5. All the evidence presented at such length by their lawyers does not seriously ____________________ the case against the accused.

6. I was an extremely sensitive child, and the death of my beloved mother certainly had a(n) ____________________ effect upon me.

7. More than anything else, the ability to create distinctive characters and make them come alive on the page is the ____________________ of a great novelist.

8. For years, Churchill's warnings about Hitler were dismissed as alarmism; only after the outbreak of World War II did people appreciate his ____________________.

9. And such are the quirks of fate that there Maria was, after all her mishaps and blunders, firmly ____________________ as the president of the firm.

10. Though the guests at the gala benefit tried to maintain an air of cheer, the ____________________ news of the international crisis hung like a pall over the gathering.

End Set B

Synonyms

*Choose the word or form of the word from this Unit that is the same or most nearly the same in meaning as the **boldface** word or expression in the phrase. Write that word on the line. Use a dictionary if necessary.*

1. undone by a lack of **foresight** ______
2. moved by the **sentimental** story ______
3. one debater's **scurrilous** remarks ______
4. lives by the **maxim** "first do no harm" ______
5. began the story **in the middle** ______
6. **moderate** the tones of the flute ______
7. the **trade** for services rendered ______
8. the **benchmark** of a good film ______
9. the **debauched** Mardi Gras celebration ______
10. would **undermine** all our achievements ______
11. lived through a **horrifying** experience ______
12. scared by the **ominous** dream ______
13. **murderous** disputes between the Hatfields and the McCoys ______
14. **clumsy** efforts at reconciliation ______
15. a **beneficial** aspect of the trip ______

Antonyms

*Choose the word or form of the word from this Unit that is most nearly opposite in meaning to the **boldface** word or expression in the phrase. Write that word on the line. Use a dictionary if necessary.*

1. **displace** herself and move away from home ______
2. a **dour** group waiting at the ticket window ______
3. **conceal** rumors that school is cancelled ______
4. supported his **orthodox** ideas ______
5. a **successful** attempt to scale the wall ______

Writing: Words in Action

In "Origins of Anarchism" (pages 80–81) the writer asks, "How can people who passionately object to social organization come together to act as a coherent political force?" Write an essay explaining whether such people can come together and, then, how they can or why they cannot. Use three or more words from this Unit.

*Some of the words you have studied in this Unit appear in **boldface** type. Read the passage below, and then circle the letter of the correct answer for each word as it is used in context*

It was to have been a relaxing break from the Washington routine. In the late summer of 1901, President William McKinley, his wife Ida, and several senior aides were to visit Buffalo, New York, the site of the Pan-American Exposition, a spectacular world's fair. At the height of his power, McKinley had overseen a return to economic prosperity and a swift victory in the Spanish-American War, and in 1900, he had won re-election to a second term, despite another **abortive** attempt by the silver-tongued Democratic candidate, William Jennings Bryan, to unseat him.

Yet George B. Cortelyou, Secretary to the President, was apprehensive. Anarchist plots were **bruited** everywhere. The previous summer, King Umberto I of Italy had been assassinated by an Italian American immigrant, Gaetano Bresci. It would not have been **waggish** to claim that terrorism was in the air. In 1907, the acclaimed novelist Joseph Conrad would write *The Secret Agent*, a novel whose plot revolved around anarchist violence; the novel itself was set in London in 1886.

On Friday, September 6, President McKinley, comfortably **ensconced** in the Buffalo mansion of John G. Milburn, president of the Exposition, enjoyed a **salubrious** morning walk along scenic Delaware Avenue. Then he and Ida set off on a sightseeing trip to Niagara Falls. At four o'clock in the afternoon, on the grounds of the Exposition, McKinley greeted the public at the Temple of Music. It was at this theater, when he extended his hand in greeting, that he was shot twice at point-blank range. One shot was **maladroit,** barely grazing McKinley; the other, however, entered his abdomen and was never found by the doctors attending him. Eight days later, the President died of gangrene poisoning.

---

1. What is the meaning of **abortive** as it is used in paragraph 1?

a. premature **c.** fruitless
b. latent **d.** unintentional

2. What is the meaning of **bruited** in the context of the passage?

a. reported **c.** forecast
b. denounced **d.** emphasized

3. What is the meaning of **waggish** as it is used in paragraph 2?

a. ambiguous **c.** excessive
b. droll **d.** resonant

4. What does **ensconced** most likely mean as it is used in paragraph 3?

a. enclosed **c.** settled
b. included **d.** hidden

5. In paragraph 3, what does **salubrious** suggest about the morning walk?

a. It was lengthy. **c.** It was solitary.
b. It was wholesome. **d.** It was frustrating.

6. What characteristic is suggested by **maladroit** in paragraph 3?

a. clumsiness **c.** impulsiveness
b. precision **d.** dexterity

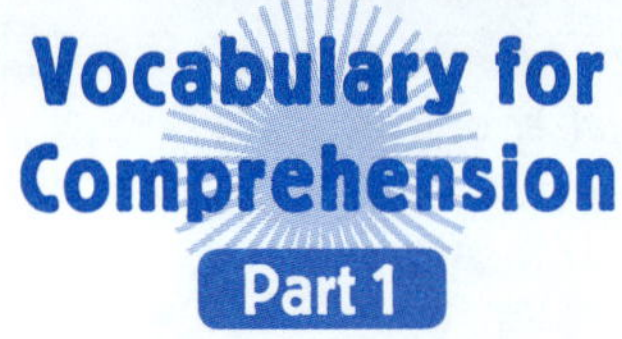

*Read this passage, which contains words in **boldface** that appear in Units 4–6. Then choose the best answer to each question based on what is stated or implied in the passage. You may refer to the passage as often as necessary.*

Questions 1–10 are based on the following passage.

On December 24, 1938, a tall man was rushing up the spiral staircase of an apartment block in a comfortable but undistinguished *barrio*, or neighborhood, of Buenos Aires. It was the kind of quietly inhospitable *barrio* whose real virtues were a secret known to the people who lived there and not many others. This man, Jorge Luis Borges, was thirty-nine years old, was an **aficionado** about the *barrios* of Buenos Aires and knew so much about them that people could never be sure the stories he told about the barrios could be true.

Borges's **punditry** covered many areas of expertise, but all his life he had been consumed by an insatiable curiosity about the city. His voracious appetite for reading was supported by an extraordinarily retentive memory, and at the age of fourteen his deteriorating eyesight spurred him to invent a system of mental classification, a **mnemonic** device so powerful that he would always be able to remember everything he had ever read. He was a born librarian. For him, cross-referencing was part of the process of reading. Everything he read enriched the meaning of everything he knew, and lent plausibility to everything he constructed. Every piece of knowledge, however humble, obscure, implausible, or manifestly bogus, had the potential to illuminate some unexamined area of our shared humanity.

Borges wanted to be a writer, but literary success had eluded him in every **genre** he tried. But now he yearned to provide the missing mythology of Buenos Aires. His writing would have nothing to do with **tendentious** military history, or with the flying reptiles that figured so prominently in the ancient cultures of the continent. He would give wings to the dreams of the *barrios*, reveal their mystical **affinities**, and expose the forces that gave each *barrio* its own life and magic.

On this cold winter day, Borges planned to disclose what slept beneath the terrible grey hush of this peaceful, well-maintained *barrio*. Tears stung his eyes, and he tried to rub them away as he ran to meet his friend. Being late made him self-conscious.

He did not have a chance to see the window swing open directly above him. The impact caused the glass to shatter, and several filthy shards embedded themselves in his head. Septicemia set in, and for two weeks he suffered from nightmares and delirium that were **corollary** effects of the fever. For days he was perilously close to death. His accident proved **portentous**. After a protracted convalescence he was not the same writer—he had broken through the **parameters** of conventional prose. His last book before his illness had sold thirty-seven copies. The first book he wrote after his illness, *Ficciones* (1943), is widely regarded as the most influential collection of fantasy short stories ever published in Spanish. Its startling originality and web of fantasy ensconced Borges among the greatest of the twentieth century's writers and as a primary influence on the development of a genre that came to be called magic realism.

1. What is the author's purpose in the first paragraph?
- **A)** to convey a clue to Borges's literary methods
- **B)** to establish the impression that Borges is hiding
- **C)** to give a brief introduction to Borges and his interests
- **D)** to convey an accurate impression of Borges's appearance

2. As it is used in line 23, "mnemonic" most nearly means
- **A)** knowledgeable.
- **B)** advanced.
- **C)** reminder.
- **D)** writing.

3. As it is used in line 38, "genre" most nearly means
- **A)** location.
- **B)** publisher.
- **C)** subject.
- **D)** type.

4. It can reasonably be inferred that the "system of mental classification" (lines 22–23) Borges developed
- **A)** influenced the way he expressed his ideas in his novels.
- **B)** would be unnecessary in the modern world.
- **C)** was irrelevant and impossible for anyone else to grasp.
- **D)** often meant he memorized things of little interest or relevance.

5. Paragraph 3 (lines 36–47) demonstrates
- **A)** Borges's fondness for acting out fictional versions of himself.
- **B)** how easily Borges is distracted by his private obsessions.
- **C)** how earnestly Borges wanted to express his feelings about Buenos Aires.
- **D)** the comic futility of Borges's way of life and attempts at being a writer.

6. As it is used in line 41, "tendentious" most nearly means
- **A)** unproven, or questionable.
- **B)** intended to glorify one faction.
- **C)** intended to provoke civil unrest.
- **D)** splendidly victorious.

7. It can reasonably be inferred that Borges used his vast knowledge of Buenos Aires to
- **A)** praise his fellow citizens.
- **B)** invent folklore and legend.
- **C)** enrich his writing.
- **D)** write the history of the *barrios*.

8. Which choice provides the best evidence for the answer to the previous question?
- **A)** Lines 8–14 ("This man ... true")
- **B)** Lines 15–18 ("Borges's ... the city")
- **C)** Lines 31–35 ("Every piece ... humanity")
- **D)** Lines 36–38 ("Borges ... he tried")

9. It can reasonably be inferred that Borges's illness
- **A)** was brought on by his deteriorating eyesight.
- **B)** was made worse by the nightmares he had.
- **C)** made him take his writing and his life more seriously.
- **D)** brought about a change that greatly influenced his writing style.

10. The primary purpose of this narrative is to
- **A)** explain the circumstances of Borges's sudden transformation as a writer from obscurity to greatness.
- **B)** tell the story of how Borges became world famous by writing an account of the accident that changed his life.
- **C)** show how an inexplicable accident inspired Borges to write fiction.
- **D)** demonstrate how Borges was able to turn a deeply unfortunate event into a stroke of good luck.

Vocabulary for Comprehension Part 2

*Read these passages, which contain words in **boldface** that appear in Units 4–6. Then choose the best answer to each question based on what is stated or implied in the passages. You may refer to the passages as often as necessary.*

Questions 1–10 are based on the following passages.

Passage 1

Child prodigy Maria Gaëtano Agnesi was born into a wealthiest families in eighteenth-century Milan. Maria's father, Pietro Agnesi Mariami, was an important man in Milan. He recognized Maria's genius, and hired the best tutors for her.

It was Maria's misfortune that her father put her gifts on display to enhance his own prestige. He **bruited** her talents and turned her fluency in seven languages into entertainment. Guests at Pietro's soirees embodied the intellectual glamor, political power, and cultural influence to which he aspired. He would pay a distinguished mathematician an **emolument commensurate** with his eminence, and this hired star would initiate the entertainment by stating an original mathematical proposition in Latin. Maria would make a counter-proposition, and they would continue until Maria won, but she found such exhibitions **traumatic**.

In 1727, when she was just nine years old, Maria published a Latin discourse in defense of higher education for females, which showed extraordinary intellectual **prescience**. She begged to be released from performing, but her father refused. However, he granted her three hours per day for private study. It took her ten years to write her *Philosophical Propositions* (1738), and *Analytical Methods for Young Italians,* which she also began in childhood, was published in 1748. When her father died in 1752, Maria abandoned mathematics, gave her fortune to the poor and devoted her life to helping the sick.

Passage 2

Daisy Ashford was 36 years old when one day in 1917 she found an old exercise book in a drawer. It contained the manuscript she had written and lost twenty-seven years earlier. She had been a prolific author as a child, but the urge to write had left her in her teenage years.

The manuscript Daisy found was titled *The Young Visiters* (sic), a comedy of manners about "an elderly man of forty-two" called Alfred Salteena and his efforts to smooth the path of love for two friends as well as his heroic struggle to rise from the **hoi polloi** and become a gentleman. The adult Daisy showed the manuscript to her friends, and its reputation spread. It was published in 1919 with the author's childhood misspellings left intact. The book became a comic sensation. Some critics said that it could not have been written by a child, while others said the comedy sprang from the child's **risibly** grandiose misconceptions of adult fears and dreams.

Daisy Ashford would have been a prodigy even if she had never written a word. As a child she had no appetite for children's books, but her vast consumption of adult literature ran the **gamut** from the peaks of Tolstoy to the depths of Victorian melodrama. She found the behavior of adults **ineffably** funny, and paid tribute to their absurdity in *The Young Visiters.* It is the work of a person of genius. Fortunately, Ashford's fame came later in life, and the nine-year-old author was free to enjoy her childhood.

1. As it is used in line 9, "bruited" most nearly means
A) sold.
B) advertised.
C) mocked.
D) expunged.

2. In Passage 1, how is the main idea of the second paragraph (lines 7–22) best summarized?
A) Maria's performances made her famous.
B) Pietro financed Maria's research with the income from her shows.
C) Pietro exploited Maria's gifts to boost his own social status.
D) Maria's linguistic skills were more popular than her mathematical prowess.

3. As it is used in line 22, "traumatic" most nearly means
A) liable to cause nightmares.
B) vividly effective.
C) damaging to her health and well-being.
D) exciting.

4. As it is used in line 59, "risibly" most nearly means
A) demonstrably.
B) laughably.
C) wittily.
D) mistakenly.

5. As it is used in line 66, "gamut" most nearly means
A) menu.
B) marathon.
C) gauntlet.
D) entire range.

6. In Passage 2, the author quotes from *The Young Visiters* in order to show
A) Daisy's misuse of vocabulary.
B) Daisy's ignorance of human evolution.
C) Daisy's youth creates accidental humor.
D) that the book really is funny.

7. In Passage 1, the author emphasizes the emotional stress of being gifted, while the author of Passage 2 indicates
A) that Ashford handled the stress because of her sense of humor.
B) that prodigies should accept all praise, because it is well-meant.
C) that child prodigies would always be misunderstood and ill-treated.
D) that Ashford was fortunate that her childhood gifts were not discovered until she was an adult.

8. Which choice provides the best evidence for the answer to the previous question?
A) Lines 55–60 (The book ... dreams)
B) Lines 61–63 (Daisy Ashford ... word)
C) Lines 63–67 (As a child ... melodrama)
D) Lines 71–73 (Fortunately ... childhood)

9. The author of Passage 1 describes the exploitation of a talented child, while the author of Passage 2 investigates
A) the true author of *The Young Visiters*.
B) the unique perspective of a child prodigy and how it is expressed.
C) how Ashford's childhood would have been if her genius had been known.
D) the influence of the works of other authors on any work of fiction.

10. In which ways did Gaëtano and Ashford value their accomplishments?
A) Gaëtano flourished under pressure from her father, while Ashford believes her writing resulted from her free will.
B) Gaëtano believes her gifts ruined her life, while Ashford believes that writing illuminated her childhood.
C) Gaëtano is glad to be rid of her obligation to perform for her father's friends, while Ashford is glad to publish the book of the brilliant child she was.
D) Gaëtano envies Ashford for the casual way she gave up writing as a teenager, while Ashford admires Gaëtano for her enduring devotion to mathematics.

Synonyms

*From the word bank below, choose the word that has the same or nearly the same meaning as the **boldface** word in each sentence and write it on the line. You will not use all of the words.*

affinity	**divination**	**obloquy**	**salubrious**
commensurate	**hoi polloi**	**obsequies**	**systemic**
elixir	**in medias res**	**portentous**	**vicissitude**
derring-do	**internecine**	**prurient**	**volte-face**

1. If only curing sickness in real life were as simple as in fairy tales, where a **tonic** can bring the ill back to full health. ____________
2. The **savage** battles of the American Civil War cost more lives than any other American conflict and nearly tore the country in two. ____________
3. Her enrollement in art school was a complete **turnabout** from someone who had always stated her ambitions to become a lawyer. ____________
4. After a long and dreary day, spending time with my oldest friend and laughing over memories had an **invigorating** effect. ____________
5. Your bank account may suffer if you continue to indulge in your **penchant** for exclusively buying designer clothes. ____________
6. The parents wondered how such **lewd** content was allowed to be shown on daytime television, when children may be watching. ____________
7. I visit my general practitioner when I'm sick, as I know he'll take a more **comprehensive** look at my health than a specialist would. ____________
8. The **fluctuations** in fortune that she has experienced have taught her to enjoy the moment, as everything may change in an instant. ____________
9. We wondered why such a smart woman has that low-level job instead of a career **comparable** with her level of intelligence. ____________
10. The press had heaped such **opprobrium** on the suspect before the trial that it would be impossible to find impartial jury members. ____________
11. When I realized the author had begun the story **in the middle,** I realized that the plot would soon become clear to me. ____________
12. He claimed to have the gift of **prophecy** after he predicted exactly what would happen in the movie, but I suspect he had seen the film previously. ____________

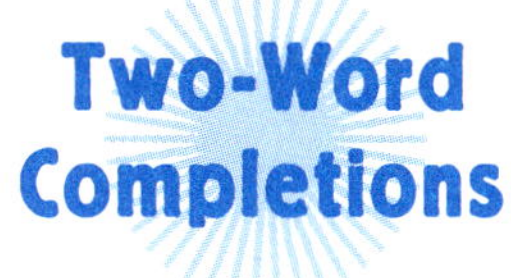

Select the pair of words that best completes the meaning of each of the following sentences.

1. Famous for his daring ________________ deep behind Northern lines, J. E. B. Stuart, the South's most colorful cavalry commander, led his men on one dangerous mission after another with all the ________________ and style of one of Charlemagne's legendary paladins.

   a. forays ... panache
   b. philippics ... derring-do
   c. obsequies ... persona
   d. emoluments ... prescience

2. Though I can't say that I relish the thriller as a literary form, I'm a real ________________ of the detective ________________.

   a. iconoclast ... matrix
   b. aficionado ... genre
   c. persona ... folderol
   d. pundit ... touchstone

3. Because French, Spanish, and Italian are ________________ languages, in college I quickly and happily ________________ myself in the study of Romantic languages, as I had studied Spanish in middle school and high school.

   a. maudlin ... vitiated
   b. persiflage ... plethora
   c. cognate ... ensconced
   d. interstices ... liturgy

4. My aunt delighted in creating ________________ comic strips that made visual the moral principles she valued; however, she made sure that her readers did not feel as if she were delivering a weekly ________________.

   a. saturnalian ... prescience
   b. contumelious ... quid pro quo
   c. bilious ... corollary
   d. waggish ... homily

5. When he realized that flattery was getting him nowhere, he attempted to ________________ me into acquiescence; but, here again, his efforts proved ________________.

   a. browbeat ... abortive
   b. bruit ... risible
   c. modulate ... maladroit
   d. vitiate ... tendentious

6. My late night ________________ on the meaning of my life and my role as office worker, I fear, are ________________ of a general displeasure with my current position.

   a. mnemonics ... ineffable
   b. lucubrations ... symptomatic
   c. obsequies ... portentous
   d. emoluments ... insouciant

7. In one of her more devastating ________________, Dorothy Parker is reputed to have once observed that an incompetent actor's interpretation of a role ran the ________________ of emotions from A to B.

   a. lucubrations ... mnemonic
   b. homilies ... parameters
   c. dicta ... gamut
   d. corollaries ... cul-de-sac

Denotation and Connotation

Words always have **denotations**, or dictionary definitions. Words can also have numerous **connotations**, or subjective meanings. A word often has a *positive* or *negative* connotation.

Skilled writers use nuance in denotation and connotation to communicate carefully. For example, to describe a confident character, a writer might describe her as *bold, daring, presumptuous, reckless, audacious,* or *plucky*. Each word conveys a different message.

Consider these synonyms for the relatively negative word *maudlin*:

sentimental *effusive* *mushy* *mawkish*

Sentimental has a somewhat neutral connotation, suggesting someone who can easily become emotional. *Effusive* often has a positive connotation and can show approval or abundance of emotion. *Mushy* has a negative connotation, and *mawkish* is so negative that it conveys a feeling of disgust.

Look at these examples of words that are similar in denotation but have different connotations.

NEUTRAL	POSITIVE	NEGATIVE
authority	**aficionado**	**fanatic**
compel	**suggest**	**browbeat**
inexpert	**amateur**	**maladroit**

Expressing the Connotation

Read each sentence. Select the word in parentheses that expresses the connotation (positive, negative, or neutral) given at the beginning of the sentence.

positive **1.** The (**ineffable, indescribable**) beauty of Lake Superior may only be expressed in poetic verse.

positive **2.** Your words of kindness were the necessary (**elixir, remedy**) that gave me, at once, both hope and peace.

negative **3.** The black and (**portentous, ominous**) gathering storm clouds reflected the darkness our family faced.

neutral **4.** The teachers' effectiveness was (**vitiated, weakened**) when the class sizes were increased.

negative **5.** The (**obloquy, reproach**) endured by the journalist caused him to resign.

negative **6.** The mayor delivered a (**lecture, philippic**) urging workers to end the strike.

positive **7.** Her (**sheer, diaphanous**) dress was sleeveless and wowed the media.

neutral **8.** My speech concerning the proposed law was (**partisan, tendentious**) but honest.

Classical Roots

gen—race, kind, class; origin, birth

This root appears in **genre**, "a type, class, or variety, especially with relation to literary composition or painting" (page 74). Some other words based on the same root are listed below.

carcinogen	**degenerate**	**generic**	**genocide**
congenital	**genealogy**	**genesis**	**homogeneous**

From the list of words above, choose the one that corresponds to each of the brief definitions below. Write the word in the blank space in the illustrative sentence below the definition.

1. the systematic extermination of a racial, political, or cultural group
During the regime of Pol Pot (1975–1979), Khmer Rouge forces in Cambodia conducted a ____________________ of unprecedented proportions.

2. to deteriorate or decline physically or morally; exhibiting such decline; a morally degraded person
The judge condemned their ____________________ behavior by imposing a stiff sentence.

3. a record or account of a family's or a person's descent; lineage; the studyof ancestry and family histories
Using online resources, he was able to trace his ____________________ back ten generations.

4. relating to an entire group or class; not protected by trademark, nonproprietary
We know many products by their brands but not by their ____________________ names.

5. cancer-causing substance
Food additives cannot be used unless they pass tests proving that they are not ____________________.

6. uniform in composition; like in nature or kind
The Latin Club is comprised of a remarkably ____________________ group of students.

7. existing at birth; constituting an essential characteristic as if by birth, inherent
No amount of guidance and counseling could overcome the fact that she was simply a ____________________ liar.

8. creation, origin; the coming into being of something
No one is entirely sure of the ____________________ of the idea that became the Internet we know today.

UNIT 7

Read the following passage, taking note of the ***boldface*** *words and their contexts. These words are among those you will be studying in Unit 7. It may help you to complete the exercises in this Unit if you refer to the way the words are used below.*

On the Edge

<First-Person Narrative>

"There's nothing in the world like a Class V river after spring melt," my friends assured me, recounting tales of **picaresque** adventures on the river last spring.

"It's living on the edge," they said, and I really couldn't tell if they were trying to get me scared or pumped up.

As we unpacked our kayaks, they were hollering and laughing, frenetic, **gamboling** around the site; I was excited too, but less boisterous, trying to concentrate my energy. It would be my first time on a river this rough, but if I was nervous, I wasn't **ambivalent**: I'd been envisioning this moment for years, and could not wait to hit the water. Besides, I knew my friends wouldn't give me **carte blanche**; they'd lead the way, and I'd follow, guided by the greater experience of my companions.

From the moment we put into the river, I was **imbued** with a profound awe at its power—I mean, I'm fit and strong, but it took every ounce of strength to control that boat, **refractory** under the river's influence, till after ten minutes of wrestling against the vessel and the water I was exhausted. Looking ahead, I took some comfort from the sight of my friends' boats skipping over the rolling foam.

That moment of consolation might have broken my focus, because, before I could react, an **inchoate** wall of froth raged up from the river, an angry ghost, and the whole world disappeared. I couldn't see my friends, or the banks, or the cliffs beyond—worse, I didn't see that execrable hole coming, that roiling **cataclysm** of backwash, till it had already snatched and swallowed me whole. Fierce currents slapped me from every side; I flapped, helpless, like a salmon in grizzly

jaws; upright, underwater, upright, underwater, upside-down, I don't know how many times that kayak and I capsized and came right again.

Beleaguered by surging waters, my normal, everyday brain chemistry fallen into **abeyance**, I was running on pure adrenaline. Staring into the icy eyes of the abyss, my body wrestled with the river, which seemed a living thing, pushing against me, forcing me deeper underwater, torturing that **malleable** kayak till I thought it would snap like a toy. But with a furious final slap my bow dove deep, we caught a downstream current, and I lurched out of the hole.

My strength was sapped, my stomach **queasy**, and a fast glance downriver did nothing to revive my spirits. White water churned through a bouldery maze; my friends were gone from sight. I'd already taken a pounding, and the stretch ahead seemed just as rough. I could have **opted** to swim to the bank but decided against it: If I got out of that kayak, one of the approaching boulders might prove too quick a **nemesis**.

Those scraggy boulders nearly got me anyway, but I worked my way through them in a frantic blur of paddling. Relieved, I exhaled hard, groaning and laughing in one breath—unaware that I was out of the frying pan and into the fire. My ears, still ringing from the ordeal in the hole, didn't hear the commotion of the approaching roar, and my gaze was riveted on my friends, just now come into view, standing and gesticulating wildly on the left bank. They'd seen the waterfall ahead, and—normally none too **fastidious** about avoiding risks—they'd judged the drop too dangerous and paddled ashore rather than chance the fall. Too late to join them—the swirling current swept me over the brink.

One good thing about plunging over a waterfall is that it doesn't take long. There were three drops, and I went airborne three times, and somehow I thwacked miraculously down and upright into splashing water at each drop's end. I can hardly take credit for it, but to any observer the feat must have seemed accomplished with some **éclat**.

"You all right?" my friends shouted, scrambling down the rocks to where I finally returned to the bank.

The reply rolled from my lips with euphoric **savoir-faire**.

"Living on the edge is fine," I panted, "but don't ever go over it."

Audio

For iWords and audio passages, go to SadlierConnect.com.

Definitions

Note the spelling, pronunciation, part(s) of speech, and definition(s) of each of the following words. Then write the appropriate form of the word in the blank space in the illustrative sentence(s) following.

1. ambivalent (am biv′ ə lənt)
(*adj.*) having opposite and conflicting feelings about someone or something
Despite their deeply ____________ attitudes, the scientists went ahead with the program.

2. beleaguer (bi lē′ gər)
(*v.*) to set upon from all sides; to surround with an army; to trouble, harass
Sherman's division arrived by train, then positioned itself to ____________ the city's fortress.

3. carte blanche (kärt′ blänsh′)
(*n.*) full freedom or authority to act at one's own discretion
The boss gave us ____________ in the matter of how we were going to approach the client.

4. éclat (ā klä′)
(*n.*) dazzling or conspicuous success or acclaim; great brilliance (of performance or achievement)
Dazzled by the ____________ of the performance, critics heaped praise on the troupe.

5. gambol (gam′ bəl)
(*v.*) to jump or skip about playfully
The children began to ____________ like fawns in a meadow.

6. inchoate (in kō′ it)
(*adj.*) just beginning; not fully shaped or formed
At first a molten and ____________ mass, it soon grew, picked up speed, and destroyed all in its path.

7. lampoon (lam pün′)
(*n.*) a malicious satire; (*v.*) to satirize, ridicule
Their ____________ of his speech impediment did not amuse the dictator.
The intent was to ____________ the senator.

8. philistine (fil′ i stēn)
(*adj.*) lacking in, hostile to, or smugly indifferent to cultural and artistic values or refinements; (*n.*) such a person
Their ____________ contempt for art is something the curator simply cannot abide.
The mayor is seen as a ____________ by the members of the city's arts community.

9. picaresque (pik ə resk′) (*adj.*) involving or characteristic of clever rogues or adventurers

Reviewers cited the ____________ element in the novel as its best feature.

10. refractory (ri frak′ tə rē) (*adj.*) stubborn; hard or difficult to manage; not responsive to treatment or cure

Caring for the ____________ patient left us exhausted and drained.

Using Context

*For each item, determine whether the **boldface** word from pages 102–103 makes sense in the context of the sentence. Circle the item numbers next to the six sentences in which the words are used correctly.*

1. The doctor gained fame for his success with several seemingly **refractory** cases.
2. It is a common complaint of parents that as soon as they lay their children down to sleep, the children begin to **beleaguer** them with questions and requests.
3. The wealthy client set no spending limits and expressed no preferences, so the architect had **carte blanche** for designing the house.
4. The walrus is a massive creature that moves on land with great **éclat**.
5. The editor identified the parts of the essay that were vague and **inchoate** and strongly suggested a major revision.
6. Earthquakes, hurricanes, and avalanches are all examples of the **ambivalent** power of nature.
7. It was painful to watch the long-distance runner **gambol** and then fall down in exhaustion just a few feet before the finish line.
8. The fact that someone doesn't like a particular style of art doesn't necessarily make him or her a **philistine**.
9. The mayor promised to **lampoon** all available resources in order to provide immediate help to those affected by the power failure.
10. Like Cervantes's *Don Quixote*, the novel on which it is based, the musical *Man of La Mancha* recounts the **picaresque** adventures of a landowner who sets out to live like a heroic knight.

Set A

*Select the **boldface** word that better completes each sentence. You might refer to the passage on pages 100–101 to see how most of these words are used in context. Note that the choices might be related forms of the Unit words.*

1. During World War II, in the (**gamboled, beleaguered**) city of Leningrad, employees and citizens worked tirelessly to protect art in the State Hermitage Museum.

2. Because Thurber combines humor and pathos so masterfully, we might say that the mood of his stories is (**inchoate, ambivalent**).

3. Since they had always been reasonably well-behaved, I was utterly taken aback by the twins' (**ambivalent, refractory**) behavior.

4. With all the misplaced confidence of inexperienced youth, I set out to make a million dollars by (**gamboling, lampooning**) in the not-so-verdant pastures of Wall Street.

5. Although we disagreed with much of what you said, we could not help admiring the rhetorical brilliance and (**carte blanche, éclat**) of your writing style.

6. Although his poetry is somewhat crude and (**inchoate, picaresque**), it has a primitive energy and drive that many readers find extremely appealing.

7. She was bewildered by the exhibition of abstract art, but, fearing to be labeled a (**lampoon, philistine**), she pretended to understand what she was looking at.

8. The student-run university newspaper is decidedly a(n) (**éclat, lampoon**), and their reporters relish poking fun at the student government and the administration.

9. Mary Bennett's (**philistine, picaresque**) taste in music is so well known that her sisters cringe every time she approaches the pianoforte.

10. Perhaps you hope to divert our attention from your own misconduct by maliciously (**lampooning, gamboling**) a sincere and able public official.

11. With plenty of free time and with an excellent library at my disposal, I gave myself (**philistine, carte blanche**) to read anything I wanted.

12. In spite of his courage and love of adventure, he lacks the stature of a true hero; his character might better be described as (**picaresque, refractory**).

Choose the word from the word bank that best completes each of the following sentences. Write the correct word or form of the word in the space provided.

ambivalent	**carte blanche**	**gambol**	**lampoon**	**picaresque**
beleaguer	**éclat**	**inchoate**	**philistine**	**refractory**

1. A host of creditors ________________ the hapless businessman with demands for payment and threats of legal action.

2. Should we expect the needs and purposes of a true poet to be understood by such a thoroughgoing ________________?

3. The young pianist dazzled the audience with the ________________ and verve of his performance.

4. Because I had unlimited faith in their honesty and discretion, I felt no qualms about giving them ________________ to do whatever they thought was necessary.

5. You made some rather clever suggestions at the meeting, but on the whole, your ideas were far too ________________ to serve as the basis for a workable plan.

6. Her equivocal answers to my questions about going to college in the fall clearly revealed her ________________ attitude toward leaving home.

7. The entire issue of the magazine was designed as a(n) ________________ satirizing the follies and futilities of mass-consumption advertising.

8. Instead of settling down to a job and a family, Tom seems to be modeling his life on the career of some rogue out of a(n) ________________ novel.

9. As we turned in to the ranch, we saw two young foals ________________ playfully in the open field.

10. Though Jane's mount was as docile as a newborn lamb, mine proved to be the most ________________ animal I had ever ridden.

End Set A

Definitions

Note the spelling, pronunciation, part(s) of speech, and definition(s) of each of the following words. Then write the appropriate form of the word in the blank space in the illustrative sentence(s) following.

1. **abeyance** (ə bā′ əns) — (*n.*) a state of being temporarily inactive, suspended, or set aside

   The administrators and staff reluctantly agreed to hold the matter in ________________.

2. **cataclysm** (kat′ ə kliz əm) — (*n.*) a sudden, violent, or devastating upheaval; a surging flood, deluge

   Diplomacy could not stop the ________________ of World War I.

3. **debauch** (di bôch′) — (*v.*) to corrupt morally, seduce; to indulge in dissipation; (*n.*) an act or occasion of dissipation or vice

   Those who would ________________ the innocent deserve our wrath.

   The ________________ began at midnight.

4. **fastidious** (fa stid′ ē əs) — (*adj.*) overly demanding or hard to please; excessively careful in regard to details; easily disgusted

   Known for her ________________ taste, the decorator was always in great demand.

5. **imbue** (im byü′) — (*v.*) to soak or stain thoroughly; to fill the mind

   The celebrated teacher strove to ________________ her students with the desire to succeed.

6. **malleable** (mal′ ē ə bəl) — (*adj.*) capable of being formed into different shapes; capable of being altered, adapted, or influenced

   The ________________ minds of the young students were at the mercy of the charismatic professor.

7. **nemesis** (nem′ ə sis) — (*n.*) an agent or force inflicting vengeance or punishment; retribution itself; an unbeatable rival

   Calculus proved to be my ________________.

8. **opt** (opt) — (*v.*) to make a choice or decision

   We had to ________________ for the cheaper model.

9. queasy
(kwē′ zē)

(*adj.*) nauseated or uneasy; causing nausea or uneasiness; troubled

The remarks gave me a ____________________ feeling in the pit of my stomach.

10. savoir-faire
(sav wär fâr′)

(*n.*) the ability to say and do the right thing in any situation; social competence

The experienced and wily ambassador handled the delicate affair with her usual ____________________.

Using Context

*For each item, determine whether the **boldface** word from pages 106–107 makes sense in the context of the sentence. Circle the item numbers next to the six sentences in which the words are used correctly.*

1. The gory scenes made some of the moviegoers so **queasy** that they had to step out of the theater for some fresh air.
2. As I watched the footage of a recent tsunami on the news, my heart ached for the victims of this **cataclysm**.
3. You can **opt** to receive the monthly updates by email or text message.
4. I try to **imbue** all thoughts from my mind when I meditate at night, but it's often difficult not to focus on the stressful projects I have at work.
5. The audience cheered when the superhero finally captured her **nemesis** and foiled his evil plan for destruction.
6. I was afraid that I would make a bumbling display of **savoir-faire** with my inexperience at interviewing such high-ranking officials.
7. He is a **malleable** child who does not adapt easily to new situations or changes in his daily routine.
8. The officials decided to temporarily suspend the plans to build the new bridge, but promised to return the matter to **abeyance** once the public's questions were resolved.
9. A group of parents is petitioning the network not to include such mature content in its programming, which, they say, will **debauch** their children's innocent minds.
10. The author is known for her **fastidious** way of writing, ensuring that all details are accurate and that there are no plot holes throughout the series.

Set B

*Select the **boldface** word that better completes each sentence. You might refer to the passage on pages 100–101 to see how most of these words are used in context. Note that the choices might be related forms of the Unit words.*

1. James Thurber's stories are extremely funny, but they are also (**imbued, debauched**) with a profound sense of the pathos of the human condition.

2. Would it not be a gross miscarriage of justice to prosecute us under a law which, for all practical purposes, has been in (**abeyance**, **savoir-faire**) since the early years of the last century?

3. Their (**fastidious, queasy**) preoccupation with minor details of style is not to be confused with a genuine appreciation of language.

4. Instead of endless lamentations about how bad things are, let us try to look realistically at the (**cataclysms, options**) open to us.

5. Scientists have synthesized a new and durable metal compound that is both magnetic and extremely (**fastidious, malleable**) at room temperature.

6. Refusing to become flustered, she handled the embarrassing situation with the finesse and (**queasiness, savoir-faire**) of a born diplomat.

7. Another world war would be a (**savoir-faire, cataclysm**) on so vast a scale that it is doubtful whether civilization could survive it.

8. Perhaps she felt disturbed at the prospect of having to betray her friends, but she seems to have overcome her (**queasiness, cataclysm**) without too much trouble.

9. I think the widespread use of technology in schools (**debauches, imbues**) the youth.

10. Their obsession with military conquest, leading them to waste their vast resources on armaments and endless wars, proved to be their (**nemesis, abeyance**).

11. It is one thing to be open-minded and (**queasy, malleable**); it is quite another to be without fixed ideas or principles of any kind.

12. Although I intended to host a movie night, my parents worried it would turn into a(n) (**debauch, abeyance**).

Completing the Sentence

Choose the word from the word bank that best completes each of the following sentences. Write the correct word or form of the word in the space provided.

abeyance	**debauch**	**imbue**	**nemesis**	**queasy**
cataclysm	**fastidious**	**malleable**	**opt**	**savoir-faire**

1. They showed such a deplorable lack of ____________________ in handling that difficult situation that they converted a mere unpleasantness into a social disaster.

2. I was confident that I would do well in the scholarship examination, but my hopes were dashed by my old ____________________, mathematics.

3. The purpose of the course in American history is to ____________________ young people with a genuine understanding of what this country stands for.

4. Why would they have ____________________ themselves by joining in that obscene celebration?

5. Many scientists are fearful that the West Coast may someday suffer a(n) ____________________ as violent as the earthquake that devastated San Francisco in 1906.

6. I freely confess that just the sight of a roller coaster is enough to make me feel ____________________.

7. Such capacity for growth and self-improvement can be expected only in the ____________________ years of the teens and early twenties.

8. Oscar's careless housekeeping and sloppy habits were an endless source of exasperation to his ____________________ roommate.

9. Perhaps once in a generation, a people is faced with a great moral crisis in which it must ____________________ for good or evil, war or peace, life or death.

10. There are circumstances under which it is desirable to make decisions swiftly and unequivocally, but there are other cases in which it is wise to hold decisions in ____________________.

End Set B

Synonyms

*Choose the word or form of the word from this Unit that is the same or most nearly the same in meaning as the **boldface** word or expression in the phrase. Write that word on the line. Use a dictionary if necessary.*

1. **instill** the troops with courage ________
2. proceeded to **ridicule** the speaker ________
3. **harass** the messenger of bad news ________
4. dresses in a **meticulous** manner ________
5. an **equivocal** response ________
6. a tale of a **roguish** adventure on the high seas ________
7. a town devastated by the **catastrophe** of the overflowing river ________
8. felt **unsettled** by the motion of the boat ________
9. **choose** to eat either cake or pie for dessert ________
10. vowed to defeat his **adversary** ________
11. welcomed the **deferment** ________
12. handled the interview with his usual **finesse** ________
13. attempted to sway the **impressionable** undecided voters ________
14. was in its **rudimentary** form at that time ________
15. offered us **free rein** ________

Antonyms

*Choose the word or form of the word from this Unit that is most nearly opposite in meaning to the **boldface** word or expression in the phrase. Write that word on the line. Use a dictionary if necessary.*

1. a **dutiful** employee ________
2. asked to **trudge** across the stage ________
3. to **inspire** the youth by good example ________
4. a family of **aesthetes** who read voraciously ________
5. critiqued the **mediocrity** of the actor's performance ________

Writing: Words in Action

Consider the risks and the thrill of kayaking or canoeing in white water, and then consider at least two other extreme sports. Write a descriptive essay that discusses the risks and the thrills of these sports. Use at least three details from the passage (pages 100–101) and three or more words from this Unit.

*Some of the words you have studied in this Unit appear in **boldface** type. Read the passage below, and then circle the letter of the correct answer for each word as it is used in context*

Kayak—the palindromic word itself (try spelling it backwards) hints unmistakably at the canoe's malleable design. First used by subarctic hunters such as the Inuit and Aleut, kayaks today come with and without cockpits, appended air chambers, and foot-powered rotational propellers; moreover, at the risk of **lampoon**, it must be admitted that some kayaks are now being sailed, as well as powered by outboard gas engines or small electric motors. The original kayakers, as well as some contemporary devotees, would doubtless spurn such accoutrements as tasteless, or even **philistine—**tokens of **debauched** oarsmanship.

For **fastidious** kayak owners, the design of their canoes is imbued in trade-offs. Longer kayaks, for instance, are typically faster. Touring and sea kayaks may measure 16 to 19 feet. But if you are in the market for a new kayak, the issue of maneuverability may make you **ambivalent**, and a whitewater kayak depending primarily on river current for forward motion will rarely exceed 8 feet in length.

Similarly conflicting considerations arise with the issue of beam profile, as the stability of a single-hulled kayak depends primarily on the width of its cross-section. If you **opt** for a V-shaped hull, you will find traveling straight (tracking) easier, but maneuvering (turning) harder, while flat-bottomed hulls make turning easier but traveling in a constant direction harder.

And finally there is the issue of rocker, or the lengthwise curvature of a kayak. Heavily rockered kayaks have a shrunken effective waterline, since the bow and stern lie out of the water. In general, a moderate rocker may improve handling and make the kayak more maneuverable.

---

1. What is the meaning of **lampoon** as it is used in paragraph 1?

a. hyperbole
b. understatement
c. metonymy
d. ridicule

2. What is the meaning of **philistine** in the context of the passage?

a. boorish
b. peremptory
c. ludicrous
d. impertinent

3. What is the meaning of **debauched** as it is used in paragraph 1?

a. recrudescent
b. corrupted
c. inefficient
d. immature

4. In paragraph 2, what does **fastidious** suggest about the kayak owners?

a. They are ignorant
b. They are impulsive
c. They are finicky
d. They are indecisive

5. What does **ambivalent** most likely mean as it is used in paragraph 2?

a. restless
b. ambitious
c. supercilious
d. conflicted

6. What does **opt** most likely mean as it is used in paragraph 3?

a. select
b. research
c. plan
d. propel

Read the following passage, taking note of the ***boldface*** *words and their contexts. These words are among those you will be studying in Unit 8. It may help you to complete the exercises in this Unit if you refer to the way the words are used below.*

Target This!

<Persuasive Essay>

Your laptop is in cahoots with companies to get you to buy stuff. Think the idea is farfetched or something out of a dystopian novel? Think again. It's no **aberration**. When you click on a popular website or click to a new link, that information is captured by sophisticated tracking software that sends data to businesses or organizations eager to sign you up as a customer, client, or member. And it's not just when you use your desktop computer: More and more online marketers are using apps to track and collect data from smartphone users. This practice is called targeted advertising, or behavioral targeting, and it's a multibillion-dollar industry that's growing fast. E-commerce is booming, and experts say online tracking technology is only the beginning, a **harbinger** of things to come. Is this form of niche marketing a **de facto** deception and a **depredation**—or a forward-thinking way to help you discover the goods and services that might interest you?

Online retailers are tracking consumers in order to pinpoint and engage potential customers, get an e-edge, and boost **lackluster** sales. Advertisers use "cookies" to keep track of your browsing and shopping habits, tastes,

Accept cookies

preferences, and behaviors and then display ads that correspond to your past clicks or purchases; social-networking sites collect user actions in the form of comments, clicks, and profile updates. The newest technologies are able to predict, often to an uncanny degree of accuracy, what your next steps online might be. Customer profiles can include information like age, gender, race, income, marital status, and more. With this information, advertisers are able to drill down into niches and target subniches. They can use tracking information to create relevant advertisements and content that they think people might want to see, to **pander** to even the most unusual **peccadilloes** and whims of the consumer. Meanwhile, some online retailers are working to earn their customers' confidence and are taking steps to safeguard personal data. And some believe that the **pièce de résistance** is a seal of approval from a trusted third party, such as the Better Business Bureau, which has strict standards for bestowing accreditation. Marketers maintain that personal privacy isn't violated because Web site visitors aren't identified by name, but not everyone agrees with that assertion.

The amount of information gathered about unsuspecting consumers is frightening, and computer users need to know about it. While there is **empathy** for businesses needing to think creatively and create buzz for their brand, consumer concerns are increasing and are the **bane** of advertisers. The advice, "Let the buyer beware," is something every computer user should heed. Privacy-rights groups and opponents of targeted niche advertising aren't merely noisy **malcontents** forming **ad hoc** protests. They have plenty of powerful allies: Congress has stepped into the fray, with a few **cantankerous** lawmakers questioning online sellers' ethics and **casuistry** and pushing for more regulation and consumer protection. The issue has also been **remanded** to the Federal Trade Commission for review.

Are you willing to give up your privacy every time you access news, music, and entertainment sites? Do you want to hand over details of your life to a grasping retailer who will use your own data against you? Write to your congressperson to demand stricter Web-data-collecting regulations!

Audio

For iWords and audio passages, go to SadlierConnect.com.

Write a review

Note the spelling, pronunciation, part(s) of speech, and definition(s) of each of the following words. Then write the appropriate form of the word in the blank space in the illustrative sentence(s) following.

1. aberration (ab ə rā′ shən)
(*n.*) a departure from what is proper, right, expected, or normal; a lapse from a sound mental state

In an ____________________ of judgment, the coach chose not to call a critical time-out.

2. ad hoc (ad′ häk′)
(*adj.*) for this specific purpose; improvised; (*adv.*) with respect to this

An ____________________ committee was formed immediately.

We met, ____________________, to consider the issue.

3. bathos (bā′ thos)
(*n.*) the intrusion of commonplace or trite material into a context whose tone is lofty or elevated; grossly insincere or exaggerated sentimentality; the lowest phase, nadir; an anticlimax, comedown

After wallowing in ____________________, the writer returned to her novel in earnest.

4. casuistry (kazh′ ū is trē)
(*n.*) the determination of right and wrong in questions of conduct or conscience by the application of general ethical principles; specious argument

The professor's ideas, once highly regarded, now appear to be nothing more than ingenious ____________________.

5. de facto (dē fak′ tō)
(*adj.*) actually existing or in effect, although not legally required or sanctioned; (*adv.*) in reality, actually

The dictator's wife is the ____________________ head of state.

It appears that, ____________________, the information is true.

6. empathy (em′ pə thē)
(*n.*) a sympathetic understanding of or identification with the feelings, thoughts, or attitudes of someone or something else

The grandparents felt ____________________ for the aspirations of their grandchildren.

7. hedonism (hē′ də niz əm)
(*n.*) the belief that the attainment of pleasure is life's chief aim; devotion to or pursuit of pleasure

A beach bum's mindless ____________________ may appeal to all working people at one time or another.

8. nepotism (nep′ ə tiz əm)
(*n.*) undue favoritism to or excessive patronage of one's relatives

To avoid any hint of ____________________, the owner of the team refused to hire any of his relatives.

9. pièce de résistance (pē əs də rā zē stäns′)

(*n.*) the principal dish of a meal; the principal event, incident, or item; an outstanding accomplishment

The ____________ of the remarkable repast was the dessert, a ten-tiered cake adorned with spun sugar.

10. syndrome (sin′ drōm)

(*n.*) a group of symptoms or signs that collectively characterizes or indicates a disease, disorder, abnormality, etc.

With ubiquitous computer use, carpal tunnel has become a decidedly modern ____________.

Using Context

*For each item, determine whether the **boldface** word from pages 114–115 makes sense in the context of the sentence. Circle the item numbers next to the six sentences in which the words are used correctly.*

1. After studying several of the best silent movies from the 1920s, I no longer look upon these films as works of melodrama and **bathos** but regard them as genuine works of art.

2. It takes years of training to reach the level of **casuistry** needed to secure a place on the Olympic team.

3. The popular downtown café has become the **de facto** headquarters of three different reading groups.

4. The social worker had a particular sense of **empathy** for the city's foster children because she had once been in the same situation herself.

5. The only way to settle this **aberration** is to hire a lawyer and go to court.

6. Scientists raced to develop a **syndrome** for the previously unknown virus that had broken out and sickened thousands of people.

7. It takes a great deal of **hedonism** as well as practical knowledge to complete this three-day hiking excursion.

8. A special prosecutor was appointed to investigate the charges of bribery and **nepotism** within the governor's office.

9. The winter festival's **pièce de résistance**, a life-size mammoth sculpted from ice, did not disappoint the record-setting crowd that attended.

10. When it began to rain heavily during our hike, we used the space under a large rock ledge as an **ad hoc** shelter.

Set A

*Select the **boldface** word that better completes each sentence. You might refer to the passage on pages 112–113 to see how most of these words are used in context. Note that the choices might be related forms of the Unit words.*

1. So strong is my (**empathy, casuistry**) with the poems of Robert Frost that I often feel as though I could have written them myself.

2. Since you've been spending time with these new friends, I sense in you a sort of mental (**pièce de résistance, aberration**) that both worries and disappoints me.

3. The (**syndrome, bathos**) of poverty, drug addiction, and crime that afflicts our cities calls for remedial action on a truly national scale.

4. Then came Miss Bolton's cornet solo, which we all recognized immediately as the (**pièce de résistance, casuistry**) of that long musical evening.

5. Although the law forbids residential separation of the races, we all know that a state of (**de facto, ad hoc**) segregation exists in some communities.

6. In all aspects of their behavior, Raina and Joe showed the self-indulgence and gross indifference to others that is characteristic of the true (**syndrome, hedonist**).

7. In many respects it is a good movie, but sadly, the director has allowed sentiment to spill over into sentimentality, and sentimentality into (**bathos, casuistry**).

8. The negotiators agreed not to try to draw up an overall treaty but to deal with each specific problem on a(n) (**de facto, ad hoc**) basis.

9. We must not assume that their behavior, however (**aberrant, empathetic**) by conventional standards, is a sign of mental illness.

10. Your efforts to prove that because "no one is perfect," all moral standards are relative and therefore meaningless, struck me as sheer (**casuistry, hedonism**).

11. "Am I to be accused of (**casuistry, nepotism**)," queried the mayor, "just because my wife, daughter, brother, and nephew happen to be the best applicants for the jobs?"

12. Our fundraising committee formed (**de facto, ad hoc**) in order to more efficiently help the displaced or uninsured families that were affected by the floods.

Completing the Sentence

Choose the word from the word bank that best completes each of the following sentences. Write the correct word or form of the word in the space provided.

aberration	**bathos**	**de facto**	**hedonism**	**pièce de résistance**
ad hoc	**casuistry**	**empathy**	**nepotism**	**syndrome**

1. How is one to explain that strange ____________________ from the habits and standards that he had followed for so many years?

2. Though he had embraced a creed of unabashed ____________________ in his youth, he ended his life among a group of ascetics living in the desert.

3. Her visits to the nursing home are motivated not by a detached sense of duty but by a genuine ____________________ for those who are lonely.

4. A high temperature, yellowish complexion, and general feeling of fatigue are all characteristic of the mononucleosis ____________________.

5. Would it be ungracious of me to suggest that the ____________________ of the feast, given on the menu as "filet mignon," had the taste and texture of old shoe leather?

6. Yes, I believe in helping out relatives, but I haven't spent a lifetime building this business to make it a monument to ____________________.

7. As there was no agency concerned with race relations, the Mayor created a(n) ____________________ committee to deal with such matters.

8. The history of the world teaches us that we should never let ourselves be blinded by the meretricious ____________________ of a demagogue, no matter how appealing it may appear at first glance.

9. Those sentimentalized effusions introduced a note of ____________________ into what should have been an occasion marked by dignity and restraint.

10. I find myself in the position of ____________________ supervisor; now I would like to have the title, salary, and privileges that go along with the job.

End Set A

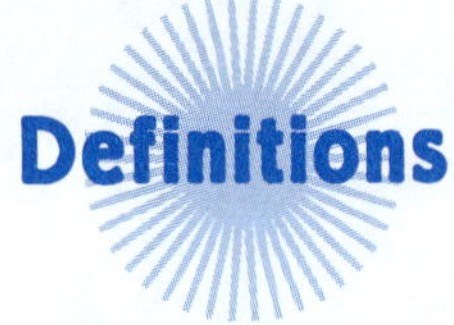

Definitions

Note the spelling, pronunciation, part(s) of speech, and definition(s) of each of the following words. Then write the appropriate form of the word in the blank space in the illustrative sentence(s) following.

1. **bane** (bān)
(*n.*) the source or cause of fatal injury, death, destruction, or ruin; death or ruin itself; poison
Rain, the ____________________ of picnics, was forecast for the day we had scheduled ours.

2. **cantankerous** (kan taŋʹ kə rəs)
(*adj.*) ill-tempered, quarrelsome; difficult to get along or deal with
The ____________________ machine befuddled the team of technicians assigned to repair it.

3. **depredation** (dep rə dāʹ shən)
(*n.*) the act of preying upon or plundering
The ____________________ of the invaders left scars that will take years to heal.

4. **harbinger** (härʹ bən jər)
(*n.*) a forerunner, herald; (*v.*) to herald the approach of
Daffodils in bloom are a ____________________ of spring.
Crocuses, too, ____________________ the approach of spring.

5. **lackluster** (lakʹ lus tər)
(*adj.*) lacking brilliance or vitality; dull
The weary soldier's ____________________ stare haunted the photographer, who captured it with her lens.

6. **malcontent** (malʹ kən tent)
(*adj.*) discontented with or in open defiance of prevailing conditions; (*n.*) such a person
The ____________________ transit workers went out on strike.
The angry mayor referred to the strikers as a group of vocal, lazy ____________________.

7. **mellifluous** (mə lifʹ lü əs)
(*adj.*) flowing sweetly or smoothly; honeyed
The folk singer's ____________________ voice appealed to young and old the world over.

8. **pander** (panʹ dər)
(*v.*) to cater to or provide satisfaction for the low tastes or vices of others; (*n.*) a person who does this
The hosts proceeded to ____________________ to every whim of their delighted guests.
His brother was a ____________________ who ran a cheap pool hall on the outskirts of town.

9. peccadillo (pek ə dil′ ō)

(*n.*) a minor sin or offense; a trifling fault or shortcoming

If you will overlook my ____________________, I will ignore yours.

10. remand (ri mand′)

(*v.*) to send or order back; in law, to send back to jail or to a lower court

The outlaw was ____________________ to the custody of the sheriff.

Using Context

*For each item, determine whether the **boldface** word from pages 118–119 makes sense in the context of the sentence. Circle the item numbers next to the six sentences in which the words are used correctly.*

1. My boss says that our mobile phones are the **bane** of productivity and insists that we turn them off while at work.
2. Although it is still terribly cold outside, I take comfort in the chirping of birds as the **harbinger** of warmer weather.
3. The restaurant hostess asked the group to **remand** in the lobby while she found them an unoccupied table.
4. His **lackluster** reaction to the good fortune of his friend hinted that he may have been feeling a little jealous.
5. My **cantankerous** neighbor always greets me warmly and enthusiastically when I pass her on the street.
6. Although the actor is talented, no director wants to work with a **malcontent** who is never happy with his circumstances.
7. The administrator was charged with the disgraceful **peccadillo** of embezzling more than $1 million from the organization.
8. Even though I know reality shows simply **pander** to their audience's taste for drama, I admit I enjoy watching them when I don't want to think too much.
9. The grandmother could calm any child with her **mellifluous** voice, whether she was singing or simply whispering some soothing phrases.
10. Our school participates in many programs to help people in the community, such as food and clothing drives and other acts of **depredation**.

Set B

Choosing the Right Word

*Select the **boldface** word that better completes each sentence. You might refer to the passage on pages 112–113 to see how most of these words are used in context. Note that the choices might be related forms of the Unit words.*

1. Said Churchill to the British people after the Munich agreement: "We must reject these (**mellifluous, malcontent**) assurances of 'peace in our time.'"

2. The (**peccadillos, depredations**) of the terrible disease could be seen only too clearly in her extreme emaciation and feebleness.

3. We learned with dismay that our application had been neither approved nor rejected, but (**pandered, remanded**) to a "higher authority for further consideration."

4. The car was forever breaking down, but its owner seemed to derive a sort of perverse satisfaction out of battling with the (**mellifluous, cantankerous**) old heap.

5. True, we won the game, but I think our team gave a rather (**lackluster, malcontent**) performance in beating a weak opponent by so narrow a margin.

6. How can you compare a mere social (**peccadillo, depredation**) with a misdeed that has caused such great harm to other people?

7. The (**baneful, mellifluous**) looks that they directed at us made it only too clear that we had little hope for mercy at their hands.

8. A candidate for high public office should seek to debate the issues on an objective level, instead of (**remanding, pandering**) to the prejudices of the times.

9. We may find (**malcontents, harbingers**) annoying, but the fact is that they often serve as "gadflies" to bring about desirable changes.

10. The man in the gray cap is a (**pander, bane**) who engages in all kinds of illegal activities but somehow never gets caught.

11. The (**mellifluous, malcontent**) citizens formed a committee to disseminate a petition, to organize a general strike, and to monitor legislative proceedings.

12. With the extreme cold and the deep snows still holding on, the gradual lengthening of the days was the only (**bane, harbinger**) of spring.

Choose the word from the word bank that best completes each of the following sentences. Write the correct word or form of the word in the space provided.

bane	**depredation**	**lackluster**	**mellifluous**	**peccadillo**
cantankerous	**harbinger**	**malcontent**	**pander**	**remand**

1. Like everyone else, I was charmed by the ____________________ tones of the speaker, but later I could extract very little real meaning from what she had said.

2. Those cases that call for further attention will be ____________________ to the proper agencies.

3. Yes, you have scored a quick commercial success, but you have done it only by ____________________ to low and depraved tastes.

4. It was hard to believe that the eager, vibrant youth I had known was now this shabby derelict, staring into space with ____________________ eyes.

5. I think you are showing poor judgment in condemning them so severely for what is, after all, little more than a(n) ____________________.

6. Because they have followed a policy of bringing in executives and supervisors from the outside, instead of promoting from within their own ranks, the office is filled with grumbling ____________________.

7. He had been happy-go-lucky as a young man, but years of disappointment and misfortune have turned him sour and ____________________.

8. It took years for that country to recover from the ____________________ wrought by the Second World War and its concomitant social and economic dislocations.

9. The pitcher's lightning fastball has proved the ____________________ of many a celebrated home-run hitter.

10. Is it too optimistic to hope that your willingness to undertake that thankless task is the ____________________ of a new maturity and a more responsible attitude?

Synonyms

*Choose the word or form of the word from this Unit that is the same or most nearly the same in meaning as the **boldface** word or expression in the phrase. Write that word on the line. Use a dictionary if necessary.*

1. struck me as utter **quibbling** __________
2. suffers from a recognizable **group of symptoms** __________
3. seen by scientists as an **irregularity** __________
4. was the **spoiler** of our crops __________
5. quickly formed a **makeshift** group to combat bullying __________
6. the complaints of an **agitator** against the French nobles __________
7. presented the **showpiece** of the concert __________
8. **return** to custody before the trial __________
9. felt **compassion** for the injured dog __________
10. refused to **indulge** the whims of the children __________
11. uninspired by the dancer's **vapid** performance __________
12. the **ornery** old goat __________
13. committed an **indiscretion** __________
14. a **herald** of the coming of winter __________
15. victims of the **pillage** __________

Antonyms

*Choose the word or form of the word from this Unit that is most nearly opposite in meaning to the **boldface** word or expression in the phrase. Write that word on the line. Use a dictionary if necessary.*

1. awakened by the **shrill** sound __________
2. the refreshing **impartiality** of the manager __________
3. recognized as **de jure** sovereign by the people __________
4. the **sublimity** of the story's conclusion __________
5. never experienced **self-denial** __________

Writing: Words in Action

In "Target This!" the writer asks, "Are you willing to give up your privacy every time you access news, music, and entertainment sites?" Write your own answer to this question, using specific examples from your studies, reading (pages 112–113), or personal experience. Use three or more words from this Unit.

Some of the words you have studied in this Unit appear in ***boldface*** *type. Read the passage below, and then circle the letter of the correct answer for each word as it is used in context*

At the risk of incurring **bathos**, it is no exaggeration to claim that tracking, recognition, and inventory play outsized roles in hundreds of different spheres and arenas, ranging from supermarkets to hospitals. For decades now, the most common tool to accomplish such tasks was the barcode, which still remains ubiquitous, but a noteworthy challenge to barcodes has arisen from RFID technology.

Hardly a **mellifluous** acronym, RFID stands for Radio-Frequency Identification. This small electronic system, which does not require batteries, consists of three parts: a scanning antenna, a transceiver with a decoder, and a transponder, which is the RFID tag itself. The antenna emits radio-frequency signals that communicate with the transponder and also provide the tag with the energy to communicate. Although more expensive than barcodes, RFIC tags have advantages which, in the mind of an inventory manager, might suggest **hedonism**. Unlike barcode readers, RFID readers do not require a direct line of sight to the tag; they can pull information at distances up to 300 feet, as opposed to 15 feet, and they can read 40 or more tags a second; they are substantially more durable than barcodes, and they possess read-write capability.

The assets of RFID are so compelling that most managers would risk accusations of **nepotism** to retain these small electronic wonders. Implementation of RFID technology in healthcare and libraries is growing steadily, and hospitals can reduce their supply overstock and match drugs with prescription information to forestall harmful **syndromes.** About 30 million library items worldwide now contain RFID tags. Tags can be read while books are in motion, and a stack of books can be read simultaneously. It would be **casuistry** not to like RFID.

---

1. What is the meaning of **bathos** as it is used in paragraph 1?

a. ridicule
b. anticlimax
c. satire
d. censure

2. What is the meaning of **mellifluous** in the context of the passage?

a. euphonious
b. strident
c. grating
d. comprehensive

3. What is the meaning of **hedonism** as it is used in paragraph 2?

a. nostalgia
b. puritanism
c. pleasure-seeking
d. asceticism

4. In paragraph 3, what does the word **nepotism** suggest about the managers?

a. They are judicious.
b. They are not impulsive.
c. They are not impartial.
d. They are prudent.

5. What does **syndromes** most likely mean as it is used in paragraph 3?

a. breakdowns
b. patterns
c. competitions
d. barriers

6. What characteristic is suggested by **casuistry** in paragraph 3?

a. speciousness
b. precision
c. stinginess
d. presumption

UNIT 9

*Read the following passage, taking note of the **boldface** words and their contexts. These words are among those you will be studying in Unit 9. It may help you to complete the exercises in this Unit if you refer to the way the words are used below.*

Volunteer Profile: Jennifer Yoder

<Profile>

In the 40 years since its foundation, the nonprofit organization People's Habitat has worked to eliminate poverty-housing and homelessness from the world and to make decent housing a matter of conscience and action. The organization's efforts are **ecumenical** in scope, with active programs across the globe. People's Habitat has provided over 450,000 affordable homes and served over 2,100,000 people to date, earning **kudos** from presidents, community leaders, and activists alike.

People's Habitat could not function without the thousands of volunteers who donate their time and labor to the organization—volunteers like Jennifer Yoder. Now a lawyer in her early thirties, Jennifer first heard of People's Habitat in college, when a roommate **inveigled** her into attending a People's slide show presentation one evening.

"I have to admit, I was reluctant at first," Jennifer recalls with a sheepish laugh, "but the more I learned about what PH does, the more passionate I became about the organization."

Her increasingly **fervid** interest in the group came to a head in the summer of 2005, when Hurricane Katrina devastated the Gulf Coast Region.

"I'd never heard of such a **gargantuan** storm in my life," says Jennifer of the Category 5 hurricane, "and the early news did not **bode** well for the people down there on the coast."

In the wake of Katrina, PH quickly initiated a special Gulf Coast Emergency program. Jennifer decided to take a semester off from law school and pitch in.

"Everywhere I looked," she explained, "I saw damaged property and battered **infrastructure**. Most of the houses left standing in coastal Mississippi were rotten, full of mold and **dank, fetid** air."

People's Habitat shipped pre-constructed housing components to the region, assembled them in areas less stricken by the storm, and installed them at recovery sites in record time. The rapid progress gave many residents the strength not to **truckle** to despair, so often a **bête noire** for disaster victims.

"Gulf Coast Emergency was the **heyday** of my participation with People's Habitat," beams Jennifer, "and I really gained so much from the experience. I don't mean to sound like a **sycophant**, but with People's Habitat you really do give a little to get a lot."

A lot has changed for Jennifer in the years since Gulf Coast Emergency. She graduated from law school and currently works for a medium-sized law firm in her hometown of Akron, Ohio.

"Most of my volunteer work is spent behind a desk lately, and on the phone," she confesses, "because I mainly focus on fundraising nowadays."

Women volunteers help build homes for the needy.

Asked if she misses getting her hands dirty, Jennifer laughs. "Sure I do. The memory of working together with all those volunteers and family members to build homes, it brings up such a positive feeling, like a deep sense of **beatitude**."

Fortunately, it sounds as if Jennifer will soon be back building houses. She's promised her niece and **protégé**, Tula, that they'll work together on a local Women Construct project nearby in Summit County before Tula heads off to college next fall. PH's Women Construct projects typically involve an all-female crew of construction volunteers, with men invited to participate as onsite assistants and teachers. "Tula's been talking about it all year, and I'm pretty excited about it myself. We'll have an opportunity to help a hard-working family in need—and it'll be a great bonding experience, too!"

Audio

For iWords and audio passages, go to **SadlierConnect.com**.

Flooded homes in New Orleans, September 2005

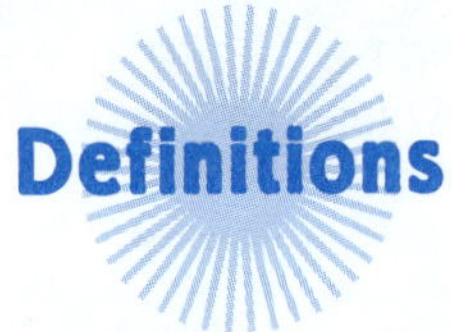

Definitions

Note the spelling, pronunciation, part(s) of speech, and definition(s) of each of the following words. Then write the appropriate form of the word in the blank space in the illustrative sentence(s) following.

1. avatar (a′ və tär)

(*n.*) an embodiment (as of a concept or philosophy) often in a person; an electronic image that represents and is manipulated by a computer user

Once users choose __________________ for the application, they can virtually connect with friends.

2. bête noire (bet nwär′)

(*n.*) someone or something that one especially dislikes, dreads, or avoids

Spinach used to be the __________________ of my diet, but that was before I tasted blood sausage.

3. dank (daŋk)

(*adj.*) unpleasantly damp or wet

Mold can grow in a __________________ basement.

4. fervid (fər′ vid)

(*adj.*) burning with enthusiasm or zeal; extremely heated

Using __________________ words of praise, the coach gave the team a pep talk before the big game.

5. gargantuan (gär gan′ chü ən)

(*adj.*) of immense size, volume, or capacity; enormous, prodigious

The spirited artist had a __________________ thirst for life.

6. incubus (iŋ′ kyə bəs)

(*n.*) a demon or evil spirit supposed to haunt human beings in their bedrooms at night; anything that oppresses or weighs upon one, like a nightmare

I dreamt that an __________________ entered my room.

7. kudos (kü′ dōs)

(*n.*) the acclaim, prestige, or renown that comes as a result of some action or achievement

The poet received all the __________________ due a Nobel laureate.

8. prolix (prō lix′)

(*adj.*) long-winded and wordy; tending to speak or write in such a way

The father of the bride regaled anyone who would listen with a __________________ description of the wedding.

9. protégé (prō′ tə zhā) (*n.*) someone whose welfare, training, or career is under the patronage of an influential person; someone under the jurisdiction of a foreign country or government

The _________________ of the ex-champion may one day be a champion herself.

10. tautology (tô tol′ ə jē) (*n.*) needless repetition of an idea by using different but equivalent words; a redundancy

Filled with endless _________________ and solecisms, the lengthy book is a tiresome read.

Using Context

*For each item, determine whether the **boldface** word from pages 126–127 makes sense in the context of the sentence. Circle the item numbers next to the six sentences in which the words are used correctly.*

1. To someone who is not trained in law, legal documents seem impossibly dense and **prolix**.
2. Reactions to the new play were mixed; **kudos** from one critic and praise from another.
3. If cold winter weather is your **bête noire**, you should definitely give up on the idea of accepting a job in Stockholm, Sweden.
4. Once a young **protégé** in the kitchens of several French famous restaurants, he is now a renowned chef who mentors today's students of French cuisine.
5. This unsuccessful day of apartment hunting has yielded nothing but rentals in the dark, **dank** basements of homes.
6. According to a basic principle of management science, a task that seems **gargantuan** becomes workable if it is broken into a set of smaller, more attainable tasks.
7. After prying open the door of the ancient **avatar**, the explorers were stunned to find the interior intact.
8. The theater workshop has been the **incubus** for many first-time playwrights who went on to have remarkably successful careers.
9. As we begin to age, said the beauty expert, our skin may sag as it loses its **tautology**.
10. Ever since the age of ten, when she first learned that such a physical challenge existed, she has had a **fervid** desire to swim across the English Channel.

Set A

Choosing the Right Word

*Select the **boldface** word that better completes each sentence. You might refer to the passage on pages 124–125 to see how most of these words are used in context. Note that the choices might be related forms of the Unit words.*

1. The Hindu god Vishnu is most often associated with ten (**avatars, protégés**), while the god also has about 10,000 names.

2. She was such a (**prolix, fervid**) supporter of the Los Angeles Dodgers that she seemed unable to speak of anything else.

3. His zest for life and his boundless optimism were expressed perfectly, it seemed to me, in his (**gargantuan, dank**) smile.

4. The crashing thunder and piercing lightning seemed to summon a(n) (**tautology, incubus**) that haunted the child in her sleep.

5. Our goal as a nation and as a society must be to free ourselves completely of the (**kudos, incubus**) of racial prejudice.

6. My criticism of his statement is not merely that it is (**prolix, fervid**), but that it uses words to obscure rather than to reinforce the meaning.

7. I have no desire to be known as a nonconformist, but I am not going to allow fear of public disapproval to become my (**avatar, bête noire**).

8. Her composition was seriously weakened by (**tautologies, kudos**) such as "an older woman who is approaching the end of her life span."

9. The emergency room nurse is the very (**avatar, tautology**) of patience and generosity, as he or she often stays at the hospital late to comfort patients.

10. In the twilight of her long career, she began to receive the (**bête noire, kudos**) that her brilliant but unconventional writings so richly deserved.

11. I felt that I could not continue to live any longer in that (**dank, gargantuan**) atmosphere of prejudice and hostility.

12. You did nothing to help me, but now that I have achieved some success, you have the gall to claim me as your (**protégé, bête noire**).

Completing the Sentence

Choose the word from the word bank that best completes each of the following sentences. Write the correct word or form of the word in the space provided.

avatar	dank	gargantuan	kudos	protégé
bête noire	fervid	incubus	prolix	tautology

1. The memory of my ghastly blunder and of the harm it had done to innocent people weighed on my spirit like a(n) ____________________.

2. In *David Copperfield*, Dickens described with heartbreaking realism the period of his own childhood that he spent toiling in a(n) ____________________ cellar.

3. As the ____________________ of one of the great violinists of our times, she has had an unrivaled opportunity to develop her musical talents.

4. To maintain that, because human beings are aggressive animals, they will always be involved in conflicts seems to me a mere ____________________.

5. Once I created an inexact ____________________ for the new dancing video game, I became inexplicably motivated to exercise.

6. I consider the vogue use of "hopefully" illogical, inept, and pretentious; it has become my linguistic ____________________.

7. After I read one of your ____________________ and repetitive reports, I always have the feeling that you have never heard the expression "less is more."

8. Falstaff is a behemoth personality, whose ____________________ appetites, especially for sack and sleep, never seem to be satiated.

9. I think it was terribly naive of us to expect to get a fair hearing from such ____________________ partisans of the opposing party.

10. May I say, in all modesty, that I don't deserve such ____________________ just because I was all-state in football and led my class academically.

End Set A

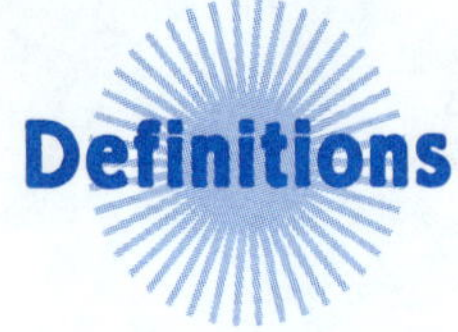

Definitions

Note the spelling, pronunciation, part(s) of speech, and definition(s) of each of the following words. Then write the appropriate form of the word in the blank space in the illustrative sentence(s) following.

1. beatitude (bē at′ ə tüd)
(*n.*) a state of perfect happiness or blessedness; a blessing
Do you think that not having to worry about money is the consummate ________________ of being wealthy?

2. bode (bōd)
(*v.*) to be an omen of; to indicate by signs
With a smile that ________________ well, the teacher enters the room and greets the students.

3. ecumenical (ek yu men′ i kəl)
(*adj.*) worldwide or universal in influence or application
An ________________ council meets on the third Tuesday of each month.

4. fetid (fet′ id)
(*adj.*) having an unpleasant or offensive odor
The stale, ________________ air of the windowless room was an irritation to all who had to be there.

5. heyday (hā′ dā)
(*n.*) the period of greatest power, vigor, success, or influence; the prime years
During the ________________ of the clipper ship, these graceful vessels were the swiftest on the seas.

6. infrastructure (in′ frə strək chər)
(*n.*) a basic foundation or framework; a system of public works; the resources and facilities required for an activity; permanent military installations
The city's aging ________________ was beginning to become a problem that needed to be addressed.

7. inveigle (in vā′ gəl)
(*v.*) to entice, lure, or snare by flattery or artful inducements; to obtain or acquire by artifice
The planning committee chair ________________ us to join them by promising good seats at the ceremony.

8. lagniappe (lan′ yap)
(*n.*) an extra or unexpected gift or gratuity
To reward their loyal customers, the grateful store handed out ________________ to all the day's shoppers.

9. sycophant (sik′ ə fənt) (*n.*) someone who attempts to win favors or advance him- or herself by flattery or servile behavior; a slanderer, defamer

The actor, angered by his manager's constant false flattery, called him a two-faced ________________.

10. truckle (truk′ əl) (*v.*) to yield or submit tamely or submissively

The knight would ________________ to no one.

Using Context

*For each item, determine whether the **boldface** word from pages 130–131 makes sense in the context of the sentence. Circle the item numbers next to the six sentences in which the words are used correctly.*

1. If you are looking for an apprentice who will **truckle** to your orders without asking questions, I am the wrong person for the job.
2. Unfortunately, our small school does not have the **infrastructure** to support such sophisticated, state-of-the-art educational technology.
3. Let's try to avoid discussing **ecumenical** issues that only matter to a few people.
4. As soon as I drove onto the highway, I encountered a traffic jam—yet another **lagniappe** that made me late for my interview!
5. To stroll through the community flower garden is a wondrous experience filled with colorful sights and **fetid** fragrances.
6. The closing of a huge manufacturing plant in our city does not **bode** well for our community's economic future.
7. In the **heyday** of advertising, commercials were thought to be nearly as entertaining as the television programs themselves.
8. It's one thing to treat your superiors with respect and courtesy, but quite another to relentlessly butter them up in the manner of a **sycophant**.
9. The newlyweds' sense of **beatitude** quickly faded once they returned from their honeymoon and had to face the pressures of the real world again.
10. I am not going to allow your rude behavior and harsh criticisms to **inveigle** me any more than they already have.

Set B

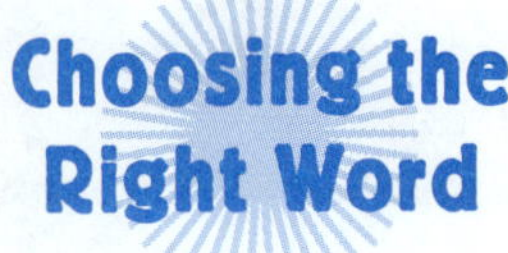

Choosing the Right Word

*Select the **boldface** word that better completes each sentence. You might refer to the passage on pages 124–125 to see how most of these words are used in context. Note that the choices might be related forms of the Unit words.*

1. Scientists have for some time been correlating the functions of human consciousness with the neural (**lagniappe, infrastructure**) of the brain.
2. After a long investigation, detectives arrested two con artists who had (**truckled, inveigled**) many elderly victims into giving the con artists their life savings.
3. The corporate (**sycophant, lagniappe**) did succeed in climbing the ladder of success for a few years, but his repellent behavior eventually caught up with him.

4. To choose giving over receiving is to reap eternal (**lagniappe, beatitude**).
5. The lowering clouds and mounting winds did not (**bode, truckle**) well for our hopes for perfect beach weather.
6. Surrounded from childhood by flattering courtiers, the monarch grew to adulthood unable to distinguish a friend from a (**beatitude, sycophant**).
7. When the sanitation strike continued into a second week, people began to complain about the (**fetid, ecumenical**) smell that hung over the sweltering city.
8. Surely you can make an honest effort to please your employer without (**boding, truckling**) to the vanity of the person who pays your salary.
9. When I saw the beautiful girl you had brought to the prom, I understood the reason for your smile of (**fetid, beatific**) self-satisfaction.
10. In all the great philosophies, we find common standards that must be regarded as (**fetid, ecumenical**) values, equally valid at all times and in all places.
11. I was paid generously for my work, but the kind smile and gracious words were a delightful (**lagniappe, heyday**).
12. We can now recognize that many institutions that seemed, at a particular time, to be in their (**sycophant, heyday**) were actually already on the decline.

Completing the Sentence

Choose the word from the word bank that best completes each of the following sentences. Write the correct word or form of the word in the space provided.

beatitude	ecumenical	heyday	inveigle	sycophant
bode	fetid	infrastructure	lagniappe	truckle

1. Was it just our imagination, or was the room still ____________ with the smell of stale cigar smoke?

2. The atmosphere of mistrust and hostility did not ____________ well for the outcome of the peace talks.

3. The lame-duck president looked back with nostalgia on the power he had wielded during the ____________ of his administration.

4. I was happy enough when she agreed to go to the prom with me, but her suggestion that we use her car was an unexpected ____________.

5. The speaker emphasized that in the modern world the barriers between different groups are rapidly being broken down and that we must try to think in truly ____________ terms.

6. At the risk of losing the election, I refused to ____________ to the fleeting passions and prejudices of a small part of the electorate.

7. Like most people, I enjoy flattery, but I can't be ____________ into doing something that in my heart I know is wrong.

8. It was a subject of heated debate in the early nineteenth century whether the federal government should play any part at all in building the ____________ to support the fledgling American economy.

9. In the dreamy ____________ of their first love, nothing I might have said would have had the slightest effect on them.

10. Far better to receive sincere criticism, no matter how severe, than to endure the groveling adulation of a(n) ____________.

End Set B

Synonyms

*Choose the word or form of the word from this Unit that is the same or most nearly the same in meaning as the **boldface** word or expression in the phrase. Write that word on the line. Use a dictionary if necessary.*

1. a **zealous** follower of the guru _______________
2. known throughout the town as a **flunky** _______________
3. a great champion in her **prime** _______________
4. considered kryptonite Superman's **nemesis** _______________
5. the spoiled eggs' **putrid** smell _______________
6. was **beguiled** by promises of lower taxes _______________
7. could **foreshadow** disaster for all involved _______________
8. received **accolades** for his performance _______________
9. was an **apprentice** of the famous shoemaker _______________
10. refused to **grovel** at her feet _______________
11. has a **huge** ego _______________
12. the **burden** of famine and disease _______________
13. a computer user's **virtual identity** _______________
14. a document of **worldwide** significance _______________
15. a tottering **foundation** _______________

Antonyms

*Choose the word or form of the word from this Unit that is most nearly opposite in meaning to the **boldface** word or expression in the phrase. Write that word on the line. Use a dictionary if necessary.*

1. wrote a **terse** passage _______________
2. a carefully constructed and **concise statement** _______________
3. descended the stairs to the **dry** basement _______________
4. in a state of complete **despair** _______________
5. **penalty** for returning the book late _______________

Writing: Words in Action

Suppose you have just returned from a two-week trip working with People's Habitat, and you want to convince a friend to go with you next time. Write an argument, using at least three details from the passage (pages 124–125), that might help you convince someone to volunteer. Use three or more words from this Unit.

Some of the words you have studied in this Unit appear in ***boldface*** *type. Read the passage below, and then circle the letter of the correct answer for each word as it is used in context.*

In the welter of distressing news that haunts modern media like an **incubus**, a beacon of hope has shone steadily since 1976. That was the year when the American philanthropist Millard Dean Fuller and his wife Linda founded Habitat for Humanity International. Over its first three decades, this **lagniappe** of an organization, often simply referred to as Habitat, has built more than 350,000 houses for 1.75 million people. Funded primarily by private donations, Habitat is an organizational **avatar** of the Golden Rule. At the risk of **tautology**, the Fullers aspired to translate the values of unselfishness, practicality, and neighborliness into bricks and mortar. Such a challenge might seem to have been a **gargantuan** task, except for the fact that Habitat has succeeded so admirably and has garnered such kudos in doing so.

Habitat skillfully channels donated funds, materials, and labor to build modest-sized houses, which it then sells at reduced prices to people in need. New homeowners must be certified as being in need but must also be able to pay their mortgages. Habitat realizes no profit from the home sales and uses the homeowners' monthly payments to build additional houses. The organization is active in all 50 states and in 90 foreign countries. **Prolix** encomia aside, Habitat's worldwide recognition is due in no small measure to its most celebrated supporters and participants: former president Jimmy Carter and his wife Rosalynn. Every year, the Carters lead a weeklong building project that attracts volunteers from all over the world.

---

1. What is the meaning of **incubus** as it is used in paragraph 1?

a. éclat
b. savoir-faire
c. evil spirit
d. protégé

2. What is the meaning of **lagniappe** in the context of the passage?

a. bonus
b. snack
c. octopus
d. mirage

3. In paragraph 1, what does the word **avatar** suggest about Habitat?

a. It is an embodiment.
b. It represents a rule.
c. It is an organization.
d. It is a donation.

4. What does **tautology** most likely mean as it is used in paragraph 1?

a. hyperbole
b. redundancy
c. flattery
d. confusion

5. In paragraph 1, what does the word **gargantuan** suggest about the task?

a. It is unrealistic.
b. It is complex.
c. It is opaque.
d. It is immense.

6. What characteristic is suggested by **prolix** in paragraph 2?

a. generosity
b. foolishness
c. wordiness
d. naïveté

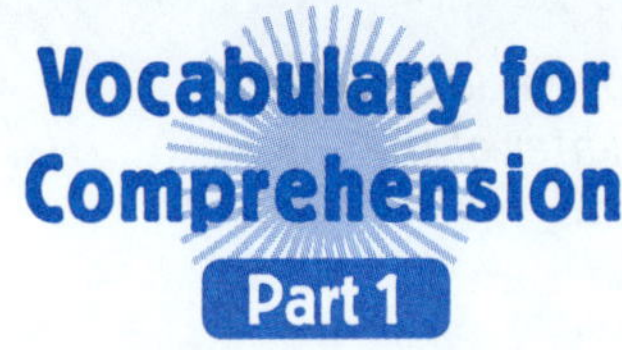

*Read this passage, which contains words in **boldface** that appear in Units 7–9. Then choose the best answer to each question based on what is stated or implied in the passage. You may refer to the passage as often as necessary.*

Questions 1–10 are based on the following passage.

This passage is adapted from *Don Quixote,* by Miguel de Cervantes. Translation published in 1880.

In a village of La Mancha, the name of which I have no desire to call to mind, there lived not long since one of those gentlemen that keep a lance in the lance-rack, an old buckler[1], a lean hack, and a greyhound for coursing. A pot of rather more beef than mutton, a salad on most nights, scraps on Saturdays, lentils on Fridays, and a pigeon or so extra on Sundays, made away with three-quarters of his income. The rest of it went in a doublet[2] of fine cloth and velvet breeches and shoes to match for holidays. On week-days he made a brave figure in his best homespun. He had in his house a housekeeper past forty, a niece under twenty, and a **protégé** for the field and market-place, who used to saddle the hack as well as handle the bill-hook[3]. The age of this gentleman of ours was bordering on fifty; he was of a hardy habit, spare, gaunt-featured, a very early riser and a **fervid** sportsman. Historians will have it his surname was Quixada or Quesada (for here there is some **ambivalence** among the authors who write on the subject), although from reasonable conjectures it seems plain that he was called Quexana.

You must know, then, that the above-named gentleman whenever he was at leisure (which was mostly all the year round) **opted** to read **picaresque** books of chivalry with such ardour and avidity that he almost entirely neglected the pursuit of his field-sports, and even the management of his property. To such a pitch did his eagerness and infatuation go that he sold many an acre of tillageland to buy books of chivalry to read, and brought home as many of them as he could get. But the **pièces de résistance** were those of the famous Feliciano de Silva's composition. Their lucidity of style and complicated conceits were as pearls in his sight, particularly when in his reading he came upon courtships and cartels. Here he often found **prolix** passages like "the reason of the unreason with which my reason is afflicted so weakens my reason that with reason I murmur at your beauty." Or again, "the high heavens, that of your divinity divinely **imbue** you with the stars, render you deserving of the desert your greatness deserves." Over **casuistry** of this sort the poor gentleman lost his wits, and used to lie awake striving to understand them and worm the meaning out of them; what Aristotle himself could not have made out or extracted had he come to life again for that special purpose. He was not at all easy about the wounds which the character Don Belianis gave and took. It seemed to him that, great as were the surgeons who had cured this avatar of chivalry, he must have had his face and body covered all over with seams and scars. He commended, however, the author's way of ending his book with the promise of that interminable adventure. Many a time was he tempted to take up his pen and finish it properly as is there proposed, which no doubt he would have done, and made a successful piece of work of it too, had not greater and more absorbing thoughts prevented him.

---

[1] small shield
[2] men's jacket
[3] cutting or pruning tool

1. The first paragraph suggests that the gentleman was a
A) wealthy landowner.
B) retired knight.
C) person of limited means.
D) professional sportsman.

2. Which choice provides the best evidence for the answer to the previous question?
A) Lines 1–6 ("In a … for coursing")
B) Lines 6–11 ("A pot ... his income")
C) Lines 15–19 ("He had ...bill-hook")
D) Lines 20–23 ("The age ... sportsman")

3. What point does the narrator make by including several possible surnames for the gentleman (lines 24–29)?
A) The gentleman was supposedly a historical figure about whom various authors had written.
B) The gentleman lived too long ago for his name to be known with certainty.
C) There is disagreement among scholars about the gentleman's name.
D) The gentleman's actual name is not important to the story.

4. As it is used in line 17, "protégé" most nearly means
A) ward.
B) servant.
C) farmhand.
D) professional.

5. It can reasonably be inferred from the second paragraph that books of chivalry were
A) easily attainable.
B) widely read.
C) rare and costly.
D) popular but sophisticated.

6. As it is used in line 42, "pièces de résistance" most nearly means
A) main dishes.
B) outstanding accomplishments.
C) fitting examples.
D) centerpieces.

7. When the narrator describes the books' "lucidity of style" (lines 44– 45), he is using
A) satire.
B) exaggeration.
C) irony.
D) imagery.

8. As it is used in line 56, "casuistry" most nearly means
A) solid reasoning.
B) specious argument.
C) confusion.
D) passages.

9. According to the narrator, what caused the gentleman to lose his mind?
A) He had too much free time.
B) He became a collector of books of chivalry.
C) He neglected his interests and property to have more time to read.
D) He tried to make sense of impenetrable passages in books of chivalry.

10. Which of the following statements best summarizes the passage?
A) A gentleman squanders his estate in order to collect books of chivalry.
B) A gentleman becomes obsessed with books of chivalry and would write one himself except that he has bigger things on his mind.
C) Books of chivalry cause a gentleman to lose his social position and sanity.
D) After reading many books of chivalry, a gentleman decides to write an ending for his favorite.

Vocabulary for Comprehension Part 2

*Read this passage, which contains words in **boldface** that appear in Units 7–9. Then choose the best answer to each question based on what is stated or implied in the passage. You may refer to the passage as often as necessary.*

Questions 1–10 are based on the following passage.

This passage is adapted from *The Last Man*, by Mary W. Shelley. Published in 1826.

I AM the native of a sea-surrounded nook, a cloud-enshadowed, **dank** land, which, when the surface of the globe, with its shoreless ocean and trackless continents, presents itself to my mind, appears only as an inconsiderable speck in the **gargantuan** whole; and yet, when balanced in the scale of mental power, far outweighed countries of larger extent and more numerous population. . . . England, seated far north in the turbid sea, now visits my dreams in the semblance of a vast and well-manned ship, which mastered the winds and rode proudly over the waves. In my **inchoative** days she was the universe to me. When I stood on my native hills, and saw plain and mountain stretch out to the utmost limits of my vision, speckled by the dwellings of my countrymen, and subdued to fertility by their labours, the earth's very centre was fixed for me in that spot. The rest of her orb was as a fable, to have forgotten which would have cost neither my imagination nor understanding an effort.

My fortunes have been, from the beginning, an exemplification of the power that **malleability** may possess over the varied tenor of man's life. With regard to myself, this came almost by inheritance. My father was one of those men on whom nature had bestowed to prodigality the envied gifts of wit and imagination, and then left his bark[1] of life to be impelled by these winds, without adding reason as the rudder, or judgment as the pilot for the voyage. His extraction was obscure. But circumstances brought him early into public notice, and his small paternal property was soon dissipated in the splendid scene of **hedonism** in which he was an actor. During the short years of thoughtless youth, he was adored by the high-bred triflers of the day, nor least by the youthful sovereign, who escaped from the intrigues of party, and the arduous duties of kingly business, to find never-failing amusement and exhilaration of spirit in his society. My father's **refractory** impulses perpetually led him into difficulties from which his ingenuity alone could extricate him. The accumulating pile of debts of honour and of trade, which would have bent to earth any other, was supported by him with a light spirit and tameless hilarity; while his **savoir-faire** was so necessary at the tables and assemblies of the rich, that his derelictions were considered **peccadilloes**, and he himself received with intoxicating flattery.

This kind of popularity, like every other, is evanescent: and the difficulties of every kind with which he had to contend, increased in a frightful ratio compared with his small means of extricating himself. At such times the king, in his **empathy** for him, would come to his relief, and then kindly take his friend to task. My father gave the best promises for amendment, but his social disposition, his craving for the usual diet of admiration, and more than all, the prudent man's **bête-noir**, gambling, which fully possessed him, made his good resolutions transient, his promises vain. With the quick sensibility peculiar to his temperament, he perceived his power in the brilliant circle to be on the wane.

[1] small sailing ship

1. The main purpose of this passage is to
A) explain the downfall of the narrator's father.
B) provide details about the narrator's background.
C) criticize the culture of the king's court.
D) paint a nostalgic portrait of a past era in English history.

2. It can reasonably be inferred from the first paragraph that
A) England is at the height of its naval power.
B) the narrator is critical of the British empire.
C) the narrator no longer sees himself as English.
D) the narrator's view of the world has widened since the time he describes.

3. According to the narrator, he inherited from his father
A) a weakness for gambling.
B) little wealth but good connections to important people.
C) a life characterized by change and adaptation.
D) debt.

4. Which choice provides the best evidence for the answer to the previous question?
A) Lines 25–28 ("My fortunes ... man's life")
B) Lines 36–40 ("His extraction ... an actor")
C) Lines 40–47 ("During ... his society")
D) Lines 50–54 ("The accumulating ... hilarity")

5. In lines 33–36, the narrator uses which of the following literary devices to describe the narrator's father?
A) Hyperbole
B) Metaphor
C) Analogy
D) Foreshadowing

6. As it is used in line 47, "refractory" most nearly means
A) disobedient.
B) difficult to manage.
C) not responsive to treatment.
D) lower.

7. As it is used in line 54, "savoir-faire" most nearly means
A) knowledge.
B) tact.
C) suavity.
D) presence.

8. Which of the following statements about the narrator's father is supported by the last paragraph?
A) He realized that his social position would not endure.
B) He knew that the king would always get him out of trouble.
C) He took the king's help for granted.
D) He was unaware of the troubles he caused.

9. As it is used in line 70, "bête-noir" most nearly means
A) lure.
B) dark pleasure.
C) excitement.
D) nemesis.

10. According to the passage, why could the narrator's father not change the direction of his life?
A) He had accumulated too much debt.
B) He felt constrained by the king's empathy.
C) He wished to follow his dreams.
D) He enjoyed his social status and gambling too much.

Synonyms

*From the word bank below, choose the word that has the same or nearly the same meaning as the **boldface** word in each sentence and write it on the line. You will not use all of the words.*

ad hoc	**éclat**	**imbue**	**queasy**
avatar	**empathy**	**inchoate**	**refractory**
bane	**fastidious**	**infrastructure**	**savoir-faire**
cataclysm	**fervid**	**kudos**	**syndrome**

1. Now that the **underpinning** for the new subway line has been laid out, the actual construction can begin. ____________

2. Just thinking about riding on a rollercoaster makes me feel **unsettled**. ____________

3. The music festival opened with a dazzling amount of **celebrity,** and the performances continued to thrill the audience for hours. ____________

4. Before you start playing this computer game, you must choose a **virtual identity**, such as unicorn, a dragon, or an owl. ____________

5. During the war, army surgeons turned the grand old train station into a **makeshift** hospital. ____________

6. If anyone deserves **praise**, it is surely the volunteers who risked their lives to put out the wildfire. ____________

7. What is the best way to show **compassion** for a friend who is dealing with a serious illness? ____________

8. The **unruly** protestors refused to leave the premises until their demands were heard. ____________

9. Because I am the first person in my family to attend college, I know my graduation ceremony will **infuse** my parents and relatives with pride. ____________

10. The scientists are studying a rare physical **complex** that they think might be caused by naturally occurring toxins. ____________

11. Even though my roommate has **precise** housekeeping habits and I am fairly messy, we get along quite well. ____________

12. The dramatic mural depicted the **catastrophe** that is widely believed to have caused the abrupt extinction of the dinosaurs. ____________

Two-Word Completions

Select the pair of words that best completes the meaning of each of the following sentences.

1. Richard Wagner considered the average operagoer of his day a blatant ____________________, to whose benighted musical tastes he would in no way ____________________.

a. hedonist ... remand
b. protégé ... truckle
c. philistine ... pander
d. sycophant ... opt

2. David Bohm, an American physicist and ____________________ of Albert Einstein, has concluded that space and time are formulations of the human mind, and while some believe these ideas a(n) ____________________, he bases his hypotheses in science.

a. lagniappe ... abeyance
b. nemesis ... bathos
c. casuistry ... beatitude
d. protégé ... aberration

3. In the ____________________ of network television in the United States, many people tuned in to watch police dramas or situation comedies; however, today's television is widely criticized for ____________________ its viewers with "reality" programming.

a. nepotism ... boding
b. incubus ... inveigling
c. carte blanche ... truckling
d. heyday ... debauching

4. Miguel de Cervantes's *Don Quixote*, his magnificent and ____________________ novel, ____________________ just about every aspect of life—from the nobility to the common farmer—in sixteenth century Spain.

a. picaresque... lampooned
b. truckled... lackluster
c. remanded... gargantuan
d. gamboled... ecumenical

5. Our ____________________ and aging professor of history had his moments of brilliance, but so often had such a ____________________ presence in the classroom that students eventually learned to avoid his classes altogether.

a. mellifluous ... de facto
b. cantankerous ... lackluster
c. ecumenical ... fetid
d. ambivalent ... malleable

6. In the spring of that year, bands of marauding Goths broke into the province, ____________________ the governor in his own capital, and committed such ____________________ that the economy of the region did not recover for a generation.

a. debauched ... tautologies
b. remanded ... abeyances
c. beleaguered ... depredations
d. lampooned ... peccadillos

7. At the court of an autocratic ruler, free speech is usually replaced by the obsequious twaddle of self-seeking toadies and ____________________, eager to get ahead by ____________________ to the opinions of their all-powerful master.

a. sycophants ... truckling
b. lagniappes ... debauching
c. harbingers ... pandering
d. malcontents ... lampooning

WORD STUDY

In the passage "Volunteer Profile: Jennifer Yoder" (see pages 124–125), the writer points out that Yoder's interest in volunteering "came to a head" after Hurricane Katrina. As a whole, this simple phrase has an altogether different meaning when compared to the literal meanings of each word examined alone.

This kind of phrase is an **idiom**. In the unit opener passage, the phrase "came to a head" means to reach the highest point.

Choosing the Right Idiom

Read each sentence. Use context clues to figure out the meaning of each idiom in ***boldface*** *print. Then write the letter of the definition for the idiom in the sentence.*

1. After the statement, the press secretary had to answer the journalists' questions **off the cuff**. ______
2. The weekend is over. Tomorrow is Monday, and we go **back to the salt mines**. ______
3. His analysis of the personal computing industry is **wide of the mark** and doesn't impress me. ______
4. Mr. Lee is overconfident and tends to forget that he is only a **big fish in a small pond**. ______
5. Because I trust you completely, I will give you **free rein** to develop and manage the project to the end. ______
6. The mayor is using this issue as a **red herring** to divert attention from the teachers' strike. ______
7. The school's organic garden was a **labor of love** that took five full years to realize. ______
8. **In one fell swoop**, the child stepped on the dog's tail, pulled down the bookshelf, and broke the radio. ______
9. Our boss says you are a bit **green around the gills**. You should go home and rest. ______
10. The restaurant manager left her job **under a cloud**, as she was accused of mishandling funds. ______

a. complete freedom

b. something that distracts or misleads

c. most important person in a small group

d. off target

e. without planning

f. something done only for the satisfaction

g. sickly looking

h. under suspicion

i. time to return to something unpleasant, such as work

j. all at once

This root appears in **malcontent** (page 118), which means "one who is dissatisfied with conditions." Some other words based on the same root are listed below.

maladapted	malfeasance	malfunction	malingerer
malaise	malformation	malice	malodorous

From the list of words above, choose the one that corresponds to each of the brief definitions below. Write the word in the blank space in the illustrative sentence below the definition. Use an online or print dictionary if necessary.

1. unsuited or poorly suited for a particular purpose or situation
   The storage area was large enough, but it was __________________ for use as a classroom.

2. a vague feeling of physical or mental discomfort
   For no evident reason, she was too beset by __________________ to attend class.

3. a desire to cause harm or suffering; deep-seated ill will
   Legally, murder is distinguished from manslaughter by the element of __________________ aforethought.

4. wrongdoing or misconduct in public office
   The politician was accused of __________________ when the crooked scheme became public knowledge.

5. a failure to operate correctly or in a normal manner; to operate poorly or imperfectly
   Radio contact was lost for over an hour because of a technical __________________.

6. having a bad odor; ill-smelling; highly improper
   To my sensibilities, all blue-veined cheeses are unbearably __________________.

7. one who pretends to be ill in order to escape duty or work
   He was fired from the squad because he proved to be a shiftless __________________.

8. an abnormal or faulty bodily structure or part
   The disease caused an unsightly __________________ of the patient's face.

UNIT 10

*Read the following passage, taking note of the **boldface** words and their contexts. These words are among those you will be studying in Unit 10. It may help you to complete the exercises in this Unit if you refer to the way the words are used below.*

A River of English

<Humorous Essay>

Language is no **monolithic** edifice, hatched full-formed at the dawn of time, unchanging through the ages. A language is a living creature, sprung from the mouths and minds of the men and women who speak it. From one generation, from one neighborhood, from one speaker to the next, the river of language keeps flowing—and you can't step in the same river twice.

Things move fast in our modern world, and our language is one of those fast-moving entities, spurred by a rush of economic productivity and technological innovation. Each day, hoards of marketers assemble to coin new and improved brand names, catchy slogans, **fulsome** phrases fine-tuned to **dissimulate** the profit motive and manufacture demand. Scientists convene to agree on appropriate names for late-discovered organisms, particles, or **empirical** techniques. Each invention and discovery wants a catchy name. Each profession maintains a trendy lexicon of **apocryphal** jargon. Creative artists from Shakespeare to the latest song writer have increased the stock of our language in their quest for the **mot juste**.

The course of English is altered by wordsmiths in business, science, and art. But at its heart, linguistic change is driven by the accretion of unpredictable, near **imperceptible** transformations in the way we speak—and the way we speak is changing all the time.

Words enter our language, pass into common usage, and shift in meaning through the years. Four hundred years ago, highbrow English chefs borrowed from the French, using the word

"**liaison**" to characterize ingredients that hold a sauce together; today we're more likely to use the word to refer to people who facilitate cooperation among parts of an organization. Medieval alchemists steeped in Latin adopted the word "**sublimate**" to describe the act of heating liquid into vapor; centuries later, a psychologist with a metaphorical bent took the same word to name mental acts by which we refine our baser impulses into acceptable behavior. In the days of horse-powered transportation, the footman who ran errands for his master was called a **lackey**; we've retained the word to refer to slavish subordinates, or anyone who behaves like one and accepts unjust social **disparity**.

Among the most telling contributions to the language are simple, common phrases that color speech efficiently, without the obtrusiveness of more **flamboyant** locutions. In the nineteenth century, people who had to wait tried to "hold on," while those who aimed to hide sought to "hole up." Early twentieth-century English speakers who wanted a good look were the first to take a "gander," and those who heard a great deal were the first to have heard an "earful." Fresh colloquialisms often reflect the times they crop up in: As the gears of the industrial age churned ahead full steam, speakers thought to call a dull routine a "grind." By the mid-twentieth century, a project that was going well was "cooking with gas," while one faring poorly was going "down the tubes."

Bleary-eyed scholars peruse dusty tomes to determine the history of words and phrases in our language, as well as shifts in meaning over time. Occasionally they bring remarkable **acumen** to bear in **adjudicating** academic disputes about origins and rectifying **anachronisms** in the record. Fortunately, it takes less effort for most speakers to keep abreast of the twists and turns of the language. We just open our mouths, and the words come pouring out.

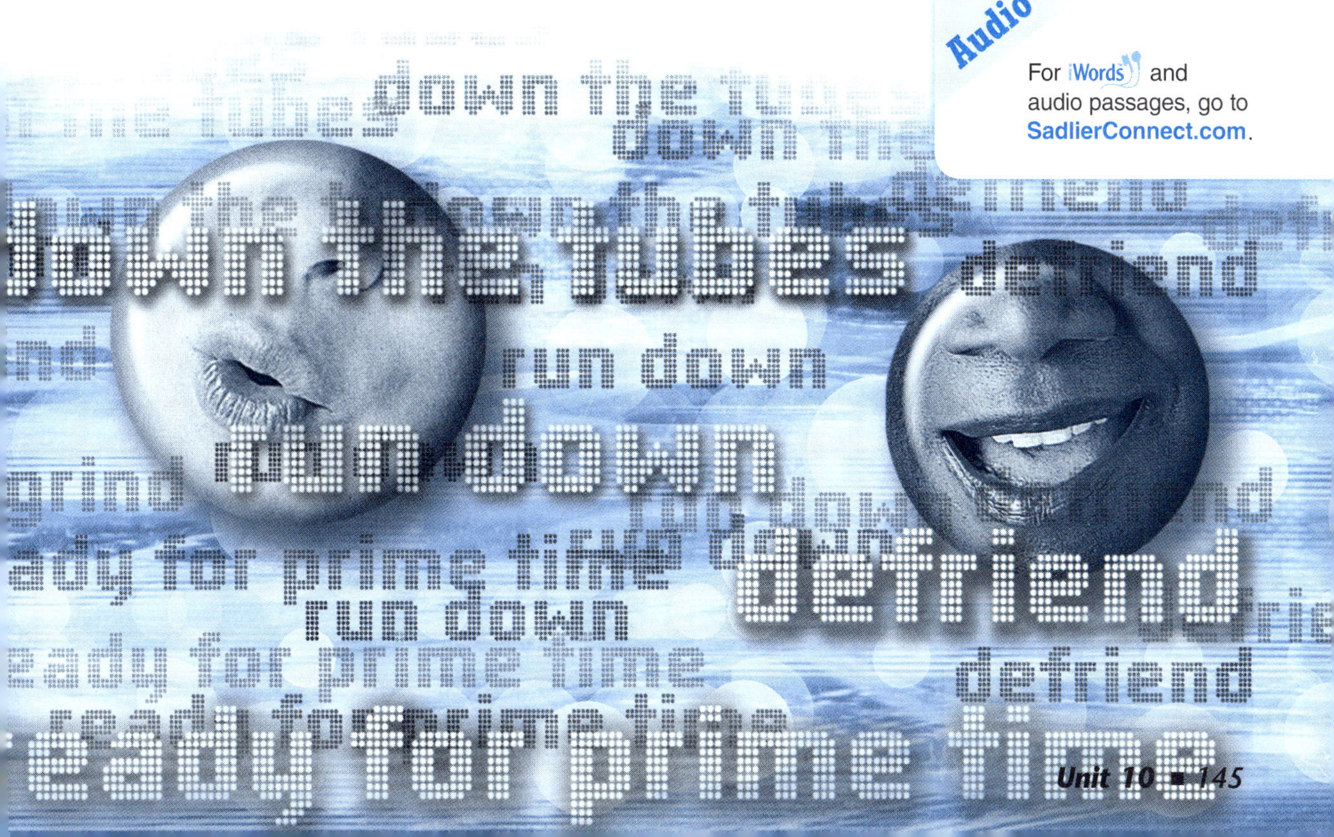

Audio

For iWords and audio passages, go to SadlierConnect.com.

Note the spelling, pronunciation, part(s) of speech, and definition(s) of each of the following words. Then write the appropriate form of the word in the blank space in the illustrative sentence(s) following.

1. anachronism (ə nak' rə niz əm) — (*n.*) a chronological misplacing of events, objects, customs, or persons in regard to each other

To avoid introducing ____________________ into their work, authors of historical novels must do painstaking research.

2. apocryphal (ə pok' rə fəl) — (*adj.*) of doubtful or questionable authenticity

Although his tales of youthful derring-do are probably ____________________, they are very entertaining.

3. dissimulate (di sim' yə lāt) — (*v.*) to hide or disguise one's true thoughts, feelings, or intentions

In awkward social situations, it is sometimes more courteous to ____________________ than to be straightforward.

4. flamboyant (flam boi' ənt) — (*adj.*) highly elaborate or ornate; vividly colored; strikingly brilliant or bold

We were dazzled by the ____________________ plumage of the birds in the tropical rain forest.

5. imperceptible (im pər sep' tə bəl) — (*adj.*) extremely slight; incapable of being perceived by the senses or the mind

When two candidates agree on most issues, voters may find the differences between them ____________________.

6. lackey (lak' ē) — (*n.*) a uniformed male servant; a servile follower

A wealthy Victorian household generally included numerous maids, ____________________, and other domestics.

7. mot juste (mō zhüst') — (*n.*) the most suitable or exact word or expression

The erudite film and theater critic always managed to find the ____________________ to sum up her opinion.

8. patrician (pə trish' ən) — (*n.*) a member of the ruling class; a person of high rank; (*adj.*) belonging to, befitting, or characteristic of such a person

Though her origins were humble, she had the assurance and bearing of a ____________________.

Many scions of ____________________ families feel obliged to choose a life of public service.

9. propitiate (prō pish′ ē āt)

(*v.*) to make someone or something favorably inclined toward oneself; to conciliate, satisfy, or appease

Many ancient peoples practiced rituals involving offerings and sacrifices to ____________________ their gods.

10. sic (sik)

(*adv.*) thus so; intentionally written so

When you see ____________________ in a book, it is usually parenthetical, and it means that an obvious error was from an original text and thus to be left as is.

*For each item, determine whether the **boldface** word from pages 146–147 makes sense in the context of the sentence. Circle the item numbers next to the six sentences in which the words are used correctly.*

1. It is relatively easy to tell how babies are feeling at any given moment because, unlike older children and adults, they have not yet learned to **dissimulate**.

2. For our American history project, we decided to explore the question of whether the story of the famous folk hero Johnny Appleseed is **apocryphal** or based in fact.

3. Some musicians are known for their **flamboyant** appearance as for their music.

4. The trail became wider—nearly **imperceptible**—we had no choice but to turn back.

5. The biography told the story of an American heiress who married into a **patrician** English family and spent the rest of her life in English high society.

6. In the fairy tale "Cinderella," the main character is at first treated as a lowly household servant, but is later transformed into a magnificent **lackey**.

7. The director did not choose to set Chekov's *The Cherry Orchard* in the present day for the sake of mere novelty; instead, the **anachronism** was meant to encourage audiences to consider how the play's themes apply to today's world.

8. It would be exceedingly harsh to blame someone for an occasional **mot juste**, since just about everyone has said or done something socially awkward at one time or another.

9. The editor inserted the word ***sic*** after each of the three misspellings in the famous artist's letter that she was preparing for publication.

10. Several leading economists warned that lowering interest rates would **propitiate** rather than mitigate inflation in the country.

Set A

*Select the **boldface** word that better completes each sentence. You might refer to the passage on pages 144–145 to see how most of these words are used in context. Note that the choices might be related forms of the Unit words.*

1. The London Eye, the famous Ferris wheel in Great Britain that opened to the general public in 2000, is both a(n) (**imperceptible, flamboyant**) display and a brilliant achievement.

2. As she is descended from a long line of (**lackeys, patricians**), at a fine restaurant she expects haute cuisine, attentive and meticulous waitstaff, and a resident wine steward.

3. Those solemn religious ceremonies are intended to protect the tribe from disasters by (**propitiating, dissimulating**) the gods who control natural phenomena.

4. There is probably nothing worse than having (**patrician, apocryphal**) tastes on an income better suited to the lifestyle of a pauper.

5. She is so concerned with words that she seems to think the only thing that is needed to deal with a problem is to find the (**mot juste, anachronism**) to describe it.

6. The story about Bunker Hill with its warning, "Don't fire until you see the whites of their eyes," may be (**flamboyant, apocryphal**), but I'm going to continue believing it.

7. In a campaign speech, the candidate said, "My opponent has flaunted (**[sic], mot juste**) all of the principles of sound fiscal management."

8. It's no wonder he's got such a swelled head when all those (**patricians, lackeys**) tagging along after him do nothing but sing his praises.

9. Because deadly carbon monoxide gas can be neither seen nor smelled, its presence is practically (**apocryphal, imperceptible**).

10. Most students failed the midterm exam, but they were able to (**dissimulate, propitiate**) their teacher by forming study groups for second semester.

11. The main character is a bumbling inventor who has accidentally transported himself back to the past, there to suffer the misadventures of a hapless (**lackey, anachronism**).

12. When you say that your rival has a talent for (**propitiation, dissimulation**), what you really mean is that he is an out-and-out phony.

Choose the word from the word bank that best completes each of the following sentences. Write the correct word or form of the word in the space provided.

anachronism	**dissimulate**	**imperceptible**	**mot juste**	**propitiate**
apocryphal	**flamboyant**	**lackey**	**patrician**	**sic**

1. Then she leaned toward me and said confidingly, "Between you and I ________________, I didn't believe a word he said."

2. His efforts to ________________ his feelings of inadequacy by pretending to be bored and indifferent are a sign of immaturity.

3. Although these stories have been widely accepted for many years, we now have ample evidence to show that they are completely ________________.

4. During the early years of the Roman Republic, plebeians vied bitterly with ________________ for political dominance.

5. In calling them "stinkers," I may not have been too refined; but in view of their disgraceful conduct, I think I applied the ________________.

6. The able auctioneer acknowledged bids from the audience that were so discreet as to be ________________ to the untrained eye.

7. One would expect such ________________ behavior from an attention-seeking celebrity, not from a normally shy, unassuming person.

8. We need not try actively to ________________ the opponents of our candidate, but we can certainly take reasonable precautions to avoid antagonizing them.

9. As the duke's coach drew up, two ________________ in splendid livery stepped forth to open the carriage door.

10. Having the Civil War general sign documents with a ballpoint pen struck me as the most ludicrous ________________ in the whole miniseries.

End Set A

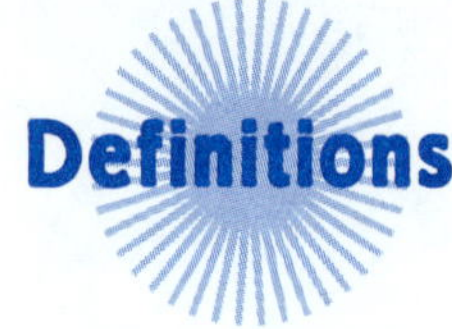

Note the spelling, pronunciation, part(s) of speech, and definition(s) of each of the following words. Then write the appropriate form of the word in the blank space in the illustrative sentence(s) following.

1. acumen
(a kyü′ mən)

(*n.*) keenness of insight; quickness or accuracy of judgment

Stars who enjoy long careers generally choose their roles with remarkable ________________.

2. adjudicate
(ə jüd′ i kāt)

(*v.*) to act as judge in a matter; to settle through the use of a judge or legal tribunal

An arbitrator may sometimes ________________ a civil suit involving a relatively small sum of money.

3. disparity
(dis par′ ə tē)

(*n.*) a difference or inequality in age, rank, degree, amount, or quality; a dissimilarity, unlikeness

The growing ________________ between the rich and the poor is a matter of grave concern.

4. empirical
(em pir′ i kəl)

(*adj.*) derived from, dependent upon, or guided by practical experience, observation, or experiment, rather than by theory; so verifiable

The compilation of ________________ data is an essential part of sound scientific research.

5. fulsome
(fu̇l′ səm)

(*adj.*) offensively insincere or excessive; disgusting, sickening

It is best to take the ________________ praise that appears in film previews with a grain of salt.

6. immolate
(im′ ə lāt)

(*v.*) to kill as a sacrifice, especially by fire; to destroy or renounce for the sake of another

When the Aztecs took captives, they enslaved some and ________________ others.

7. liaison
(lē′ ə zon)

(*n.*) the contact or means of communication between groups; someone acting as such a contact; any close relationship; a thickening or binding agent used in cooking

Block associations serve as ________________ between neighborhoods and city governments.

8. monolithic
(mon ə lith′ ik)

(*adj.*) characterized by massiveness, solidness, and total uniformity

The government buildings in the state's capital can best be described as ________________ in style.

9. nihilism (nī′ əl iz əm)
(*n.*) a total rejection of existing laws; extreme radicalism
Those who rebel against the restraints imposed by society may be attracted to ________________.

10. sublimate (səb′ lə māt)
(*v.*) to redirect the energy of a biological or instinctive impulse into a higher or more acceptable channel
If we are to live in harmony with one another, we must learn to ________________ our aggressive impulses.

Using Context

For each item, determine whether the ***boldface*** *word from pages 150–151 makes sense in the context of the sentence. Circle the item numbers next to the six sentences in which the words are used correctly.*

1. I hope to work as a broadcaster one day, so I am thrilled to be appointed the media **liaison** between the school and local news outlets.

2. He is one of the most pleasant talk-show hosts on television because of the **fulsome** language he uses when interviewing his guests.

3. I had many questions about the lecture, but I kept my mouth shut for fear that I would reveal my **acumen** on the subject.

4. She attempted to **sublimate** her guilt for the damage to the car with many excuses, but I was able to see right through her.

5. Declaring that you believe in **nihilism** in a courtroom will not make you immune to punishment if you have actually broken the law.

6. **Monolithic** dormitories and lecture halls appeared to loom intimidatingly from the enormous university campus.

7. Teachers must be prepared to **adjudicate** disagreements between students as justly as possible.

8. It is important for parents to show no **disparity** between what they say and what they do, or they will not be good role models for their children.

9. Although I initially disagreed with the author's point, she was able to **immolate** her opinion so effectively in the article that I eventually came around to her side.

10. The detective could not find enough **empirical** evidence to prove that his suspect was guilty, but his instincts told him to keep looking.

Set B

*Select the **boldface** word that better completes each sentence. You might refer to the passage on pages 144–145 to see how most of these words are used in context. Note that the choices might be related forms of the Unit words.*

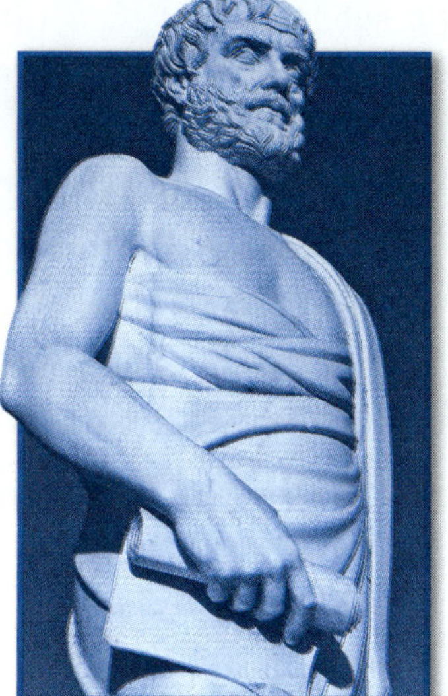

1. Though Plato's approach to philosophy often seems somewhat mystical, Aristotle's is decidedly (**empirical, fulsome**).

2. In a pluralistic democracy, such as the United States, there is little chance that a(n) (**empirical, monolithic**) public opinion will ever develop on any controversial issue.

3. A breeder of dogs, my uncle was asked to (**adjudicate, immolate**) at the local dog show.

4. There seemed no point in the author's gratuitous use of such (**fulsome, monolithic**) language other than to offend the taste of the reader.

5. The cost of (**adjudication, nihilism**) often exceeds the amount of the award.

6. No country can survive the threats of foreign invasion and domestic insurrection unless it is governed by leaders with extraordinary political (**acumen, disparity**).

7. Some psychologists theorize that genius in any field represents a special kind of (**immolation, sublimation**) of capacities, drives, and needs that are in all of us.

8. We are not suggesting that students should run the school, but we believe that the administration should maintain a (**nihilism, liaison**) with the students.

9. I agree that there are imperfections in our society, but I cannot accept your (**monolithic, nihilistic**) belief that the entire past must be discarded.

10. People who engage in self-destructive behavior seem to have a desire to (**sublimate, immolate**) themselves.

11. There is often a (**liaison, disparity**) between what people aspire to do and what they are equipped to do by natural endowment and training.

12. It is said that the sun will (**immolate, adjudicate**) a vampire.

Choose the word from the word bank that best completes each of the following sentences. Write the correct word or form of the word in the space provided.

acumen	disparity	fulsome	liaison	nihilism
adjudicate	empirical	immolate	monolithic	sublimate

1. The fate of individuals accused of war crimes may be ____________________ by an international court.

2. A major political party in the United States represents a coalition of many different views and interests, rather than a(n) ____________________ structure.

3. During the campaign in West Virginia in 1861, Robert E. Lee acted as the ____________________ between the commanders of the two independent Confederate brigades operating in the area.

4. I know you're trying to curry favor with the boss, but must you greet every one of his bright ideas with such ____________________ flattery?

5. Their blanket rejection of the standards and values on which our society is founded seems to be little short of senseless ____________________.

6. Though I believed their promises at first, I soon came to realize the great ____________________ between their words and their deeds.

7. It is one thing to spin out ingenious theories; it is quite another to find ____________________ confirmation for them.

8. The company's profits increased remarkably last year, thanks mainly to the new president's exceptional business ____________________.

9. The aggressive drive can be channeled into antisocial forms of behavior or ____________________ into loftier, more worthwhile endeavors.

10. What a shock it was for her to discover the unworthiness of the cause for which she had ____________________ her youth, her talents, and her hopes of happiness.

End Set B

Synonyms

*Choose the word or form of the word from this Unit that is the same or most nearly the same in meaning as the **boldface** word or expression in the phrase. Write that word on the line. Use a dictionary if necessary.*

1. known for wearing **garish** outfits ____________________
2. sought to **placate** their supervisor ____________________
3. place **exactly as written** in the margin ____________________
4. noticed the **chronological error** in the history book ____________________
5. spun many **fictitious** tales ____________________
6. based on **experiential** evidence ____________________
7. noticed the **discrepancy** in their answers ____________________
8. needed an **intermediary** between the principal and the students ____________________
9. heaped with an **inordinate** amount of flattery ____________________
10. appointed to **mediate** the dispute ____________________
11. held up by **massive** columns ____________________
12. a strong **perspicacity** to pick the best performing stocks ____________________
13. sought the **right word** with which to end the speech ____________________
14. has a tendency to **dissemble** ____________________
15. learned to **rechannel** their impulses ____________________

Antonyms

*Choose the word or form of the word from this Unit that is most nearly opposite in meaning to the **boldface** word or expression in the phrase. Write that word on the line. Use a dictionary if necessary.*

1. a plan to **rescue** the hostages ____________________
2. a group that espouses **political caution** ____________________
3. willingly worked hard for his **employer** ____________________
4. descended from **peasants** ____________________
5. made **conspicuous** movements ____________________

Writing: Words in Action

Think about the slang and phrases that young people commonly use today. Also consider slang and phrases that were common among previous generations. Write an essay examining youth language and slang then and now. Use at least two details from the passage (pages 144–145) and three or more words from this Unit.

Vocabulary in Context

Some of the words you have studied in this Unit appear in ***boldface*** *type. Read the passage below, and then circle the letter of the correct answer for each word as it is used in context.*

Whenever the dark clouds of **nihilism** threaten to descend, consider the **acumen**, determination, and perseverance of the lexicographer James Augustus Henry Murray. Born in 1837 in southern Scotland, Murray became the third and by far the most influential editor of the *Oxford English Dictionary*, a project so monumental as to virtually defy belief, with 414,825 words, 1,827,000 citations, 16,000 pages, a total production cost of £300,000 [**sic**]. Murray himself labored from 1879 until his death in 1915; the first edition of the *OED* would not be completed until 1928.

Although he was a precocious polymath, Murray did not enjoy an auspicious start in life. Scarcely **patrician**, the Murrays could not afford to send their son to university, and he left school at fourteen. In London, where he became a schoolteacher, luck led him to the Philological Society, which had envisioned a new dictionary of the English language as far back as 1857. When he learned of the project, Murray told Frederick Furnivall, the befuddled second editor in search of a successor, "I rather wish I could have a go at it."

After an interview at Oxford, Murray was entrusted with one of the most daunting challenges in the history of the written word. Throughout his labors, however, he retained a certain humility. He had no intention of **immolating** himself on the altar of lexicography. As if to **propitiate** the shade of his revered predecessor, Samuel Johnson, Murray reproduced Johnson's words in the preface to his great *Dictionary* of 1755: "I saw that one enquiry only gave occasion to another, that book referred to book, that to search was not always to find, and to find was not always to be informed."

---

1. What is the meaning of **nihilism** as it is used in paragraph 1?

a. paralysis **c.** languor
b. deception **d.** rejection

2. What is the meaning of **acumen** in the context of the passage?

a. congeniality **c.** perspicacity
b. dexterity **d.** obtuseness

3. What is the meaning of **sic** as it is used in paragraph 1?

a. approximately **c.** for example
b. thus so **d.** the same

4. What does **patrician** most likely mean as it is used in paragraph 2?

a. commercial **c.** aristocratic
b. scholarly **d.** reclusive

5. What does **immolating** most likely mean as it is used in paragraph 3?

a. preserving **c.** accusing
b. accommodating **d.** killing

6. What characteristic is suggested by **propitiate** in paragraph 3?

a. conciliation **c.** scrutiny
b. alienation **d.** compensation

UNIT 11

*Read the following passage, taking note of the **boldface** words and their contexts. These words are among those you will be studying in Unit 11. It may help you to complete the exercises in this Unit if you refer to the way the words are used below.*

Remarks Prepared for Delivery Before Congress

<Script for Political Speech>

Esteemed colleagues and fellow citizens, good morning:

Our nation faces a stark choice between entering, ill-advisedly, into a war against an amorphous enemy, or remaining at peace. Before we rush to send citizens into harm's way, before we commit resources for years to come, we must let the lessons of history guide us.

Twenty-eight centuries ago, after years of fighting, the Athenian and Trojan armies were at an **impasse** until the Greeks employed a bold and **parlous** tactic. Unable to penetrate King Priam's Troy by force, the Greek army breached the walls with **bravado** and cunning. They built a colossal hollow wooden horse, left it outside the fortress, and feigned departure. Many Trojan leaders suspected treachery and reasoned that receiving an offering from their ruthless enemy was a **non sequitur**. Nonetheless, in a calamitous example of **quixotic** thinking, Priam had the horse pulled inside. This gift **metamorphosed** into a treacherous trick. Athenian warriors emerged from within the hollow horse that night and opened the gates of Troy for their army, which was poised to continue the **vendetta**.Troy was ransacked.

This legendary episode exemplifies a trait of governments that historians deem "folly." Despite leaders' capacity for wisdom, even brilliance, a puzzling **dichotomy** exists: Governments chronically act in a manner contrary to their own interests, despite the availability of viable alternatives.

Take Montezuma, who made a fateful decision that cost him dearly. Five centuries ago, he ruled a wealthy, sophisticated Mesoamerican empire of five million people. Despite warnings from advisors, he fell prey to Cortez and his 600 soldiers, 17 horses, and 10 cannon. While a huge Aztec army stood by, Montezuma, fooled by the Spaniard's **mystique** into thinking him a returning god, gave the conquistador safe passage into the city, and soon after found himself captured.

President Obama looks at a speech, 2009.

State of the Union Address, 2009

Consider the ill-advised choice the British government made in dealing with its disconsolate American colony, where there was no clear **consensus** for revolt. Options in England abounded for compromises that could have **constricted** the increase in grievances and mended fences, but instead, its government opted to use force. Suppressing an independence movement in a colony more than 1000 miles long and 3000 miles away proved to be an expensive miscalculation for the British.

And lastly, remember Pearl Harbor. The Japanese should have learned from a fateful blunder the German Kaiser made in World War I when, by attacking American shipping, the Kaiser made a reluctant nation his enemy. The United States sent two million soldiers to Europe, thus ending Germany's attempt to dominate that continent. Japan, in its zeal to establish an Asian Pacific empire, repeated the Kaiser's folly when, despite having reasonable alternatives, its government opted for bombing the U.S. Pacific fleet. It was a terrible miscalculation. Instead of gaining the empire it sought, Japan enjoyed a moment of **euphoria**, but then suffered catastrophic defeat.

When individuals exhibit a lack of normal prudence or foresight, it's regrettable, but when governments do, it's tragic. Whatever causes folly—impulse, ambition, prejudice, hubris—is antithetical to the **sine qua non** of government: to rule reasonably in the interest of its people. And that's what we *must* do right here in this chamber. Look no further than our recent **quagmires** abroad to see the disheartening results of past folly—we dare not repeat such mistakes this day. Say "No" to the **effusive** beating of the drums of war and let us not follow the dangerous path that has tempted so many of our predecessors. Thank you.

Audio

For iWords and audio passages, go to **SadlierConnect.com**.

Definitions

Note the spelling, pronunciation, part(s) of speech, and definition(s) of each of the following words. Then write the appropriate form of the word in the blank space in the illustrative sentence(s) following.

1. bravado (brə vä' dō)
(*n.*) a display of false or assumed courage
The challenger's boast that he would knock the champ out in the first round was sheer ____________.

2. constrict (kən strikt')
(*v.*) to make smaller or narrower, draw together, squeeze; to stop or cause to falter
An accident or road repairs might ____________ the flow of traffic on a busy highway.

3. dichotomy (dī kot' ə mē)
(*n.*) a division into two contradictory or mutually exclusive parts; a branching or forking in an ancestral line
Many of the world's great works of literature examine the ____________ between good and evil.

4. gothic (goth' ik)
(*adj.*) characterized by or emphasizing a gloomy setting and grotesque or violent events; such a literary or artistic style; a type of medieval architecture
In many a ____________ novel, the life of the brooding protagonist is blighted by a dark secret.

5. impasse (im' pas)
(*n.*) a dead end; a position from which there is no escape; a problem to which there is no solution
When negotiations reached an ____________, the workers went out on strike.

6. mystique (mi stēk')
(*n.*) an aura or attitude of mystery or veneration surrounding something or someone
A ____________ still clings to some of the great movie stars of the past.

7. non sequitur (non sek' wi tər)
(*n.*) an inference or conclusion that does not follow logically from the facts or premises
When it was the next debater's turn, he confounded us with an argument undermined by ____________.

8. parlous (pär' ləs)
(*adj.*) full of danger or risk, perilous
In a televised speech, the president warned the nation that it would face ____________ times.

9. quagmire (kwag′ mīr)
(*n.*) soft, soggy mud or slush; a difficult or entrapping situation
After a week of heavy rain, the farmer's fields were reduced to a ____________________.

10. sine qua non (sin ə kwä nōn′)
(*n.*) an essential or indispensable element or condition
The ____________________ for a successful party is a group of interesting and sociable guests.

*For each item, determine whether the **boldface** word from pages 158–159 makes sense in the context of the sentence. Circle the item numbers next to the six sentences in which the words are used correctly.*

1. The search party reached an **impasse** along the treacherous, snow-covered mountain trail, and unfortunately, they had to turn back.

2. The band debated whether signing a contract with a major record company would allow them greater freedom to produce music or would **constrict** their creativity.

3. As the dangerous storm approached, the governor warned residents to evacuate coastal areas for more **parlous** regions of the state.

4. The glamorous movie actress's sudden withdrawal from public life only served to add to her **mystique**.

5. The speaker argued that the need to choose between economic growth and an environmentally sustainable future was, in fact, a false **dichotomy**.

6. Architectural critics praised the sleek, modern lines of the city's newest high-rise **gothic**-style office building.

7. The long, rambling essay was made up of one **non sequitur** after another.

8. Making an offensive remark in public is a **sine qua non** that should be avoided at all costs.

9. Week after week, the characters in the television drama face a **quagmire** of scheming and betrayal.

10. Although he is famous throughout the country, the celebrity often goes out into the community with such an unassuming **bravado** that locals almost overlook his presence.

Set A

*Select the **boldface** word that better completes each sentence. You might refer to the passage on pages 156–157 to see how most of these words are used in context. Note that the choices might be related forms of the Unit words.*

1. Mr. Ridley is fascinated by the Middle Ages and (**parlous, gothic**) architecture; therefore, he plans to travel around Europe this summer.

2. There is no point in trying to decide exactly which of the factors is most important for victory in the election; every one of them is a (**non sequitur, sine qua non**).

3. Perhaps her volunteering to undertake the mission was mere (**bravado, mystique**), but the fact remains that she accomplished a great deal.

4. Very few of the world's problems can be understood in terms of a simple (**bravado, dichotomy**) of right and wrong.

5. There are times when I like to read a (**gothic, parlous**) tale of gloomy castles, mysterious strangers, and unhappy romances.

6. After the downpour the first night, our camping trip became nightmarish, as we had to drag our supplies through fallen limbs and trudge through a (**bravado, quagmire**).

7. For a long time we lived under the illusion that "everything would come out all right," but, inevitably, we arrived at the (**dichotomy, impasse**) where we had to face realities.

8. Involvement in the long war in Vietnam led the United States into a (**sine qua non, quagmire**) from which it was extremely difficult to withdraw.

9. Space suits are designed to afford astronauts maximum protection without unduly (**constricting, dichotomizing**) their freedom of movement.

10. Our thesis was that, at this stage in their history, Americans must eschew the (**sine qua non, mystique**) of force and violence and develop new ideals of social cooperation.

11. Despite the grave risks that the rescue attempt would entail, there was no shortage of volunteers for the (**parlous, gothic**) undertaking.

12. Their analysis of the problem seemed to me extremely fallacious—full of false assumptions, dubious generalizations, and (**constrictions, non sequiturs**).

Completing the Sentence

Choose the word from the word bank that best completes each of the following sentences. Write the correct word or form of the word in the space provided.

bravado	**dichotomy**	**impasse**	**non sequitur**	**quagmire**
constrict	**gothic**	**mystique**	**parlous**	**sine qua non**

1. Each episode in the silent-movie serial *The Perils of Pauline* ended with the heroine facing another ____________________ predicament.

2. His challenge to fight was pure ____________________; inwardly he hoped that no one would take him on.

3. The rugged landscape, with the severe vertical lines of the mountains in the background, lent an air of ____________________ gloom to the entire scene.

4. You cannot duck your responsibility for negotiating an agreement simply by announcing that you have reached a hopeless ____________________.

5. To achieve an hourglass figure, fashionable ladies of the nineteenth century employed tight-fitting corsets to ____________________ their waistlines.

6. Although it may be true that hard work does not guarantee success, it is certainly a(n) ____________________ for doing well in any endeavor.

7. As the disappointing results of the poll filtered in, the candidate sank into a(n) ____________________ of doubts about the future.

8. Ernest Hemingway's *Death in the Afternoon* offers a rare insight into the ____________________ of the bullring and the attitudes that surround that ancient blood sport.

9. The speakers said that they could see little hope for world peace unless something could be done to bridge the ____________________ between the "have" and the "have-not" nations.

10. Modern military power requires great industrial resources, but to conclude from this that industrialized nations are inherently militaristic is a ____________________.

End Set A

Definitions

Note the spelling, pronunciation, part(s) of speech, and definition(s) of each of the following words. Then write the appropriate form of the word in the blank space in the illustrative sentence(s) following.

1. apostate (ə pos′ tāt)	(*n.*) one who forsakes his or her religion, party, or cause A politician who switches parties can expect to be denounced by former allies as an ____________________.
2. consensus (kən sen′ səs)	(*n.*) a collective or general agreement of opinion, feeling, or thinking After an unusually contentious debate, the council finally reached a ____________________.
3. effusive (i fyü′ siv)	(*adj.*) highly demonstrative; unrestrained I received such an ____________________ welcome from my hosts that I felt like the party's guest of honor.
4. euphoria (yü fōr′ ē ə)	(*n.*) a feeling of great happiness or well-being, often with no objective basis It is perfectly normal for a person who wins the lottery to feel an initial surge of ____________________.
5. lugubrious (lu̇ gü′ brē əs)	(*adj.*) sad, mournful, or gloomy, especially to an exaggerated or ludicrous degree The clown's ____________________ face, complete with a painted teardrop, never fails to make the audience laugh.
6. metamorphosis (met ə môr′ fə sis)	(*n.*) a complete transformation, as if by magic The beauty makeovers that we sometimes see on television are a kind of ____________________.
7. punctilio (pəŋk til′ ē ō)	(*n.*) a minute detail of conduct or procedure; an instant of time The mark of a true perfectionist is the need to check each and every ____________________ personally.
8. quixotic (kwik sot′ ik)	(*adj.*) extravagantly or romantically idealistic; visionary without regard to practical considerations Utopian fiction presents ____________________ fantasies of ideal social orders.

9. raconteur (rak on tər′)
(*n.*) a person who tells stories and anecdotes with great skill
The author, a noted ____________, was much sought after as a dinner party guest.

10. vendetta (ven det′ ə)
(*n.*) a prolonged feud, often between two families, characterized by retaliatory acts of revenge; any act motivated by vengeance
The two novelists, once good friends, have been carrying on a literary ____________ for more than two decades.

Using Context

*For each item, determine whether the **boldface** word from pages 162–163 makes sense in the context of the sentence. Circle the item numbers next to the six sentences in which the words are used correctly.*

1. The doctor said that some of the symptoms would not appear immediately, but others would show up **punctilio**.
2. He clearly thinks of himself as a great **raconteur** and does not seem to notice how dull his stories are to the rest of us.
3. When it was announced that I was the winner of the first-place award, the happiness that overcame me can only be described as **euphoria**.
4. I love the **effusive** joy with which my little cousin greets me and hope that she never outgrows expressing her emotions so enthusiastically.
5. Although our cousins always insisted they didn't intentionally exclude those relatives from holiday gatherings, we knew that there had been a **vendetta** between them for many years.
6. The **quixotic** expressions on many of the students' faces told the professor that she was not explaining the topic clearly enough for them to understand.
7. I am a true **apostate** of the belief that there is a positive relationship between optimism and good health.
8. The new diet product alleges that customers will experience a total body **metamorphosis** as soon as they begin using it, but real change in weight only comes about through the hard work of diet and exercise.
9. It was endearing to see the child's face light up with a **lugubrious** expression when he was handed the new toy.
10. With such a hostile, disagreeable member in our group, I don't see how we'll ever reach a **consensus**.

Set B

Choosing the Right Word

*Select the **boldface** word that better completes each sentence. You might refer to the passage on pages 156–157 to see how most of these words are used in context. Note that the choices might be related forms of the Unit words.*

1. In *Romeo and Juliet*, the hero's tragic death comes as the result of a long-standing (**vendetta, punctilio**) between his family and Juliet's.

2. Diana spent a year abroad her junior year, and, when she returned, I immediately recognized a complete, and pleasantly surprising, (**metamorphosis, apostate**).

3. It is impossible for me to convey the intensity of emotion that I felt at that (**lugubrious, euphoric**) moment when I learned that I had won the scholarship.

4. Though your efforts to enact a program of ecological reform in the face of strong opposition were (**quixotic, effusive**) and doomed to failure, they were inspiring.

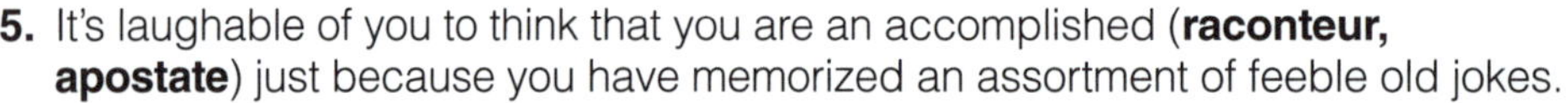

5. It's laughable of you to think that you are an accomplished (**raconteur, apostate**) just because you have memorized an assortment of feeble old jokes.

6. Aaron Burr, the third United States Vice President, concluded a (**metamorphosis, vendetta**) against Alexander Hamilton, the first United States Secretary of the Treasury, by killing him in a duel in 1804.

7. Does it seem paradoxical that, like many other great comedians, she goes about with a characteristically (**lugubrious, quixotic**) expression on her face?

8. The new assistant dean's adherence to every (**raconteur, punctilio**) in the Student Code alienated both the faculty and the student body.

9. As we learned to understand each other's needs and aspirations, a sort of unspoken (**consensus, euphoria**) developed that enabled us to work together harmoniously.

10. Your prose is (**effusive, lugubrious**), heartfelt, and unrivaled—an absolute pleasure to read.

11. Even though their son had abandoned the religion in which he had been brought up, his parents never thought of him as a(n) (**apostate, vendetta**).

12. The ordeal of the Civil War (**apostatized, metamorphosed**) Lincoln from an obscure small-town lawyer into an historical personality of universal appeal.

Completing the Sentence

Choose the word from the word bank that best completes each of the following sentences. Write the correct word or form of the word in the space provided.

apostate	effusive	lugubrious	punctilio	raconteur
consensus	euphoria	metamorphosis	quixotic	vendetta

1. When he came to the throne, the ____________________ renounced the established religion and began a vigorous campaign to reestablish paganism as the official belief system of the region.

2. How can you concern yourself with the ____________________ of protocol when your whole world is collapsing about your ears?

3. One look at the coach's ____________________ expression, and I knew that all our misgivings about the outcome of the game had been borne out.

4. The police investigation established that the victim was not an innocent bystander but the target of a gangland ____________________.

5. The man was a skilled ____________________ whose repertory of amusing anecdotes was seemingly inexhaustible.

6. It took Rome centuries to achieve the miraculous ____________________ from a minor city-state along the Tiber to the leading power in the Mediterranean world.

7. Every great president must combine various roles: the practical politician, the masterful intellectual, the tough administrator, the persuasive advocate—and at least a touch of the ____________________ visionary.

8. Though everyone in our club agreed that we had a problem, there was no group ____________________ on how to solve it.

9. Not until later did I realize that their ____________________ expressions of interest in our welfare were insincere and self-serving.

10. The mood of ____________________ brought about by our extraordinary good fortune caused us to relax our usual alertness.

End Set B

Synonyms

*Choose the word or form of the word from this Unit that is the same or most nearly the same in meaning as the **boldface** word or expression in the phrase. Write that word on the line. Use a dictionary if necessary.*

1. the glaring **division** between wealth and poverty ________________
2. a **storyteller** without equal ________________
3. a **requisite** for good health ________________
4. attend to each **fine point** myself ________________
5. underwent a truly remarkable **transformation** ________________
6. a lack of **accord** among voters ________________
7. produced feelings of **bliss** ________________
8. an analysis followed by an **illogical reference** ________________
9. her throat **contracted** from fear ________________
10. a legendary **rivalry** between the two sports teams ________________
11. had **utopian** dreams of a fantastical society ________________
12. stuck in the **bog** ________________
13. an **eerie** story of betrayal and madness ________________
14. captivated by his **aura** ________________
15. unable to break the **deadlock** ________________

Antonyms

*Choose the word or form of the word from this Unit that is most nearly opposite in meaning to the **boldface** word or expression in the phrase. Write that word on the line. Use a dictionary if necessary.*

1. has a reputation for being a **loyalist** ________________
2. **restrained** in her praise ________________
3. showed **pluck** when speaking in front of a large audience ________________
4. bought only **risk-free** stocks ________________
5. sang a **merry** ballad ________________

Writing: Words in Action

Suppose you are a legislator who was swayed by the political speech on pages 156–157. Write a statement to your constituents defending why you voted against "folly." Use at least three details from the speech, personal experiences, and prior knowledge to support your argument. Use three or more words from this Unit.

Vocabulary in Context

*Some of the words you have studied in this Unit appear in **boldface** type. Read the passage below, and then circle the letter of the correct answer for each word as it is used in context.*

The year 431 BCE was a crucial one in the history of Athens. The Delian League—the alliance of Greek city-states that had formed to fight the Persians—was fragmenting. The uneasy truce that had been struck fourteen years earlier between Athens and the **apostate** Sparta had always looked like a temporary ceasefire. As they resumed hostilities, both sides showed a fierce determination to bring the conflict to a decisive conclusion.

It was an Athenian custom in time of war to conduct funeral rites at the end of each year for those who had died in battle, and to elect a speaker to deliver an oration over the bones of the unburied dead before they were consigned to the earth. This year that solemn duty was performed by Pericles, the preeminent orator and statesman of his age, and the historian Thucydides recorded what has come to be regarded as one of the greatest speeches ever recorded.

Pericles catches the crisis of the moment with precision, but without **punctilio** or **bravado**. He does not play the **raconteur**. He praises the dead, admires their sacrifice in almost **gothic** mode, mourns their loss with a sincerity that is never **lugubrious**, and rejoices in their immortal fame—but it is when he explains what they died for that the speech bursts into a blaze of glory. More than two thousand years later, the same blaze of glory illuminated a similar oration in tribute to soldiers who had died for the same idea, but a different nation—the idea was democracy, and the nation was the United States.

---

1. What is the meaning of **apostate** as it is used in paragraph 1?

a. virtuous **c.** renegade
b. crusading **d.** evangelistic

2. What is the meaning of **punctilio** in the context of the passage?

a. propriety **c.** timeliness
b. impertinence **d.** pettiness

3. What is the meaning of **bravado** as it is used in paragraph 3?

a. courage **c.** insincerity
b. swagger **d.** overstatement

4. What does **raconteur** most likely mean as it is used in paragraph 3?

a. storyteller **c.** mourner
b. peacemaker **d.** warrior

5. What does **gothic** most likely mean as it is used in paragraph 3?

a. medieval **c.** stylistically dark
b. architectural **d.** with deliberate grandeur

6. What characteristic is suggested by **lugubrious** in paragraph 3?

a. pretentiousness **c.** cynicism
b. gloominess **d.** pessimism

UNIT 12

*Read the following passage, taking note of the **boldface** words and their contexts. These words are among those you will be studying in Unit 12. It may help you to complete the exercises in this Unit if you refer to the way the words are used below.*

Matriarchal Society

<Expository Essay>

Throughout recorded history, almost all cultures and countries have been patriarchal—controlled by men—with women relegated to second-class status. Have there been **viable** matriarchal societies in which women played important, **apposite** roles in every area of family, social, and political life? Most historians and anthropologists say no, although there have been scattered instances of quasi-matriarchal, or matrilineal, cultures in Africa, in Asia, among a few Native American tribes, and for a short time, in Hawaii. (In a matrilineal society, ancestral descent is traced through the maternal line.)

Some ancient African societies did experience periods of matriarchy, and goddess worship was common. For example, the ancient Nubians, a northern African culture of great influence and power, worshipped Isis, the all-knowing mother figure and, for a time, women dominated Nubian life. Historical evidence suggests that Nubia had an exceptionally large number of ruling queens and princesses (at least 10 have been identified). **Charismatic** warrior-queen Amanirenas is one; she led her armies into **precarious** battle against soldiers of the **narcissistic** Roman Emperor Augustus Caesar, whose **execrable**, land-grabbing behavior did not **augur** well for the Nubians.

Nubian queen Amanirenas

A theory has been posited that numerous goddess-worshipping cultures in antiquity existed—and that women ruled many places on Earth before men seized power. This theory is controversial and **impinges** on commonly held popular beliefs. While some anthropologists are convinced of its legitimacy and are exploring **labyrinthian** ancient writings and artifacts for new clues, others view the idea of women ruling the world as a false utopia, or even a **zany** myth or fantasy pushed forward by feminist **zealots**.

While examples of true matriarchies may be rare, gender-egalitarian societies and ideologies—with men and women enjoying a natural **rapport** and living on more or less equal footing—have existed and continue to exist in some parts of the world. And women have significant power, prestige, and autonomy even in cultures where men are the formal leaders. These societies have some commonalities: a strong respect for women as mothers, a closeness with nature and the natural world, an emphasis on the **utilitarian**, and a **pastiche** of gender roles. The Iroquois nations of North America have matrilineal customs, and family houses were owned by the oldest women members.

A Minangkabau woman with a traditional headdress

An Onondaga woman of the Iroquois nation

Today, in West Sumatra, Indonesia, some Minangkabau people practice a form of matriarchy, but it is not a mirror-opposite of patriarchy and it is subject to the **vagaries** of modern life. The Minangkabau follow matrilineal customs and a nature-based philosophy called "adat," which places an emphasis on nurturing growth and the maternal. Traditionally, women elders are revered and respected and women control land inheritance. But neither sex "rules"—decision-making is by consensus, with an ongoing partnership in place between the sexes for the common good.

Audio

For iWords and audio passages, go to **SadlierConnect.com**.

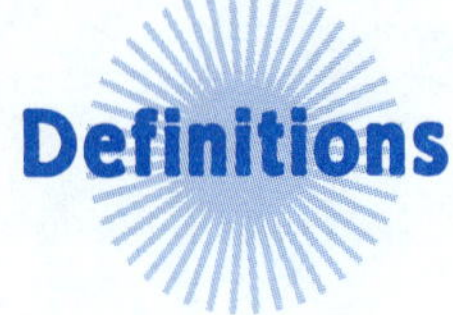

Definitions

Note the spelling, pronunciation, part(s) of speech, and definition(s) of each of the following words. Then write the appropriate form of the word in the blank space in the illustrative sentence(s) following.

1. apposite (ap′ ə zit)

(*adj.*) appropriate; suitable; apt

I did my best to give an ________________ answer to each of the interviewer's questions.

2. augur (ô′ ger)

(*n.*) a prophet or seer; (*v.*) to predict, foreshadow

The old man who lived alone in the forest was believed by the villagers to be an ________________.

The news did not ________________ well for the health of the economy in the short term.

3. charisma (kə riz′ mə)

(*n.*) the special personal magnetism that makes an individual exceptionally appealing to other people; a divinely bestowed gift or power

According to leading pundits, the dynamic young politician has the ________________ of a born leader.

4. debilitate (di bil′ ə tāt)

(*v.*) to make weak or feeble

Illness ________________ the patient so severely that she was no longer able to perform even the simplest everyday chores.

5. narcissism (när′ sə siz əm)

(*n.*) excessive self-love; absorption in oneself

Because of her ________________, she was completely unwilling to listen to other people's opinions.

6. penultimate (pe nəl′ tə mit)

(*adj.*) next to the last

In the relay race, our team was losing until the ________________ lap when our best runner swiftly moved to first place.

7. rapport (ra pôr′)

(*n.*) a close and harmonious relationship

The players in a chamber music ensemble need to develop an excellent ________________.

8. utilitarian (yü til ə târ′ ē ən)

(*adj.*) stressing practicality over other considerations; relating to the belief that what is good or desirable is determined purely by its usefulness

The layout and organization of the busy restaurant's small kitchen were strictly ________________.

9. viable (vī′ ə bəl) — (*adj.*) capable of living or developing under normal circumstances

The mayor announced a ____________ plan to reduce traffic in the downtown business district.

10. xenophobia (zen ə fō′ bē ə) — (*n.*) undue or unreasonable fear, hatred, or contempt of foreigners or strangers or of what is foreign or strange

It is sad when people who themselves were once newcomers to a land are blinded by ____________.

Using Context

For each item, determine whether the ***boldface*** *word from pages 170–171 makes sense in the context of the sentence. Circle the item numbers next to the six sentences in which the words are used correctly.*

1. A period of extreme heat and humidity can **debilitate** even the strongest and healthiest among us.
2. Because of their **apposite** nature, zebras can never be domesticated or trained in the way that other equids, or members of the horse family, can.
3. Before beginning rehearsals, the director led the cast through a set of improvisations to help them develop a sense of **rapport**.
4. Just because items such as umbrellas, raincoats, and rain boots are **utilitarian** doesn't mean they can't also be stylish.
5. According to popular superstition, finding a four-leaf clover is an **augur** of good luck, while breaking a mirror is thought to bring bad luck.
6. **Charisma** is an important trait for someone who appears on camera to have, but it is not as important for someone who works behind the scenes.
7. It takes a great deal of **narcissism** as well as courage to admit to a mistake.
8. Someone who suffers from **xenophobia** would most likely prefer climbing an open stairway to riding in an elevator.
9. A committee will examine the proposals to determine which ones are **viable** and therefore worthy of further consideration.
10. The first half hour of the movie was extremely suspenseful and exciting, but the rest of it was rather **penultimate**.

*Select the **boldface** word that better completes each sentence. You might refer to the passage on pages 168–169 to see how most of these words are used in context. Note that the choices might be related forms of the Unit words.*

1. It was the function of a Roman (**augur, rapport**) to divine the will of the gods through the interpretation of various natural phenomena, including the flight of birds.

2. Every president of our country should renew our determination to create a more (**penultimate, viable**) political and social structure for the future.

3. Even while emphasizing, as we must, (**utilitarian, narcissistic**) goals, we cannot afford to ignore ethical and aesthetic values.

4. Historians and economists fear this new gilded age might (**augur, debilitate**) badly for working-class people as the gap between rich and poor widens.

5. What we need now is not (**utilitarian, charismatic**) leadership, however inspiring, but steady, modest, and down-to-earth assistance in defining and achieving our goals.

6. The disease had such a (**debilitating, viable**) effect upon her constitution that she was unable to return to work for almost a year.

7. Anyone who spends so many hours a day primping and preening in front of a mirror can only be considered a blatant (**narcissist, xenophobe**).

8. Because the speaker before me had defined the topic so narrowly, I had to revise my notes so that only (**apposite, penultimate**) data remained.

9. True patriotism is a positive attitude and is the opposite of the negative orientation of (**charisma, xenophobia**).

10. Education is a living process that requires above all a close (**charisma, rapport**) between teacher and student.

11. It was in the (**utilitarian, penultimate**) chapter of the novel, after poring over thousands of pages, that I realized the true magnificence of the work.

12. He believed himself to be (**charismatic, xenophobic**) when in reality those who met him were put off by his frivolous small talk.

Choose the word from the word bank that best completes each of the following sentences. Write the correct word or form of the word in the space provided.

apposite	**charisma**	**narcissism**	**rapport**	**viable**
augur	**debilitate**	**penultimate**	**utilitarian**	**xenophobia**

1. The fumble by our quarterback on the opening drive, followed by a 15-yard penalty against us, did not ____________________ well for our team.

2. Oscar Wilde's famous epigram that "self-love is the beginning of a lifelong romance" is a clever comment on ____________________.

3. Luxury and self-indulgence ____________________ the once vigorous Roman people and led to the fall of the empire.

4. "Any organization that is able to survive and prosper in these trying times has indeed proven itself ____________________," she observed.

5. Their consistent attitude of hostility toward any cultural tradition different from their own cannot be excused by calling it ____________________.

6. When we asked the climbers why they wanted to scale the mountain, they gave the ____________________ reply, "Because it's there."

7. I cannot accept a purely ____________________ view of life that ignores such aspects of human experience as beauty, love, and humor.

8. Some leaders have such great personal ____________________ that they inspire an attitude akin to religious veneration in their followers.

9. Instead of sentimentalizing about the passing of rural America, we must work to achieve an effective ____________________ with our modern urban environment.

10. It was in the ____________________ year of her life that she realized she must make amends with her daughter, and so they were able to revive a mutual feeling of tenderness.

End Set A

Definitions

Note the spelling, pronunciation, part(s) of speech, and definition(s) of each of the following words. Then write the appropriate form of the word in the blank space in the illustrative sentence(s) following.

1. bilk (bilk)
(*v.*) to defraud, cheat, or swindle; to evade payment of; to frustrate, thwart

There will always be people who are only too ready to ______________ credulous individuals.

2. execrable (ek′ si krə bəl)
(*adj.*) utterly detestable, hateful, or abhorrent; extremely inferior

The crude and ______________ behavior of a few individuals spoiled the evening for the rest of us.

3. impinge (im pinj′)
(*v.*) to strike against or collide with violently; to encroach or obtrude upon; to make an impression upon

Political forces sometimes ______________ on our everyday lives.

4. labyrinth (lab′ ə rinth)
(*n.*) a bewildering maze; any confusing or complicated situation

I quickly lost my way as I wandered through the old city's ______________ of winding streets.

5. pastiche (pas tēsh′)
(*n.*) a dramatic, musical, or literary work made up of bits and pieces from other sources; a hodgepodge

The figure skater performed to a ______________ of melodies from Richard Wagner's operas.

6. precarious (pri kâr′ ē əs)
(*adj.*) very uncertain or unsure; dangerous or risky

A long period of unemployment left my friend in a financially ______________ position.

7. vacuous (vak′ yü əs)
(*adj.*) devoid of matter, substance, or meaning; lacking ideas or intelligence; purposeless

From the ______________ expression on your face, no one would guess that you have such a sharp mind.

8. vagary (vā′ gə rē)
(*n.*) an unpredictable, erratic, or seemingly purposeless action, occurrence, or notion

Who can explain the ______________ of the world of high fashion?

9. zany (zā′ nē)
(*adj.*) clownish or funny in a crazy, bizarre, or ludicrous way; (*n.*) one who plays the clown

Who doesn't love the ________________ antics of the Marx brothers?

In every sitcom, there is a goofy character who can best be described as a ________________.

10. zealot (zel′ ət)
(*n.*) a fanatical partisan; an ardent follower

When it comes to our school's hockey team, my brother can best be described as a ________________.

Using Context

*For each item, determine whether the **boldface** word from pages 174–175 makes sense in the context of the sentence. Circle the item numbers next to the six sentences in which the words are used correctly.*

1. I did not have time to review the research before the meeting, so I was worried that I would have nothing more than **vacuous** comments to offer to the discussion.
2. Confront your problems head-on rather than **impinge** them and have them resurface later.
3. He attempted to **bilk** his friends, getting them to pay for his dinner, by claiming that he forgot his wallet.
4. The activist encouraged all of her followers to help her make a difference, but she warned that she would not associate with **zealots** who would break the law in the name of their cause.
5. When the boy entered his new school and saw the **labyrinth** of hallways inside the enormous building, he was not only nervous about having to make new friends but also about finding his classes.
6. I once thought I'd be with the company long enough to reach the executive level, but the rumors of cutbacks make me fear that I'm in a **precarious** position.
7. The student's **execrable** essay received a commendation and the highest grade in the class.
8. She prefers humor that is drier and more understated than the **zany**, slapstick comedy to which I am partial.
9. Do you consider yourself spontaneous and impulsive, or predictable and prone to **vagary**?
10. He is always an excellent cook, but I think his tastiest dish is a simple **pastiche** with homemade tomato sauce and warm bread.

Set B

Choosing the Right Word

*Select the **boldface** word that better completes each sentence. You might refer to the passage on pages 168–169 to see how most of these words are used in context. Note that the choices might be related forms of the Unit words.*

1. A single clown entered the ring and comically and skillfully evaded the bull; later, a collection of (**zanies, zealots**), just as comically, failed in their evasion.
2. In condemning their (**vacuous, execrable**) conduct, let us not assume that we ourselves are completely free of blame.
3. The brand new play is a brilliant (**pastiche, labyrinth**) of Shakespearean comedies with a focus on romantic couplings that go awry.
4. I have no sympathy for those who have allowed themselves to be (**impinged, bilked**) by such an obvious get-rich-quick scheme.
5. His idea of (**zany, zealous**) behavior at a party is to wear a lampshade as if it were a hat.
6. A true work of art must be an integrated whole rather than a (**vagary, pastiche**) of discrete or incongruous elements.
7. How can you be so easily impressed by those (**vacuous, precarious**) generalizations and clichés?
8. Although I had no desire to wander through a strange town on foot, I was reluctant to trust my person to the (**vagaries, zealots**) of those wild cab drivers.
9. My dreams always lead me to the (**vagary, labyrinth**) of a dilapidated school's hallways.
10. With so many rival claimants actively engaged in trying to depose him, the monarch knew that his hold on the throne was, at best, (**zany, precarious**).
11. Your (**execrable, zealous**) enthusiasm must be matched by training and discipline if you are to achieve anything worthwhile.
12. Their optimism is so unwavering and so all-encompassing that bad news simply fails to (**impinge, bilk**) on their confidence.

Completing the Sentence

Choose the word from the word bank that best completes each of the following sentences. Write the correct word or form of the word in the space provided.

bilk	impinge	pastiche	vacuous	zany
execrable	labyrinth	precarious	vagary	zealot

1. Only later did we come to realize that there was a serious purpose behind his apparently frivolous remarks and ____________________ behavior.
2. As I lay there, drifting off to sleep, suddenly the sound of a very loud, very raucous, and very obnoxious television commercial ____________________ on on my serenity.
3. As the play is essentially a(n) ____________________ of devices and ideas drawn from many different sources, it lacks the consistency and cohesiveness of the writer's other works.
4. His ____________________ remarks revealed how little he really knew about political economy.
5. We cannot say with any confidence how long this trip will take us because our progress is dependent upon the ____________________ of the weather.
6. We recognize the need for vigorous criticism in a political campaign, but we will certainly not tolerate that kind of ____________________ character assassination.
7. Only after living and working in Washington for many years were we able to find our way through the vast ____________________ of government departments and agencies.
8. By filing false claims over a period of many years, the pair attempted to ____________________ the insurance company of large sums of money.
9. Attacked from all sides by superior forces, the army found itself in a(n) ____________________, if not totally untenable, position.
10. Our party can use the support of ardent young ____________________, but we also need the help of older and cooler heads.

End Set B

Synonyms

*Choose the word or form of the word from this Unit that is the same or most nearly the same in meaning as the **boldface** word or expression in the phrase. Write that word on the line. Use a dictionary if necessary.*

1. subject to the **whims** of fortune ______
2. **relevant** to the matter being discussed ______
3. **obtrudes** on the rights of others ______
4. friends who have a unique **bond** ______
5. **insipid** niceties and trite slogans ______
6. known for his **charm** among fans ______
7. the **next-to-last** chapter of the book ______
8. vanity and **egotism** ______
9. an exercise **fanatic** who runs 10 miles a day ______
10. guided through the **tangle** of complex tunnels ______
11. a **patchwork** of other people's ideas ______
12. entertained by the clown's **comical** antics ______
13. the prediction of the **oracle** ______
14. the tool's **practical** purpose ______
15. **duped** the unsuspecting couple ______

Antonyms

*Choose the word or form of the word from this Unit that is most nearly opposite in meaning to the **boldface** word or expression in the phrase. Write that word on the line. Use a dictionary if necessary.*

1. **fortifying** relationship with her friends and family ______
2. an **impracticable** recovery plan ______
3. **cosmopolitan** attitude toward foreign students ______
4. scored a **commendable** grade on the final exam ______
5. felt balanced on the **sturdy** perch ______

Writing: Words in Action

Imagine a modern society or government dominated by women. How would it function as compared to a male-dominated society or government? Write an essay using at least two details from the passage (pages 168–169) in which you consider how a matriarchal society would look. Use three or more words from this Unit.

*Some of the words you have studied in this Unit appear in **boldface** type. Read the passage below, and then circle the letter of the correct answer for each word as it is used in context.*

No female virtue was more admired in classical Athens than invisibility. "Great honor is hers," wrote Thucydides **vacuously**, "whose reputation among men is least, whether for praise or blame." Women were **bilked** of their rights as citizens. They had neither voice nor vote, and they could neither inherit nor own property. Athenian democracy could be misogynistic, as well as paternalistic and **xenophobic**. Girls received no formal education, but their mothers taught them the domestic duties of Athenian wives. They were underfed and deprived of sunlight to emphasize their youth, though they were never much over twelve when they married. Enormous dowries were their **penultimate** humiliation.

Spartan households were predominantly female. The men were usually on active service, and the boys left home permanently for army training at the age of seven. Slaves performed all domestic duties, so mothers taught their daughters the glories of war, self-sacrifice, and giving birth to heroes. At state day-schools, girls learned to read and write, to sing, dance, and play music. Physical training was rigorous but never **debilitating**. Sparta was not a democracy, and some of its greatest rulers were women. Men and women were equal in Spartan law. Women owned over a third of the real estate in Sparta. They never married under the age of eighteen, and dowries were regarded by all parties as insulting. According to Plutarch, the Greek biographer, when the **charismatic** Queen Gorgo was asked why Spartan women were the only women who were obeyed by their men, she replied simply, "Because we are the only mothers of real men."

---

1. What is the meaning of **vacuously** as it is used in paragraph 1?

a. misleadingly **c.** solemnly
b. thoughtfully **d.** simply

2. What is the meaning of **bilked** in the context of the passage?

a. misinformed **c.** cheated
b. ignorant **d.** burgled

3. In paragraph 1, what does the word **xenophobic** suggest about Athenians?

a. They were snobs. **c.** They hated monarchies.
b. They disliked foreigners. **d.** They feared women.

4. In paragraph 1 what does the word **penultimate** suggest about humiliation?

a. There was more than one. **c.** It was the last.
b. There were none. **d.** It was the first.

5. What does **debilitating** most likely mean as it is used in paragraph 2?

a. exhausting **c.** overheating
b. boring **d.** dispiriting

6. What characteristic is suggested by **charismatic** in paragraph 2?

a. honesty **c.** exoticism
b. magic **d.** personal magnetism

Vocabulary for Comprehension

Part 1

*Read this passage, which contains words in **boldface** that appear in Units 10–12. Then choose the best answer to each question based on what is stated or implied in the passage. You may refer to the passage as often as necessary.*

Questions 1–10 are based on the following passage.

While many children, and even adults, are drawn to the **mystique** of living in a castle, the reality of it may be less ideal than imagined. Take Highclere Castle for example—the site of the fictional residence in the British period drama *Downton Abbey.* With its 300 rooms and staff of 70, the castle costs its owners, the Carnarvon family, around one million dollars a year to run. Instead of "enchanting," the **mot juste** to describe such a residence would be "demanding." With the advent of *Downton Abbey* and its growing popularity, the Carnarvon family opened the castle's doors to tourists as well as those wishing to host momentous events at the extravagant property. Now anyone with enough money in the bank can rent the massive estate for a day and play out a fantasy of being a nineteenth-century **patrician**. Lady Carnarvon's business **acumen** is evident in her ability to see the fame brought about by the television series as an opportunity to turn the castle into a business, enabling the property to earn its keep, as the location fees from the show alone would not be enough to keep up with repairs on such an enormous estate.

However, fame and historical significance do not always translate into financial and structural stability. Such is the case of Duart Castle on the Isle of Mull, off the west coast of Scotland. Duart, owned by Sir Lachlan Hector Charles Maclean, is not only the ancestral home of the Maclean clan, it was also an important site in the history of the **vendetta** between the Maclean and Campbell clans. With needed repairs estimated at two million dollars, made worse by the 283 days of annual rainfall typical for the island, the proprietor can easily feel that he has reached an **impasse** in the process of restoring the castle. In fact, some may consider Sir Lachlan a **vacuous** man for remaining in the crumbling building without the means to repair it, but for him relinquishing the castle to the fates of Mother Nature is not really an option.

The leaky edifice is the **sine qua non** for visitors to Scotland, with visitors arriving every day from all over the world declaring their ancestral ties to the Macleans and the 600-year-old castle sitting atop a craggy cliff. Sadly, affection alone is not enough to keep the building from ruin. Even with a couple thousand visitors a month, the revenue generated by the castle is not enough to cover the costs needed to preserve the fourteenth-century edifice. Though government funds have provided for various necessary repairs, the bulk of the costs is the responsibility of the owners.

With the castle's proprietors unable to keep up with its needs, important questions emerge: Who is responsible for preserving this historical structure? Is it right for a country to allot government funds to a private residence, even if it is ancestrally and historically significant? Whatever the answers, one thing is clear: Without a stable source of funding, Duart Castle's future is **precarious.** The windfall of its starring role in *Downtown Abbey* seems to have saved Highclere Castle. Is it too late for Duart Castle to become the setting of a period drama, perhaps about the Maclean clan itself?

1. The purpose of the first sentence is to
   A) affirm that many people dream of living in a castle.
   B) dismantle some misconceptions about living in a castle.
   C) challenge the idea that everyone wants to live in a castle.
   D) disagree with the idea that living in a castle is easy.

2. The author includes facts about Highclere Castle in order to
   A) impress the reader with the size of the building and the number of people it employs.
   B) demonstrate that the building's architectural details have been thoroughly researched.
   C) illustrate a complete image of the building for the reader.
   D) emphasize the size of a castle and the amount of resources it requires.

3. As it is used in line 10, "mot juste" most nearly means
   A) inaccurate term.
   B) best expression.
   C) exact word.
   D) common phrase.

4. The author would argue that the destruction of Duart Castle would most likely be hastened by the
   A) owner's lack of interest in repairs.
   B) intense weather conditions to which it is exposed.
   C) number of tourists that walk through it every day.
   D) neglect of the government.

5. As it is used in line 43, "impasse" most nearly means
   A) a situation with no solution.
   B) a road block.
   C) a stalemate with no resolution.
   D) a permanent standoff.

6. According to the passage, the Duart Castle is
   A) significant to descendants of the Maclean clan around the world.
   B) only worth preserving for the well-being of the private residents.
   C) the sole responsibility of the owners, as the government does not wish to give aid.
   D) overrun with tourists who don't generate enough revenue to pay for repairs.

7. Which choice provides the best evidence for the answer to the previous question?
   A) Lines 50–55 ("The leaky ... craggy cliff")
   B) Lines 55–56 ("Sadly, affection ... ruin")
   C) Lines 57–61 ("Even with... edifice")
   D) Lines 61–64 ("Though ... owners")

8. The questions in the closing paragraph are meant to
   A) question a private owner's rights to government funds for repairs.
   B) pose to the reader some of the issues related to historical preservation and maintenance responsibility.
   C) clarify the difference between Highclere Castle and Duart Castle.
   D) highlight the misfortunes of Duart Castle.

9. As it is used in line 74, "precarious" most nearly means
   A) risky.
   B) sturdy.
   C) uncertain.
   D) precious.

10. Which of the following sentences best summarizes the entire passage?
   A) Only castles featured in popular television series can obtain the necessary funds to pay for their upkeep.
   B) The historical significance of castles is not relevant to their ability to raise funds.
   C) Many people dream of living in a castle, but in reality most people cannot afford the upkeep of a castle.
   D) Castle preservation is difficult for private owners, who must invent new ways to afford their building's upkeep.

Vocabulary for Comprehension Part 2

Read these passages, which contain words in ***boldface*** *that appear in Units 10–12. Then choose the best answer to each question based on what is stated or implied in the passage(s). You may refer to the passages as often as necessary.*

Passage 1

What does a nation do after a financial crisis leaves it in ruins? The island nation of Iceland built a new industry: tourism. In about a decade, tourism has become the island's top industry, offering a unique experience to all types of travelers.

For a relaxing getaway, Iceland, with its hot springs, may be a welcome change from the popular beach vacation. In the dead of winter, it is customary to walk out into the bitter cold and dip into the warmth of a geothermal pool, where you can meet both locals and other travelers. For the tourist looking for a **parlous** adventure, options abound. Imagine hiking up the side of a volcano and then descending 400 feet in a cable car into the center of the crater itself. No amount of **bravado** can mask the signs of exhilaration and fright on visitors' faces as they climb up any of Iceland's glaciers, from which the island gets its name. To **propitiate** the more cosmopolitan traveler, Reykjavik—the capital—includes a stunning concert hall and daring cuisine, such as one restaurant that draws on old Icelandic recipes for inspiration, or an ice cream parlor that serves up the country's most popular flavor: licorice.

Icelanders are aware that their most precious resource is nature itself. In order to make tourism a **viable** source of income for its citizens, the country has also placed a heavy emphasis on sustainability and preservation. Before a trip to the Nordic nation, it is important to be aware of one's own impact on the land and to care for it just as a local would. This is the message imparted by the government as it welcomes visitors to its pristine land.

Passage 2

Some may think that misgivings about tourism in one's own country is a clear sign of **xenophobia.** Yet, I would argue that it is more an expression of love for the natural beauty of one's land. The current practice of ecotourism in Iceland can only be described as pure **nihilism**. It shows a total disregard for nature, as guides shepherd along droves of visitors who carelessly trample the lush greenery beneath their hiking boots. Other tourists engage in acts of complete **narcissism** by snapping selfies in front of every volcano or waterfall they spot. While they might admire the nature scenes captured with their smartphone cameras, they nevertheless leave their trash strewn along the path, and disregard all form of regulation. At times, tourists can be found camping in empty lots or residential areas, instead of at designated sites.

The **empirical** evidence proves that ecotourism poses a serious threat to Iceland's greatest resource: its natural landscape. Furthermore, in 2015, nearly one million people visited Iceland. That is three times Iceland's total population, and every year the number of visitors climbs. Though on any given day tourists to the island well outnumber Icelanders, the citizens are the ones in charge of maintaining the land. And so, serious regulations need to be implemented!

If Iceland does not regulate its tourism, at the current rate all the land will be ravaged by the clunky hiking boots of foreigners, and **lugubrious** citizens will be left pondering how they allowed such a disaster to befall their once beautiful country.

1. As it is used in line 14, "parlous" most nearly means
A) thrilling.
B) risky.
C) tedious.
D) vigorous.

2. As it is used in line 22, "propitiate" most nearly means
A) satisfy.
B) entertain.
C) provoke.
D) challenge.

3. In Passage 1, tourism in Iceland is seen as
A) an way of averting a financial crisis.
B) a way to briefly provide employment.
C) a risky industry that is not sustainable.
D) a feasible way of boosting the economy.

4. As it is used in line 42, "xenophobia" most nearly means
A) a slight misunderstanding of cultures.
B) a strong preference for one's nation.
C) an intense dislike of foreigners.
D) a passionate aversion to travel.

5. As it is used in line 46, "nihilism" most nearly means
A) a dangerous practice.
B) disregard for the local population.
C) total destruction of natural resources.
D) dismissal of laws and regulations.

6. The author in Passage 2 is most likely concerned about
A) the fate of Iceland's natural resources.
B) tourism's economic impact.
C) Iceland's popular tourist attractions.
D) the well-being of Iceland's citizens.

7. In Passage 1, the author sees ice climbing as an exciting and dangerous tourist attraction, while in Passage 2 the author
A) sees it as a dangerous activity.
B) sees it as a threat to the glaciers.
C) sees it as equally destructive as hiking.
D) sees it as a way to teach visitors about the glaciers' value.

8. Which choice best describes the difference of opinion about Iceland's government expressed in Passage 1 and Passage 2?
A) Passage 1 analyzes the positive effects of the government's intervention in the economy; Passage 2 analyzes the negative effects.
B) Passage 1 is undecided with respect to the positive effects of tourism in Iceland; Passage 2 is certain about the negative effects of tourism in Iceland.
C) Passage 1 is enthusiastic about the impact of travelers on Iceland's natural resources; Passage 2 is skeptical about the annual number of tourists in Iceland.
D) Passage 1 has a positive view of government measures to protect the land; but Passage 2 has a negative view.

9. In Passage 1, the author emphasizes a myriad of possible activities for tourists visiting Iceland. In Passage 2, the author is much more concerned with
A) tourists who are too busy snapping photos to notice their surroundings.
B) preserving the country's natural resources, as tourism's negative effects have already been noted.
C) tourists ignoring the strict regulations implemented by the government.
D) the impact a large number of tourists has on all countries.

10. Which choice provides the best evidence for the answer to the previous question?
A) Lines 50–53 ("Other tourists ... spot")
B) Lines 53–57 ("While they ... regulation")
C) Lines 60–63 ("The ... landscape")
D) Lines 67–70 ("Though on ... land")

Synonyms

From the word bank below, choose the word that has the same or nearly the same meaning as the ***boldface*** *word in each sentence and write it on the line. You will not use all of the words.*

charisma	labyrinth	precarious	vendetta
effusive	metamorphosis	quagmire	viable
euphoria	mot juste	sic	xenophobia
imperceptible	mystique	vacuous	zany

1. The organization released a letter stating that the protesters "have made there [**intentionally so written**] point abundantly clear." ________________

2. Since I am in school and working full time, taking on any other responsibilities is just not a **feasible** solution to the problem. ________________

3. We finally found the exit sign leading the way out after wandering for an hour through the **tangle** of hallways. ________________

4. "This town will not tolerate any instances of **provincialism** and demands that all residents treat others with respect," said the mayor at the town hall meeting. ________________

5. I felt such **elation** when I received the acceptance letter to my first-choice college that I couldn't stop smiling the rest of the day. ________________

6. His sloppy bookkeeping and lack of organized financial records put him in quite a **morass** when tax season came around. ________________

7. The talk-show host is respected for her ability to balance a **comical** persona with important messages about current issues. ________________

8. Although the twins are not identical, they still look so similar that any differences in appearance are nearly **undetectable**. ________________

9. Although the applicant certainly has more **charm** than anyone else we've interviewed, he does not have enough experience. ________________

10. Though the doctors described his health as being in **dubious** condition, he made a quick recovery and was able to return home. ________________

11. The **change** that a caterpillar goes through when it turns into a butterfly is truly an amazing feat of nature. ________________

12. The **lavish** praise she bestowed on me was so over the top that I had to question her sincerity. ________________

Select the pair of words that best completes the meaning of each of the following sentences.

1. The battered war veteran taught himself to __________ his outrage and paint wondrous, fantastical, and __________ images that satirized the very political leaders who had led his country into war.
   a. sublimate … flamboyant
   b. propitiate … monolithic
   c. impinge … execrable
   d. debilitate … penultimate

2. Throughout the eighteenth and nineteenth centuries, the great __________ houses of England were staffed by armies of servants and __________, but today it is impossible for a duke or an earl to keep such a sizable domestic staff.
   a. gothic … zealots
   b. utilitarian … raconteurs
   c. patrician … lackeys
   d. monolithic … apostates

3. As her __________ lover Aeneas fled her embraces in search of his destiny on the wild and desolate shores of Italy, distraught Queen Dido __________ herself on a huge pyre atop the highest building in Carthage.
   a. fulsome … debilitated
   b. apocryphal … bilked
   c. execrable … adjudicated
   d. apostate … immolated

4. The gray and dreary walls of this office cubicle are far too __________ for my wide-eyed, __________ nature and willful disregard for authority.
   a. adjudicating … empirical
   b. debilitating … utilitarian
   c. constricting … quixotic
   d. bilking … fulsome

5. Some anecdotes about historical figures are clearly __________ because they contain __________ and other improbable elements that show the stories were written at a much later date.
   a. utilitarian … dichotomies
   b. apposite … non sequiturs
   c. empirical … disparities
   d. apocryphal … anachronisms

6. When the representatives of labor and management found that they had reached a hopeless __________ in the negotiations for a new contract, they called in an outside mediator to help break the deadlock and __________ the dispute.
   a. impasse … adjudicate
   b. rapport … dissimulate
   c. liaison … impinge
   d. consensus … debilitate

7. During your college interview, it wouldn't hurt to observe the __________ of a formal interview while also making sure to display your skills as a(n) __________ who is comfortable in a variety of contexts.
   a. augurs … rapport
   b. punctilios … raconteur
   c. non sequiturs … apostate
   d. vagaries … zealot

Denotation and Connotation

Words have both literal meanings, or **denotations**, and informal or implied meanings. These typically numerous and subjective meanings are called **connotations**. Readers or listeners bring connotations—positive, negative, or neutral—to words, while they look up the words' denotations in the dictionary.

For example, consider these synonyms for the neutral word *leave: desert, withdraw, retreat, vacate, abandon,* or *flee*. Each word conveys a different meaning. Excellent writers choose words carefully to refine their work and make it richer in meaning.

Consider these synonyms for the neutral word *impasse*:

standoff *dead end* *deadlock* *stalemate*

Standoff has a somewhat positive connotation, suggesting that the parties involved might come to an agreement. *Dead end* implies that there is no hope for agreement. *Dead end, deadlock* and *stalemate* are relatively negative and suggest little hope for progress.

Look at these examples of words with similar denotations but different connotations.

NEUTRAL	POSITIVE	NEGATIVE
hide	**pretend**	**dissimulate**
predicament	**mix-up**	**quagmire**
dispute	**squabble**	**vendetta**

Expressing the Connotation

Read each sentence. Select the word in parentheses that expresses the connotation (positive, negative, or neutral) given at the beginning of the sentence.

negative **1.** Her claims of royal ancestry are most certainly (**fraudulent, apocryphal**).

neutral **2.** Cuts in college loans will (**constrict, strangle**) students' economic futures.

neutral **3.** Will the recent court ruling (**affect, impinge on**) our everyday rights?

positive **4.** Her team produced a (**viable, possible**) plan for rebuilding the bridge.

negative **5.** The (**unintelligent, vacuous**) culture of consumption has had a deleterious effect on youth today.

negative **6.** She is a (**bigot, zealot**) who can't accept that others have a different view.

neutral **7.** The climbers' situation became (**parlous, uncertain**) as the storm raged.

neutral **8.** After the flood wrecked her home, she was in a (**precarious, perilous**) state.

Classical Roots

chron—time

This Greek root appears in **anachronism** (page 146), which means "a misplacing in time of events, objects, customs, or persons in regard to each other." Some other words based on the same root are listed below.

chronically	**chronicler**	**chronology**	**crony**
chronicle	**chronological**	**chronometer**	**cronyism**

From the list of words above, choose the one that corresponds to each of the brief definitions below. Write the word in the blank space in the illustrative sentence below the definition.

1. favoritism shown to old friends or companions in official or political appointments

The search committee accused the dean of ____________________ in his recent appointments.

2. arranged in order of time or occurrence; relating to or in keeping with the ordering of events in time

This discography is a ____________________ listing of all of the composer's recorded works.

3. a close friend or companion, chum

They planned an outing at the beach as a casual reunion of their old school ____________________.

4. an exceptionally accurate clock, watch, or other timepiece

The marine biologist especially values her underwater ____________________ when she dives.

5. one who writes or keeps a record of historical events

That magazine has long been regarded as an astute ____________________ of fashion.

6. constantly, habitually, over a prolonged period

Despite his responsibility as recording secretary, he is ____________________ late for meetings.

7. the determination of dates or of the sequence of events; the sequential ordering of dates and events; such a list or table

The documentary provides an accurate ____________________ of key battles of the last century.

8. a record of historical events presented in order of occurrence; to make or keep such a record

Anne Frank's poignant ____________________ of her years in hiding in an Amsterdam attic during World War II has been translated into scores of languages.

*Read the following passage, taking note of the **boldface** words and their contexts. These words are among those you will be studying in Unit 13. It may help you to complete the exercises in this Unit if you refer to the way the words are used below.*

Time to Clean Up Space

<Newspaper Editorial>

An artist's conception of space junk

In March 2009, when the crew of the $100 billion International Space Station was forced to implement emergency **protocols** for fleeing in an escape vehicle, the threat they sought to evade was posed not by a rogue state or an alien starship, but by a five-inch chunk of space junk. Had the debris actually struck the station, it might have depleted its entire oxygen supply. Fortunately, it missed.

We tend to think of space as **immaculate**, wide-open, and **resplendent** in its emptiness. We're proud, to the point of **vainglory**, about our extraterrestrial accomplishments, heaping **accolades** on brave astronauts and brilliant rocket scientists. But our efforts in space are **stigmatized** due to our lamentable failure to clean up after ourselves out there. As a result, a giant cloud of space junk—old rocket boosters, **vestiges** of satellites, implements discarded by astronauts, fragmentary traces of bygone collisions—now circles the planet. And this swirling junkyard poses a **chronic** threat to spacecraft, to astronauts, and to the communications satellites that our technologically driven society has come to depend on.

In decades past, scientists treated space junk as a minor nuisance; many were convinced that debris in Earth's orbit would soon wear itself down by **attrition** and fall harmlessly back to the planet, burnt up by the atmosphere. As it turns out, most space junk is likely to remain in orbit for thousands, even millions, of years. As we live, so we learn: NASA now tracks 11,000 large items of space junk, and the number is rising steadily. If nothing is done to check the increasing quantity of space junk, the risk of collision could eventually become so severe as to make space missions impracticable, perhaps permanently grounding all the world's space programs.

Thankfully, the problem is not **ineluctable**, and a range of solutions is available to address it. To begin with, spacefaring nations should come together, under their own **volition**, to develop global policies for managing space junk and producing less of it. For example, all nations should agree to a moratorium on secret tests of anti-missile weapons, as these **sub rosa** experiments and the explosions they cause in space significantly increase the volume of junk in orbit. Political agreements won't come easily, but there are good reasons to hope that relevant nations might overcome **chauvinist** bias and **factionalism** to make a deal: The growing threat from space junk is something all spacefaring nations have in common, and the threat to communications satellites should make a political solution universally appealing, at least in principle.

Technical solutions must also be tried. Robots could install rockets on dead spacecraft to knock them out of orbit and send them soaring back to Earth; powerful lasers could be used to zap smaller items of debris into oblivion. Unfortunately, as many scientists note with **acerbity**, these solutions are barely feasible today and would require significant and steady funding at a time when government support for space programs is already far too scarce and **mercurial**.

Until all the orbiting junk is cleared from the heavens, designers of spacecraft must combat space debris the old-fashioned way—by providing extra layers of protective cladding, or coating. Unfortunately, the added bulk makes satellites and vehicles heavier and far more costly. And while defensive measures like these might **palliate** matters, they do nothing to address the underlying problem. There's only one way to do that: Get the junk out of orbit.

Audio

For iWords and audio passages, go to SadlierConnect.com.

Debris from Space Shuttle Columbia is found in the field of a family home in Texas, 2003.

Computer artwork of space debris

Note the spelling, pronunciation, part(s) of speech, and definition(s) of each of the following words. Then write the appropriate form of the word in the blank space in the illustrative sentence(s) following.

1. acerbity (ə sər′ bə tē)

(*n.*) sourness or bitterness of taste; harshness or severity of manner or expression

Offended by the ____________________ of the director's remarks, the actor stormed out of the rehearsal.

2. bromide (brō′ mīd)

(*n.*) a trite or commonplace remark; a tiresome or boring person; a sedative

The usual ____________________ offered by politicians may please crowds but won't solve the nation's problems.

3. expound (ek spau̇nd′)

(*v.*) to explain in detail

The students listened attentively as their physics professor ____________________ upon the new theory.

4. factionalism (fak′ shən əl iz əm)

(*n.*) party strife and intrigue

Because of bitter ____________________ in both houses of Congress, no legislation of consequence was passed.

5. immaculate (i mak′ yə lit)

(*adj.*) spotless; without blemish or fault

After I finished washing and waxing my parents' white car, it was as ____________________ as new-fallen snow.

6. mercurial (mər kyu̇r′ ē əl)

(*adj.*) characterized by rapid and unpredictable changes of mood; fickle or inconstant

The temperamental diva is perhaps even more famous for her ____________________ behavior than for her voice.

7. palliate (pal′ ē āt)

(*v.*) to make less serious or severe by glossing over; to relieve without actually curing, mitigate

A few new laws may ____________________ the ills that plague our society but will not eradicate them.

8. stigmatize (stig′ mə tīz)

(*v.*) to brand or mark as in some way discreditable, disgraceful, or ignominious

People sometimes ____________________ innocent children because of their parents' misdeeds.

9. sub rosa (səb rō′ zə)

(*adv.*) in secret; confidentially; privately; (*adj.*) secretive

An unnamed White House source passed crucial information to reporters ____________.

At a series of ____________ meetings, the dissenting shareholders planned their next move.

10. vestige (ves′ tij)

(*n.*) a trace or visible evidence of something that once existed but now is lost or vanished

The spectacular ruins of the ancient temple are the last ____________ of a once-mighty civilization.

Using Context

*For each item, determine whether the **boldface** word from pages 190–191 makes sense in the context of the sentence. Circle the item numbers next to the six sentences in which the words are used correctly.*

1. It was hard to believe that the dusty, dirt-covered painting could be restored to such an **immaculate** condition.
2. The surgeon will carefully **expound** the scar tissue in the patient's abdomen.
3. The **acerbity** of the images that were transmitted from Mars was so astonishing that it made us marvel at the achievements of modern technology.
4. After years of **factionalism** and backbiting, the labor union was unified and able to function effectively once more.
5. The print in the footnotes of the antique book was so **mercurial** that you would need to use a magnifying glass to read it.
6. The hot tea with honey and the chicken noodle soup may **palliate** your cold for now, but I really think you need to see a doctor.
7. By law, these classified documents will remain **sub rosa** for fifty years; after that, they will be released and made available to the public.
8. If you and your teammates are genuinely dejected about losing a game, a **bromide** such as "Better luck next time" or "Win a few, lose a few" is not likely to lift your spirits.
9. In *The Scarlet Letter*, Nathaniel Hawthorne portrays a seventeenth-century New England Puritan community and a woman its members **stigmatize** for violating their moral code.
10. The Nobel Peace Prize is a **vestige** that is awarded annually to a person or organization for having made the greatest contribution to reducing strife in the world.

Set A

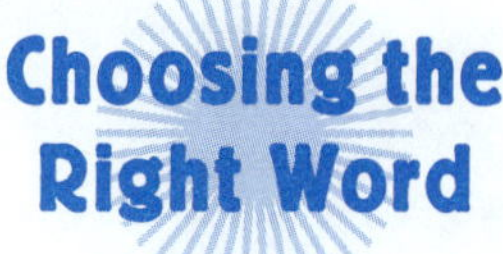

*Select the **boldface** word that better completes each sentence. You might refer to the passage on pages 188–189 to see how most of these words are used in context. Note that the choices might be related forms of the Unit words.*

1. George Washington's (**immaculate, mercurial**) reputation as a dedicated patriot has been an inspiration to many generations of Americans.

2. We are all eager to avoid the (**factionalism, stigma**) of being prejudiced and, perhaps, simultaneously unwilling to purge ourselves of our biases.

3. We spent most of the evening listening to her (**palliate, expound**) on her views on all sorts of interesting subjects.

4. My supervisor was uncomfortable with the (**mercurial, sub rosa**) meetings held in order to determine which departments would be dissolved.

5. Beneath the (**vestige, acerbity**) of their criticism, we recognized a sincere desire to help us solve our problems.

6. Although he saw himself as a wit, a bon vivant, and a man-about-town, everyone else regarded him as a hopeless (**factionalism, bromide**).

7. Though they are twins, one of them has a highly (**mercurial, vestigial**) temperament, while the other is stolid and reserved.

8. Your (**bromides, vestiges**) neither assure me nor enlighten me, and, in fact, I would like you to keep your hackneyed advice to yourself.

9. We sought desperately for some new forms of amusement to (**palliate, expound**) the boredom of those endless summer afternoons.

10. Our party can resist the attacks of its enemies from the outside, but it may fall victim to the erosion of (**bromide, factionalism**) from within.

11. In the light of the lessons of history, I am skeptical about the value of any diplomatic conferences held (**sub rosa, immaculately**).

12. The small bone at the base of the spinal column in humans is thought by biologists to be the (**vestige, bromide**) of a tail.

Completing the Sentence

Choose the word from the word bank that best completes each of the following sentences. Write the correct word or form of the word in the space provided.

acerbity	**expound**	**immaculate**	**palliate**	**sub rosa**
bromide	**factionalism**	**mercurial**	**stigmatize**	**vestige**

1. The Founding Fathers warned that without an overriding sense of national purpose, this country could be torn apart by ____________________.

2. The agreements that had been concluded ____________________ by the leaders of both parties aroused a storm of protest when they were finally made public.

3. Despite the heat and the dirt of a summer day in the city, he managed somehow to look cool and ____________________.

4. In an influential book published in 1936, the economist John M. Keynes ____________________ his theory of the causes of economic collapse.

5. Many a time-honored home remedy may indeed ____________________ the symptoms of a disease but do little or nothing to cure it.

6. His personality was so ____________________ that we never knew on any given occasion how he would react.

7. Why is it that so many theater critics are noted for the trenchancy of their perceptions and the ____________________ of their wit?

8. In spite of her advanced age and illness, one could still recognize the ____________________ of her once ravishing beauty.

9. G. B. Shaw's remark to the effect that "youth is wasted on the young" may be, as you say, an old ____________________, but it is also profoundly true.

10. Have we reached the stage where anyone who refuses to go along with the majority is to be ____________________ as a malcontent?

End Set A

Definitions

Note the spelling, pronunciation, part(s) of speech, and definition(s) of each of the following words. Then write the appropriate form of the word in the blank space in the illustrative sentence(s) following.

1. accolade (ak′ ə lād)

(*n.*) praise or approval; a ceremonial embrace or greeting

The playwright enjoyed the _______________ of both the theater critics and the public.

2. attrition (ə trish′ ən)

(*n.*) the process of wearing down by friction or gradual impairment

After many losses due to _______________, the weakened army sought an end to hostilities.

3. chauvinist (shō′ və nist)

(*adj.*) extravagantly patriotic; blindly devoted to a cause; (*n.*) such a person

During wartime, some newspapers may take an extremely _______________ stance in their editorials.

Denying that he is a male _______________, the senator cited his record of support for equal rights for women.

4. chronic (kron′ ik)

(*adj.*) continuing over a long period of time or recurring often

The president set up a blue-ribbon committee to look into the problem of _______________ unemployment.

5. imprecation (im prə kā′ shən)

(*n.*) a curse; the act of cursing

When I found myself stuck in a traffic jam, I could not resist muttering a few _______________.

6. ineluctable (in i lək′ tə bəl)

(*adj.*) not able to be avoided, changed, or overcome

Two of life's _______________ facts are death and taxes.

7. protocol (prō′ tə kôl)

(*n.*) customs and regulations dealing with official behavior and etiquette, as in a court or among diplomats; a type of international agreement; a memorandum, official account, or record

A breach of _______________ at a summit meeting of world leaders can have serious consequences.

8. resplendent (ri splen′ dənt)

(*adj.*) shining or gleaming brilliantly; splendid or magnificent

The knights, clad in _______________ armor, rode forth to engage the foe.

9. vainglory (vān′ glô rē)
(*n.*) excessive pride in and boastfulness about one's own accomplishments or qualities; a vain show or display

With insufferable ____________ the young tennis star taunted his opponent after each winning point.

10. volition (vō lish′ ən)
(*n.*) the power to choose, will, or decide; the act of choosing, willing, or deciding

Ignoring all my relatives' warnings, I chose the perilous course of my own ____________.

Using Context

For each item, determine whether the ***boldface*** *word from pages 194–195 makes sense in the context of the sentence. Circle the item numbers next to the six sentences in which the words are used correctly.*

1. We can blame the larger class sizes in our school district on the **attrition** of teachers due to budget cuts and dwindling salaries.

2. I take issue with her **chauvinist** attitude in these difficult times, when we need an optimist more than ever.

3. Even after all the praises he received for his excellent performance on the field, the football player was humble, demonstrating his **vainglory**.

4. I believe that her **chronic** sleeplessness is caused more by lifestyle choices, such as too much caffeine and not enough exercise, than it is by insomnia.

5. I find nothing more uplifting than the **resplendent** emergence of the sun after a rainfall.

6. During his acceptance speech at the awards ceremony, the actor made sure that everyone who had helped him to succeed received the proper **imprecation**.

7. Even if this turns out to be the wrong decision, at least I made the choice of my own **volition** and have no one to blame but myself.

8. The manager was tempted to fire the uncooperative employee on the spot, but she knew she had to follow **protocol** and receive approval from the human resources department.

9. During the press conference, the chief of police issued an **accolade** to everyone who had seen the crime but had done nothing to stop it.

10. The plastic surgeon understood people's desire to reverse the effects of the **ineluctable** passage of time.

Set B

*Select the **boldface** word that better completes each sentence. You might refer to the passage on pages 188–189 to see how most of these words are used in context. Note that the choices might be related forms of the Unit words.*

1. His claim to be the "greatest pole-vaulter in the world" would indeed have seemed outrageously (**chronic, vainglorious**) if it were not for the fact that he went ahead and proved it.

2. It was not until she entered the workforce in her small town in the 1950s that she realized the preponderance of male (**imprecations, chauvinists**) in positions of power.

3. My brother's (**chronic, resplendent**) tardiness is perpetually getting him into trouble at school.

4. The computer technician configured a revised (**protocol, volition**) to access new mail.

5. Critics who bestow their (**imprecations, accolades**) too easily may gain some quick popularity, but they will soon lose their credibility and influence.

6. Because the difficulty of the subject matter increases rapidly as the term proceeds, mathematics and physics courses have a high rate of student (**attrition, vainglory**).

7. They preceded her to the table, not because (**volition, protocol**) required it, but because they were eager to get at the food.

8. His talents, which had seemed so (**ineluctable, resplendent**) in his youth, now struck us as unimpressive and even pathetic.

9. Your threats and (**imprecations, protocols**) leave me unimpressed because I know that your words will not be followed by deeds.

10. "My country, right or wrong" expresses (**chauvinism, attrition**) in its most common form.

11. Although she emphasizes that she was the helpless victim of bad luck, one can recognize the effects of her own (**imprecation, volition**) in bringing about her downfall.

12. Letting the grim facts speak for themselves, the doctor explained quietly the (**ineluctable, resplendent**) tragedy that results from drug abuse.

Completing the Sentence

Choose the word from the word bank that best completes each of the following sentences. Write the correct word or form of the word in the space provided.

accolade	**chauvinist**	**imprecation**	**protocol**	**vainglory**
attrition	**chronic**	**ineluctable**	**resplendent**	**volition**

1. It was a bitter experience to have to leave the village in disgrace, followed by the jeers and ________________ of people I had tried to help.

2. No one suggested that I take an art class in my freshman year; I decided to do it purely of my own ________________.

3. ________________ in her first evening gown and her first professional hairdo, she waited impatiently for her date to escort her to the dance.

4. Since we cannot overcome the enemy by direct attack, we will wage a war of ________________ against them.

5. You may be scornful about matters of "mere ________________," as you call it, but you will soon learn that *how* things are done is often as important as *what* is done.

6. Over the years he has tried many different remedies to relieve the pain caused by his ________________ arthritis.

7. Shall I be modest and say that I simply do not deserve these extravagant ________________, or shall I be honest and admit that I do?

8. Isn't there truly an element of pathos in the certain knowledge that the ________________ and overconfidence of our youth will be laid low by "the slings and arrows of outrageous fortune"?

9. In the innocent glow of youth and inexperience, we simply assumed that we would be able to avoid the ________________ consequences of our own folly.

10. The steady and quiet devotion of people who truly love their country is very different from the noisy fulminations of mindless ________________.

End Set B

Synonyms

*Choose the word or form of the word from this Unit that is the same or most nearly the same in meaning as the **boldface** word or expression in the phrase. Write that word on the line. Use a dictionary if necessary.*

1. asked to **explicate** the meaning of the poem ____________
2. **disgraced** because of past mistakes ____________
3. an organization riven by **dissension** ____________
4. known as a **flighty** individual ____________
5. ranks depleted by **exhaustion** ____________
6. the **inescapable** ravages of time ____________
7. conveyed their plans of escape **covertly** ____________
8. did not follow the **code of conduct** ____________
9. made the decision of my own **free will** ____________
10. refused to budge on his **jingoistic** policies ____________
11. a humble person who lacked **conceit** ____________
12. the **acidity** in her tone ____________
13. an **impeccable** record of service ____________
14. preserved the **relics** of an ancient culture ____________
15. used one **cliché** after another ____________

Antonyms

*Choose the word or form of the word from this Unit that is most nearly opposite in meaning to the **boldface** word or expression in the phrase. Write that word on the line. Use a dictionary if necessary.*

1. the orator delivered **blessings** to the audience ____________
2. clad in **drab** garments ____________
3. a week of **sporadic** storms ____________
4. accepted the **criticism** with good grace ____________
5. a situation **aggravated** by the drop in temperature ____________

Writing: Words in Action

Do you think cleaning up pollution on Earth, in space, and in the oceans have the same level of urgency? Write an essay in which you consider the urgency of pollution on land, in the oceans, and in space. Use examples from your reading (pages 188–189), personal observations, and at least three words from this Unit.

*Some of the words you have studied in this Unit appear in **boldface** type. Read the passage below, and then circle the letter of the correct answer for each word as it is used in context.*

In *Superman IV: The Quest for Peace*, the Man of Tomorrow confiscates the world's entire stock of nuclear armaments and hurls it into the sun. In reality, the solution is not so easy. The Cold War has left the world with enough nuclear weaponry to destroy itself several times over, and the problem today is not so much "first use" as disuse. As the world's nuclear arsenal falls into decay, the old **protocols** no longer apply, and the old **bromides** about "mutually assured destruction" are no longer comforting, because the chances of a catastrophic accident are becoming greater than the risk of nuclear war.

Supporters of the Superman Strategy take every opportunity to **expound** it, regardless of the **imprecations** of opponents and the danger of **factionalism** within their own ranks. But why confine the strategy to nuclear weapons? Nobody has yet found a permanent solution to the **chronic** problem of nuclear waste. It is impossible to destroy outright, and storing it at the bottom of the ocean is not a permanent solution. The Superman Strategy, however, is safe and permanent—and limitless in its potential applications. We are choking ourselves with garbage. One day, those floating islands of indestructible rubbish will cover the world's oceans entirely. Can we not hurl everything we don't want into the sun?

The answer, sadly, is no—or at least, not yet. The world produces about 2.6 trillion pounds of garbage per year, and the estimated annual cost of transporting all that garbage into the sun is around $34,000,000,000,000,000 ($34 quadrillion). Economists will no doubt revisit the Superman Strategy when the technology becomes available.

---

1. What is the meaning of **protocols** as it is used in paragraph 1?

a. responses
b. prospective employees
c. codes of conduct
d. responsibilities

2. What is the meaning of **bromides** in the context of the passage?

a. theories
b. platitudes
c. digestive aids
d. slogans

3. In paragraph 2, what does the word **expound** suggest about the strategy?

a. It is inexplicable.
b. It can be elucidated.
c. It is very brief.
d. It is more faith than fact.

4. In paragraph 2, what does **imprecations** suggest about the opponents?

a. They are scientists.
b. They are undisciplined.
c. They are afraid.
d. They are vehement.

5. What does **factionalism** most likely mean as it is used in paragraph 2?

a. infighting
b. faithlessness
c. opposition
d. disloyalty

6. What characteristic is suggested by **chronic** in paragraph 2?

a. profundity
b. persistence
c. harmfulness
d. hopelessness

*Read the following passage, taking note of the **boldface** words and their contexts. These words are among those you will be studying in Unit 14. It may help you to complete the exercises in this Unit if you refer to the way the words are used below.*

A Gap Year Makes Sense

<Persuasive Essay>

This year, over two million American high school seniors will pack up laptops, smart phones, and other sundry **accoutrements** of teenage life and head off to college. Their reasons for going may be **unimpeachable**: to follow academic interests, to gain new skills, to prepare for careers. But is it possible they're in too much of a hurry? The fact is, over one-third will drop out after just one year of college. These **truncated** college careers represent a loss to the students themselves, to their colleges, and to the nation as a whole. One way to help avoid this outcome, according to an increasing number of students and educators, is to take a year off from school after high school graduation. This year has come to be known as the gap year.

Many college students start out full of optimism and enthusiasm, but any of a wide range of **disparate** factors can **supervene** to knock them off course. Some students discover they're not in the right program or school. Others, after four years of diligent work in high school, fail to apply themselves when they get to college, inclined instead to explore their new-found freedom. Insufficient preparation for college-level work, financial concerns, homesickness—the list is long, and each story is ultimately unique. But whatever the reason, dropping out of college is more than a minor **contretemps**. Many who leave regret their choice for years to come; some are burdened with student loans that they can hardly repay. And think of all the hours spent **bickering** with disillusioned parents...

Today's college-bound students report extremely high levels of stress. The most ambitious are likely to have been burning the candle at both ends, under pressure to get good grades and excel at multiple extracurricular pursuits while maintaining satisfying social lives. In such circumstances, a year off from school and a chance to revitalize oneself might seem especially **apropos**.

A gap year also affords young people more time to mature—particularly when that time is spent productively. Interning at an office

or volunteering at a local charity can provide real-life experience and broaden horizons. Working at a job has similar effects, and the income earned can be **meted** out to defray next year's tuition. Travel abroad, wilderness survival camp, exchange programs, volunteer work in a **populous** developing nation—there are many programs specifically designed to enrich the experience, confidence, and credentials of students "in the gap."

Productive "gappers" thus have an opportunity to practice self-reliance, gain self-awareness, and see how the world works outside the classroom. In the process, their gap-year experiences are likely to **coalesce** into insight that can help them **cull** their often confused notions about colleges, careers, and their skills and enable them to make wiser decisions once they return to school.

Many parents and some educators remain adamantly opposed to the gap year and decry its allegedly **noxious** effects. Their **polemics** typically rest on the claim that a single year off will inevitably expand into two or three, increasing the gapper's risk of being derailed from the college track. Happily, this concern is not generally borne out by the facts: Research demonstrates that most high-school grads who plan to go to college after a year off actually do go back to school once that year is up.

Statistics aside, the decision to take or not to take a year off before college should be approached with deliberation and **probity**, with no illusions about the character and circumstances of each student. There's no room for **dogmatic** arguments here. But there's little doubt that, for a great many college-bound high-school graduates, a gap year can provide opportunities for growth that are more likely to increase than to decrease the odds of subsequent success.

Audio

For iWords and audio passages, go to **SadlierConnect.com**.

Above: Students volunteer in a building project.

Left, top: Some students find teaching overseas rewarding.

Left, bottom: A volunteer in Ghana

Definitions

Note the spelling, pronunciation, part(s) of speech, and definition(s) of each of the following words. Then write the appropriate form of the word in the blank space in the illustrative sentence(s) following.

1. apogee (ap′ ə jē)
(*n.*) the point in the orbit of a heavenly body or artificial satellite farthest from Earth; the farthest or highest point

Many people consider the works of Michelangelo to represent the ____________________ of Renaissance art.

2. apropos (ap rə pō′)
(*adj.*) appropriate, opportune; (*adv.*) relevantly; incidentally, by the way; speaking of

When choosing a greeting card, I look for the one that is most ____________________ to the occasion.

____________________ of your plans for the summer, where are you going to spend your vacation?

3. bicker (bik′ ər)
(*v.*) to engage in a petty or peevish dispute; to move or run rapidly, rush; to flicker, quiver

If we ____________________ over every minor detail, we'll never get the job done.

4. convolution (kon və lü′ shən)
(*n.*) a rolling up, coiling, or twisting together; a sinuous folding or design

Because of its many ____________________, San Francisco's Lombard Street is called "the crookedest street in the world."

5. cull (kəl)
(*v.*) to pick out or select; to gather or collect

I will ____________________ pertinent quotations from my research to illustrate the point of my paper.

6. dogmatic (dôg mat′ ik)
(*adj.*) certain of the truth of one's own ideas; inclined to state opinions as if they were indisputable facts

People who are ____________________ are unlikely to have much tolerance for views that differ from their own.

7. noxious (nok′ shəs)
(*adj.*) harmful to physical health or morals

Firefighters wear respirator masks to protect them from smoke and ____________________ fumes.

8. probity (prō′ bə tē)
(*n.*) complete and confirmed honesty; total integrity

We should demand that our elected officials conduct themselves with the utmost ____________________.

9. supervene (sü pər vēn′) (*v.*) to take place or occur as something additional or unexpected; to follow immediately after

Events that none of us could have foreseen in our wildest imaginings ________________ to blight our hopes.

10. unimpeachable (ən im pē′ chə bəl) (*adj.*) beyond doubt or reproach; unquestionable

The members of the jury found the testimony of the key prosecution witness to be ________________.

Using Context

*For each item, determine whether the **boldface** word from pages 202–203 makes sense in the context of the sentence. Circle the item numbers next to the six sentences in which the words are used correctly.*

1. Because her credentials are **unimpeachable**, she will most likely be approved for a seat on the board of directors unanimously.

2. It was hard to believe that the small **apogee** in the rock could lead to such an enormous cave.

3. Some of the participants in the auction are antique dealers who are there to **cull** items that they can resell in their shops.

4. Your question about nerve cells in mollusks is **apropos**; in fact, I was just getting ready to discuss that particular topic.

5. You will be impressed by this housepainter's skill in painting clean, straight lines with precision and **convolution**.

6. It was refreshing to discuss foreign affairs with someone so well informed, open-minded, and **dogmatic**.

7. You must be careful not to burn any poison ivy with the rest of the yard waste because doing so could produce **noxious** fumes.

8. Rather than **bicker** over the meaning of the word, why don't we just look it up?

9. The signing of the contract has been delayed by questions about the **probity** of the bidding process.

10. A good coach is able to inspire, teach, train, motivate, and **supervene** the players on his team all at the same time.

Set A

Choosing the Right Word

*Select the **boldface** word that better completes each sentence. You might refer to the passage on pages 200–201 to see how most of these words are used in context. Note that the choices might be related forms of the Unit words.*

1. The decision by the local government to (**supervene, cull**) the white-tailed deer population this autumn is controversial and has incited protests from many groups.

2. From the roots of ancient prejudices, there grew the (**dogmatic, noxious**) plants of racial and religious hatreds.

3. The reporter assured her boss that the charges contained in her story were based on information from a(n) (**unimpeachable, noxious**) source.

4. I have neither the time nor the inclination to plough through those long, dreary books in the hope of (**supervening, culling**) a few interesting passages.

5. I agree that it is a very good book, but to say that it represents the (**apogee, convolution**) of the development of the American novel is a gross exaggeration.

6. If you are to get along in polite society, you must learn that a remark that is factually true is not necessarily (**noxious, apropos**).

7. Abraham Lincoln warned that the (**convolutions, dogmas**) of the quiet past were inadequate to the needs of the stormy present.

8. After a long silence, and when everyone was sufficiently uncomfortable, she announced, (**unimpeachable, apropos**) of nothing, that they were to be married the next weekend.

9. We expected a simple explanation, but what we got was an involved rationalization, full of all kinds of strange (**apogees, convolutions**).

10. When we least expected it, a crucial event (**culled, supervened**) that changed the outcome of our project.

11. Even the most relentless investigations by our political opponents could uncover no evidence that challenged our reputation for (**apogee, probity**).

12. I had hoped for some understanding and generosity of spirit, not this endless (**bickering, supervening**) over petty details.

Completing the Sentence

Choose the word from the word bank that best completes each of the following sentences. Write the correct word or form of the word in the space provided.

apogee	**bicker**	**cull**	**noxious**	**supervene**
apropos	**convolution**	**dogmatic**	**probity**	**unimpeachable**

1. How can we continue to live in this ____________________ atmosphere of suspicion and hatred?

2. ____________________ of your remarks on the probable effect of the law, may I quote from the column of a well-known political commentator?

3. From the vast mass of unsolicited manuscripts, the editor ____________________ the few that might be considered for publication.

4. After the noisy excitement of the big party, the eerie silence that suddenly ____________________ seemed unnatural and difficult to accept.

5. I hate to ____________________ with you over the cost of a few gallons of gasoline, but I have to because I don't have a dime to spare.

6. They possess the kind of unshakable ____________________ that not only precludes lying but also requires them to express the truth, no matter what.

7. Though her career in the movies had many ups and downs over the years, it reached its ____________________ when she won an Academy Award.

8. Although the author's conclusions are open to debate, the scholarship upon which they are based is ____________________.

9. It was absolutely impossible to follow the ____________________ of the man's tortuous reasoning as he desperately tried to prove his point.

10. You can't hope to hold a fruitful conversation if you are so ____________________ that you issue pronouncements instead of offering opinions.

End Set A

Note the spelling, pronunciation, part(s) of speech, and definition(s) of each of the following words. Then write the appropriate form of the word in the blank space in the illustrative sentence(s) following.

1. accoutrements (ə kü′ trə mənts)
(*n., pl.*) accessory items of clothing or equipment; a soldier's outfit, usually not including arms or clothing; trappings
When the new administration took office, it was accorded all the ____________________ of power.

2. coalesce (kō ə les′)
(*v.*) to blend together or fuse so as to form one body or substance
Many small tributaries ____________________ to form the mighty Amazon River.

3. contretemps (kon′ trə tä^{n})
(*n.*) an inopportune or embarrassing occurrence; a mishap
I believe in taking life's ____________________ in stride rather than making a fuss over them.

4. disparate (dis par′ ət) *or* (dis′ pər it)
(*adj.*) completely distinct or different; entirely dissimilar
Despite our ____________________ backgrounds and life experiences, we have remained the best of friends.

5. licentious (lī sen′ shəs)
(*adj.*) morally or sexually unrestrained; having no regard for accepted rules, customs, or laws
In *The Lives of the Caesars* the biographer Suetonius describes the emperor Caligula's ____________________ behavior.

6. mete (mēt)
(*v.*) to distribute or apportion by or as if by measure; to allot
Part of the job of being a parent is the responsibility to ____________________ out suitable punishment when a child misbehaves.

7. polemic (pə lem′ ik)
(*n.*) an aggressive attack on or refutation of a specific opinion or doctrine
The columnist was known for his ____________________ against those at the opposite end of the political spectrum.

8. populous (pop′ yə ləs)
(*adj.*) full of people; filled to capacity; densely populated; having a large population
Millions of people along the ____________________ Atlantic Coast fled inland as the hurricane approached.

9. repartee (rep ər tē′)

(*n.*) a swift, witty reply; conversation full of such remarks; skill in making such replies or conversation

The writers who made up the famous Algonquin Roundtable were celebrated for their sparkling ______________.

10. truncate (trən′ kāt)

(*v.*) to shorten by or as if by cutting off, lop

A family emergency forced us to ______________ our summer vacation.

Using Context

*For each item, determine whether the **boldface** word from pages 206–207 makes sense in the context of the sentence. Circle the item numbers next to the six sentences in which the words are used correctly.*

1. She claimed that she was prepared to go camping, but it wasn't until she arrived at the campgrounds that she realized that she would be in the wilderness, lacking the **accoutrements** of home.

2. When the email server began to reach maximum capacity, it would **truncate** people's messages to just a few lines.

3. Although the comedians were funny on their own, their **repartee** was so amusing to watch that they often went on tour together.

4. The best lesson I learned about acting is not to lose my **contretemps** if I make a mistake so that the rest of my performance will go more smoothly.

5. When the reporter began to realize how **disparate** the witnesses' accounts of the crime were, he took interest in the story and became determined to uncover what really happened.

6. The bank indicated that it would have to **mete** the deposit under a hold and could not make the funds available until the check cleared the other financial institution.

7. The **polemic** that the column received after it went to print gave the small paper so much publicity that it became a nationally known source of trusted news.

8. The environmental activist intended to **coalesce** his message far and wide to encourage people to reduce waste.

9. The defense lawyer argued that her client's history of **licentious** behavior had no bearing on responsibility for this particular crime.

10. Since I was accustomed to the **populous** city, it took a while to adjust to the silence that surrounded me when I moved to the country.

Set B

Choosing the Right Word

*Select the **boldface** word that better completes each sentence. You might refer to the passage on pages 200–201 to see how most of these words are used in context. Note that the choices might be related forms of the Unit words.*

1. Los Angeles supplanted Chicago as the second most (**populous, disparate**) city in the United States.

2. Unfortunately, there will always be a lawmaker accused of (**populous, licentious**) conduct, and there will always be a journalist happy to report endlessly on it.

3. What they described as a new spirit of freedom and vigorous originality seemed to me mere (**accoutrements, licentiousness**).

4. Mathematicians and students (**mete, truncate**) the infinite digits of *pi* to 3.14.

5. "Unless the various factions put aside their differences and (**coalesce, mete**) into a unified force, we will get absolutely nowhere," I said.

6. (**Repartee, Contretemps**) has been likened to a sort of verbal fencing, with the more skillful contestants driving home their weapons for the kill.

7. Because the original article was too long for our needs, we published it in a somewhat (**coalesced, truncated**) form.

8. We are all imperfect creatures, and none of us has been divinely ordained to (**truncate, mete**) out punishment to others for their transgressions.

9. Instead of taking a fresh look at the situation, they were satisfied to refute their opponents by repeating old and weary (**polemics, accoutrements**).

10. How do you expect to deal with the inevitable problems of life if you raise every (**repartee, contretemps**) to the level of a major tragedy?

11. The route of the army's retreat was littered with the discarded (**polemics, accoutrements**) of war.

12. We must not close our eyes to the flagrant (**disparities, contretemps**) between what our society aspires to be and what it actually is.

Completing the Sentence

Choose the word from the word bank that best completes each of the following sentences. Write the correct word or form of the word in the space provided.

accoutrements	**contretemps**	**licentious**	**polemic**	**repartee**
coalesce	**disparate**	**mete**	**populous**	**truncate**

1. True, you did reply to the wisecrack, but I hardly regard "Not!" as an outstanding example of devastating ____________________.

2. The lower end of the ridge had been somewhat ____________________ by the action of glacial erosion many thousands of years ago.

3. Five minutes after arriving at the dance, I upset the punch bowl—the first of many ____________________ that made the evening a nightmare.

4. There are so many ____________________ elements in her personality that I find it difficult to tell you what kind of person she is.

5. Problems such as overcrowding, traffic congestion, and air pollution are more common in big cities than they are in less ____________________ areas.

6. Their respective talents seemed to ____________________ so that they eventually developed into a well-rounded and highly productive team.

7. Does "artistic freedom" justify the making of a movie that is deliberately vulgar and ____________________ in the hope of cashing in at the box office?

8. The report was not an impartial assessment of the problems we face; it was an intemperate ____________________.

9. Our purpose is to help people in trouble, not to ____________________ out justice like a court of law.

10. Although the premier enjoyed all the ____________________ of high office, in practice he was merely a figurehead who wielded very little power.

End Set B

Synonyms

*Choose the word or form of the word from this Unit that is the same or most nearly the same in meaning as the **boldface** word or expression in the phrase. Write that word on the line. Use a dictionary if necessary.*

1. disgusted by their **wanton** behavior ____________
2. **gleaned** a few key ideas from the article ____________
3. the **toxic** effects of air pollution ____________
4. enjoyed the **trappings** of wealth ____________
5. refused to change her own **opinionated** ideas ____________
6. a flourishing and **crowded** university town ____________
7. began to **squabble** as soon as we sat down ____________
8. **parcel out** portions of food to the hungry puppies ____________
9. wrote a violent **diatribe** against his opponent ____________
10. overlooked his embarrassing **faux pas** ____________
11. one unexpected **complication** after another ____________
12. forced to **curtail** their stay ____________
13. unprepared for the disaster that **ensued** ____________
14. reached its **zenith** and then descended ____________
15. earned them a reputation for **integrity** ____________

Antonyms

*Choose the word or form of the word from this Unit that is most nearly opposite in meaning to the **boldface** word or expression in the phrase. Write that word on the line. Use a dictionary if necessary.*

1. a **dull dialogue** between the characters ____________
2. **irrelevant** to the situation ____________
3. **separate** into shallow brooks ____________
4. a person of **questionable** character ____________
5. earned **equal** compensation for the same job ____________

Writing: Words in Action

Should there be more apprenticeship programs and/or a greater number of professional choices for young people after high school? Why or why not? Support your opinion with specific examples from your studies, reading (pages 200–201), or personal experience. Use three or more words from this Unit.

Some of the words you have studied in this Unit appear in ***boldface*** *type. Read the passage below, and then circle the letter of the correct answer for each word as it is used in context.*

For many high school students, graduation is the **apogee** of the previous twelve years of education; however, some students choose to continue high-school studies even though they have graduated. This post-graduate program is a one-year academic course of study spent at an independent school. Though post-graduate programs have been extant for decades at many independent schools, they are not widely known.

There are several reasons why high school students may choose a post-graduate option: Some students may want to take an additional academic year to better prepare for college, especially if the colleges of their choice are in environments **disparate** from their own high school settings; some students may choose this option to improve their chances of being accepted to colleges of their choice; still other students may attend post-graduate programs to mature as young adults—for example, coming to understand the importance of steering away from **licentious** high school behavior.

During this post-graduate year, students are admitted as members of the senior class. Like other seniors, they will **cull** exciting classes, such as ornithology and marine biology, that may not have been available at their high schools. In addition to this curriculum, they may also take woodworking or metalworking classes, where they can make **convolutions** out of different materials. Within the classroom, they can engage in lively **repartee** with their peers and acclimate to a different educational community. Although a post-graduate year comes with an expensive price tag, it can be a beneficial option for students who discover that they are not ready for college.

---

1. What is the meaning of **apogee** as it is used in paragraph 1?

a. trough
b. pinnacle
c. initiation
d. celebration

2. What is the meaning of **disparate** in the context of the passage?

a. completely different
b. closely related
c. demographically similar
d. fairly distant

3. What is the meaning of **licentious** as it is used in paragraph 2?

a. crudely insensitive
b. carefully considered
c. ethically compromised
d. morally unrestrained

4. What does **cull** most likely mean as it is used in paragraph 3?

a. select
b. audit
c. propose
d. eliminate

5. What does **convolutions** most likely mean as it is used in paragraph 3?

a. realistic sculptures
b. intricate drawings
c. sinuous designs
d. abstract images

6. What characteristic is suggested by **repartee** in paragraph 3?

a. exuberance
b. wittiness
c. indifference
d. sarcasm

UNIT 15

Read the following passage, taking note of the ***boldface*** *words and their contexts. These words are among those you will be studying in Unit 15. It may help you to complete the exercises in this Unit if you refer to the way the words are used below.*

Justice for the Amistad

<Newspaper Article>

Washington, D.C., *Mar. 2, 1841*—With the *Amistad* case soon to hear a decision from that **apotheosis** of American justice, the United States Supreme Court, we **adumbrate** here the essentials of the case for our readers.

Two years ago, in the summer of 1839, the Spanish schooner *Amistad*, sailing along the Cuban coast, was the scene of a slave mutiny led by one Joseph Cinqué. The 57 captives on board, having unburdened themselves of their shackles by means of a secreted iron file, killed the ship's captain, took control of the vessel, and demanded return passage to their native Africa. **Beguiled** by the ship's navigator, the mutineers were instead led northward, until the *Amistad* was seized by the USS *Washington* off the Long Island coast.

The plight of these men has generated great interest among abolitionists, who quote the proverb "Oppression causeth rebellion." Under the stewardship of Lewis Tappan, a prominent New York City merchant, the Amistad Committee has raised money and attracted expertise for the legal defense of the captives. Its members have publicly **fulminated** against the injustices suffered by those men, by most accounts a veritable **jeremiad** of sorrows. Thanks in part to the Committee's efforts, Messrs. Ruiz and Montez, the Cuban slave traders and subjects of the Spanish crown who were transporting the captives aboard the *Amistad,* are now perceived by many as **opportunists** possessed of a marked cruelty and **hauteur**

At trial in a Connecticut District Court, agents of the Amistad Committee sought to **exculpate** the so-called mutineers on the grounds that they had been transported from Africa to Cuba illegally, in **contumacious** violation of international agreements outlawing the slave trade across the Atlantic. To **complement** this intention, they charged Ruiz and Montez with assault, kidnapping, and false imprisonment. Ruiz and Montez, in turn, have maintained that the captives are slaves and their own rightful property. The latter claim won quick support from the government of Spain.

The Connecticut court agreed that the transport of the slaves was illegal. It further declared that they were, therefore, not slaves at all but free men, kidnapped and held against their will, and within their rights to use force to defend their liberty. The court found, moreover, that Ruiz and Montez had made **disingenuous** claims affirming that the captives were born

Joseph Cinqué

Death of Capt. Ferrer, the Captain of the Amistad, July, 1839.

in Cuba, which is to say, on this side of the Atlantic. That false affirmation could have been naught but an **unconscionable** and willful misrepresentation of the facts. Accordingly, the District Court ruled that the *Amistad* captives were not the property of the Spanish traders and should be freed.

Evidently dissatisfied with the District Court's ruling, the federal government appealed the decision. By now the matter has worked its way up to this nation's highest court, where yesterday, after two days of legal arguments on behalf of both the *Amistad* captives and the United States government, John Quincy Adams, esteemed former President of the United States, arose to speak in defense of the captives.

The President emeritus began with a **didactic** characterization of Justice, as of necessity entailing equal regard for the rights of each individual. The atmosphere of the courtroom grew somber as the speech proceeded. On the whole, it contained little of the **fustian** and fluff that betimes overburden such orations.

Mr. Adams did not **inhibit** himself from criticizing the actions of the Executive branch, but took aim at the administration, including President Van Buren himself.

Whether his argument moved the Justices will be soon known. The Supreme Court is expected to hand down its decision within the next fortnight, after hearing closing arguments from the Attorney General.

Note the spelling, pronunciation, part(s) of speech, and definition(s) of each of the following words. Then write the appropriate form of the word in the blank space in the illustrative sentence(s) following.

1. apotheosis
(ə poth ē ō′ sis)
(*n.*) the elevation of a person to a divine rank or status; the glorification of a person as an ideal; a glorified ideal

Medieval knights were fierce warriors, but in literature they are presented as the ____________________ of chivalry.

2. bauble
(bô′ bəl)
(*n.*) a small, showy ornament of little value or use

I found a rather valuable piece of vintage costume jewelry among the ____________________ at the yard sale.

3. beguile
(bi gīl′)
(*v.*) to mislead or deceive; to cheat; to divert; to cause to vanish unnoticed

Many travelers choose to ____________________ away the long hours of a journey with an absorbing book.

4. complement
(kom′ plə mənt)
(*n.*) something that completes a whole; the quantity or number needed to make up a whole; the full number or allowance; (*v.*) to complete

The full ____________________ of dignitaries was present for the President's State of the Union Address.

She chose a hat that ____________________ her new outfit.

5. contumacious
(kon tü mā′ shəs)
(*adj.*) obstinately or willfully disobedient; openly rebellious

Teenagers who are eager to assert their independence may become quite ____________________ at times.

6. disingenuous
(dis in jen′ yü əs)
(*adj.*) lacking in sincerity or candor

____________________ individuals sometimes betray themselves in the very act of trying to appear sincere.

7. faux pas
(fō pä′)
(*n.*) a slip in manners or conduct; a social blunder

No sooner had I arrived at the party than I embarrassed myself by committing a dreadful ____________________.

8. fulminate
(ful′ mə nāt)
(*v.*) to denounce or condemn vehemently; to explode, detonate

The senator proceeded to ____________________ against foreign commitments and entanglements.

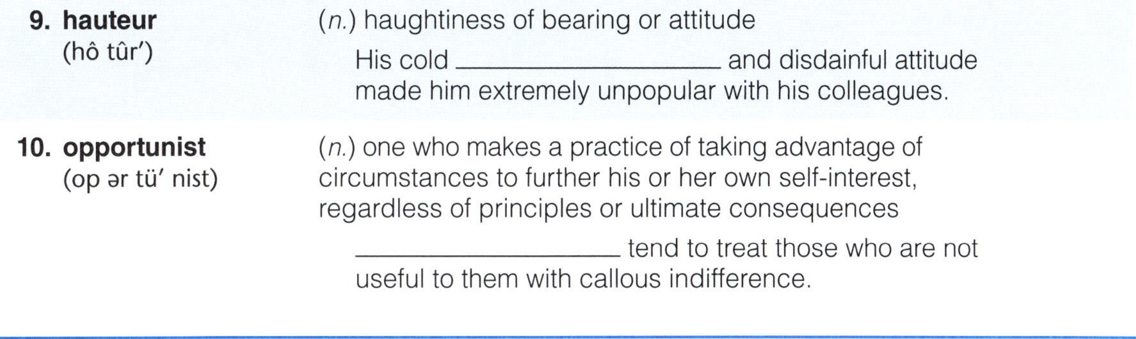

9. hauteur (hô tûr′)

(*n.*) haughtiness of bearing or attitude

His cold ____________ and disdainful attitude made him extremely unpopular with his colleagues.

10. opportunist (op ər tü′ nist)

(*n.*) one who makes a practice of taking advantage of circumstances to further his or her own self-interest, regardless of principles or ultimate consequences

____________ tend to treat those who are not useful to them with callous indifference.

Using Context

*For each item, determine whether the **boldface** word from pages 214–215 makes sense in the context of the sentence. Circle the item numbers next to the six sentences in which the words are used correctly.*

1. Flickering lights of fireflies on a summer evening never fail to **beguile** children and adults alike.

2. The landscape designer is looking for the perfect statue to **complement** the plantings in the park.

3. The community theater has put together a musical tribute to thank its longtime supporters and volunteers for their **hauteur**.

4. I would never vote for that candidate because her views are the **apotheosis** of everything I believe in.

5. The highly valuable **bauble** that once belonged to the royal family is encrusted with diamonds, emeralds, rubies, and pearls.

6. It is wiser to calmly accept train delays, traffic jams, and other annoyances over which you have no control than to **fulminate** against them.

7. The English king dispatched troops to suppress the **contumacious** American colonists.

8. Whether the case being presented is of minor or major importance, a judge is expected to be completely fair and **disingenuous**.

9. Mispronouncing someone's name is a minor **faux pas**; completely mistaking him or her for someone else is a more serious matter.

10. Some accused the industrialist of being a shameful **opportunist** who profited from war.

Set A

*Select the **boldface** word that better completes each sentence. You might refer to the passage on pages 212–213 to see how most of these words are used in context. Note that the choices might be related forms of the Unit words.*

1. The (**hauteur, apotheosis**) of the actor's career was probably when she had the opportunity to play Ophelia on the London stage.

2. They make an excellent team because his deftness in handling people effectively (**complements, fulminates**) her remarkable executive abilities.

3. The situation was rapidly becoming intolerable because some of the club members were not merely uncooperative but positively (**contumacious, opportunist**).

4. In a democracy we have no need to disguise the human failings of our leaders; we can respect them without (**beguiling, apotheosizing**) them.

5. The author found it ironic that the novel he had tossed off in his youth as a mere (**bauble, complement**) came to be viewed as his masterpiece.

6. What disappointed me was not so much your failure to complete the job but your (**contumacious, disingenuous**) efforts to avoid all responsibility for the debacle.

7. Your tactics prove that you are not just an (**opportunist, apotheosis**) but someone with a ruthless disregard for others.

8. A full and glowing moon and two shooting stars were the perfect (**opportunists, complements**) to a romantic dinner for two alongside the river.

9. When I asked him if he could dance, he looked at me with supreme (**disingenuousness, hauteur**) and asked, "Could Caruso sing?"

10. I must say that I agree with their (**apotheoses, fulminations**) against those who deface our public buildings with unsightly graffiti.

11. (**Beguiled, Fulminated**) by high-pressure sales talk, I bought a car that I did not need, could not afford, and did not even know how to drive.

12. When you have been guilty of rude conduct, do not try to minimize your guilt by referring to the incident as a mere (**hauteur, faux pas**).

Completing the Sentence

Choose the word from the word bank that best completes each of the following sentences. Write the correct word or form of the word in the space provided.

apotheosis	**beguile**	**contumacious**	**faux pas**	**hauteur**
bauble	**complement**	**disingenuous**	**fulminate**	**opportunist**

1. I won't go into that shop because the snooty salespeople treat me with the ____________________ and disdain of aristocrats dealing with their lackeys.

2. Her standards of proper behavior are so demanding that she regards every minor ____________________ as an unforgivable social offense.

3. The editorial argues that the crime-fighting situation cannot improve until the police department receives its full ____________________ of personnel.

4. Successful politicians must be alert to every favorable circumstance, but if they are no more than ____________________, it is hard to see how they will ever accomplish anything worthwhile.

5. How could a person of your knowledge and experience allow herself to be ____________________ by vague promises and empty reassurances?

6. The chairman of the Senate committee angrily threatened the witness with contempt charges because of her ____________________ attitude.

7. I wonder how many people have been taken in by those silly TV ads that attempt to pass off worthless ____________________ as valuable jewelry.

8. Though your unwillingness to make me a small loan is disappointing, what infuriates me is your ____________________ explanation that it is "for my own good."

9. It is often more effective to offer a few just words of criticism than to ____________________ long and loud against those who offend us.

10. In a rather silly painting called *The* ____________________ *of Homer*, the artist attempts to show the blind poet's reception among the gods.

End Set A

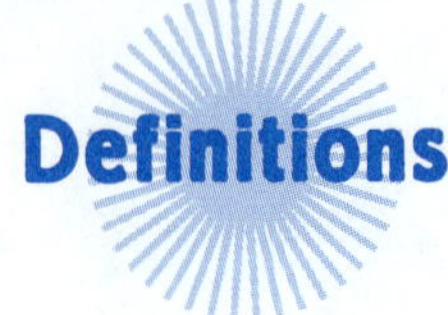

Definitions

Note the spelling, pronunciation, part(s) of speech, and definition(s) of each of the following words. Then write the appropriate form of the word in the blank space in the illustrative sentence(s) following.

1. adumbrate (ad′ əm brāt)
(*v.*) to outline or sketch broadly; to foreshadow or prefigure; to disclose partially

Writers often ____________________ key ideas right away and then elaborate on them later.

2. ascetic (ə set′ ik)
(*adj.*) practicing self-denial for the sake of personal or spiritual discipline; (*n.*) one who leads a life of self-discipline, especially to express religious devotion

Some artists and writers may find it beneficial to lead an ____________________ life free of distractions.

The life of an ____________________ supposedly repays the sacrifice of worldly things with spiritual rewards.

3. burgeon (bər′ jən)
(*v.*) to put forth new buds, leaves, or greenery; to develop rapidly or suddenly

Though it was still winter according to the calendar, our garden ____________________ in the warm, sunny weather.

4. curmudgeon (kər məj′ ən)
(*n.*) an irascible, churlish person

No matter how hard we try, nothing we do seems to please our ____________________ of a boss.

5. didactic (dī dak′ tik)
(*adj.*) intended to instruct, especially morally; inclined to moralize too much

At its best, children's literature teaches values, making it ____________________ as well as entertaining.

6. exculpate (ek′ skəl pāt)
(*v.*) to clear of guilt or blame

"I will present irrefutable evidence," the lawyer declared, "that will ____________________ my client."

7. fustian (fəs′ chən)
(*n.*) inflated or pretentious language in speech or writing; a cloth made of cotton and flax

Although the politician's speech was filled with bombast and ____________________, it was devoid of substance.

8. inhibit (in hib′ it)
(*v.*) to restrain or hold back; to hinder or arrest; to prohibit

Poor eating habits may ____________________ a young person's physical development.

9. jeremiad
(jer ə mī′ əd)

(*n.*) an elaborate or prolonged lamentation; any tale of woe

When asked about their sad plights, talk show guests often launch into tearful ________________.

10. unconscionable
(ən kon′ shən ə bəl)

(*adj.*) not guided or restrained by conscience, prudence, or reason; unscrupulous; immoderate

Top management's looting of the employees' retirement fund can only be described as ________________.

Using Context

*For each item, determine whether the **boldface** word from pages 218–219 makes sense in the context of the sentence. Circle the item numbers next to the six sentences in which the words are used correctly.*

1. Your betrayal of a loyal friend to further your own situation is **unconscionable**.

2. The **jeremiad** that arose from the audience at the end of the impressive musical number drowned out the last notes of the song.

3. The lawyer was thrilled to find footage from a security camera that would **exculpate** his client by proving he was hundreds of miles away when the crime occurred.

4. She has become so **fustian** in her older age that it is hard to convince her even to eat something new for dinner.

5. The teacher vowed that he would not let the reduced funding **inhibit** the level of education that his students receive.

6. I won't **adumbrate** you with the bothersome details, but let's just say it was not a good day!

7. We were all surprised when the surly teenager seemed to **burgeon** into a lovely and polite young woman almost overnight.

8. Although he makes a good deal of money, he prefers to donate most of it to charity and live an **ascetic** lifestyle.

9. Your **didactic** approach to cooking always produces a delicious meal, but such carefulness takes up more time than we'd like to wait for our food.

10. The neighbors warned me to steer clear of the **curmudgeon** down the street, who always has something to complain about.

Set B

*Select the **boldface** word that better completes each sentence. You might refer to the passage on pages 212–213 to see how most of these words are used in context. Note that the choices might be related forms of the Unit words.*

1. In his farewell address, President Dwight D. Eisenhower (**adumbrated, exculpated**) the necessity to beware of the rise of the "military-industrial complex."

2. The monk is a famous (**ascetic, fustian**) who sometimes appears publicly to oppose wars.

3. What is the basis for your statement that advertising costs account for an (**ascetic, unconscionable**) part of the retail price of many products?

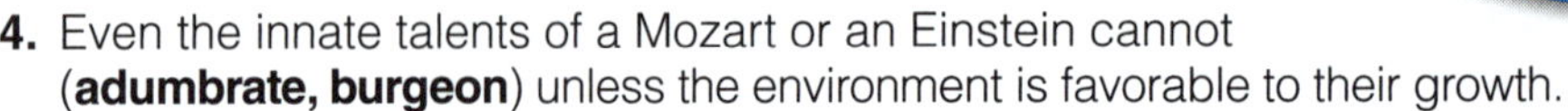

4. Even the innate talents of a Mozart or an Einstein cannot (**adumbrate, burgeon**) unless the environment is favorable to their growth.

5. The speaker referred scornfully to the "hysterical (**jeremiads, curmudgeons**) of the ecologists," but I believe that they are warning us of real dangers.

6. You have written a(n) (**didactic, unconscionable**) novel with a wealth of authentic documentation, but you have forgotten to entertain your readers.

7. Because you are usually a rather boisterous person, I was surprised by your (**ascetic, inhibited**) behavior at the party.

8. You are too young to understand how the trials of life can transform a happy-go-lucky youth into a solitary (**jeremiad, curmudgeon**).

9. The candidates underrate the electorate if they think they can win votes with that kind of antiquated (**curmudgeon, fustian**).

10. The aim of the new biography was to (**exculpate, inhibit**) its subject of charges that previous biographers had wrongfully pressed against him.

11. The ancient photograph showed my grandmother in her native Russian village, sporting a (**jeremiad, fustian**) jacket to protect her against the harsh autumn wind.

12. Unlike the Athenians, who delighted in luxury, the Spartans espoused the virtue of (**ascetic, fustian**) simplicity.

Completing the Sentence

Choose the word from the word bank that best completes each of the following sentences. Write the correct word or form of the word in the space provided.

adumbrate	**burgeon**	**didactic**	**fustian**	**jeremiad**
ascetic	**curmudgeon**	**exculpate**	**inhibit**	**unconscionable**

1. Because there was no time to go into elaborate details, all that we could do was ____________________ the general features of the plan.

2. What at first appeared to be no more than a rather favorable opinion of himself has ____________________ into unlimited conceit.

3. I find it impossible to understand how the world can stand idly by while ____________________ acts of cruelty are being committed daily.

4. While two of the accused were indicted on conspiracy charges, the third was eventually ____________________ of any involvement in the plot.

5. Instead of simply stating his case, he launched into an emotional appeal whose language degenerated into mere ____________________ and bombast.

6. At first we thought that he was just pretending to be surly, but later we discovered that he really was a(n) ____________________.

7. For the eighteenth-century moralist, art and literature had an essentially ____________________ purpose; they should teach as well as entertain.

8. We all have aggressive impulses, but in most cases our early training and conditioning tend to ____________________ the open expression of them.

9. What we need in this situation is not a lugubrious ____________________ cataloging our troubles but a workable plan for improvements.

10. After his conversion, the young man renounced his former profligacy and dissipation to lead the life of a(n) ____________________.

End Set B

Synonyms

*Choose the word or form of the word from this Unit that is the same or most nearly the same in meaning as the **boldface** word or expression in the phrase. Write that word on the line. Use a dictionary if necessary.*

1. **knickknacks** that have great sentimental value ____________
2. **outlined** their plans at a press conference ____________
3. **flourished** in that mild climate ____________
4. led an **austere** existence ____________
5. has a reputation for being a **grouch** ____________
6. the **deification** of the knight errant ____________
7. thrown out of court for being **unruly** ____________
8. works full of **grandiloquence** about high society ____________
9. a ruthless **exploiter** of any weakness ____________
10. the perfect **accompaniment** to the dinner ____________
11. dismissed as **moralistic** by most literary critics ____________
12. **rails** against the government's policies ____________
13. will **exonerate** them without further ado ____________
14. committed one **gaffe** after another ____________
15. **misled** unwary customers with vague promises ____________

Antonyms

*Choose the word or form of the word from this Unit that is most nearly opposite in meaning to the **boldface** word or expression in the phrase. Write that word on the line. Use a dictionary if necessary.*

1. gave a **sincere** response to the question ____________
2. admired for his **humility** ____________
3. attempted to **foster** good will between the two warring countries ____________
4. an obituary filled with **paeans** to the deceased ____________
5. had **justifiable** reasons for taking the money ____________

Writing: Words in Action

Is it possible—or even desirable—for a journalist to be objective when reporting on controversial or emotionally charged events? In a brief essay, support your opinion with specific examples from your studies, reading (pages 212–213), or personal experience. Use three or more words from this Unit.

*Some of the words you have studied in this Unit appear in **boldface** type. Read the passage below, and then circle the letter of the correct answer for each word as it is used in context*

Oliver Wendell Holmes, Jr. was born in 1841, the oldest child of Oliver Wendell Holmes, Sr., a famous clinician and writer who cofounded the *Atlantic Monthly.* He grew up in a wealthy and well-educated household, full of **baubles**, luxuries, and books. He attended Harvard College (now Harvard University) but was openly critical of Harvard's curriculum. Holmes apparently disrespected a professor and left college after this **faux pas** to train for the Civil War, which had recently **burgeoned**. He returned to Harvard to finish his degree and upon graduation fought in the Civil War. Although Holmes entered the war as an idealist, he left the war as a disillusioned **curmudgeon.**

Unsure of which trajectory his life would take, Holmes entered Harvard Law School in 1864 and graduated in 1866. After graduating and passing the bar, Holmes practiced law for 14 years, but his love for scholarship led him to serve as the editor of the *American Law Review* and to lecture on legal issues during this time. Displeased by his financial situation and his **ascetic** lifestyle, he also accepted an appointment to teach at Harvard Law School.

In 1902, President Theodore Roosevelt nominated Holmes to the U.S. Supreme Court. He received the nickname "the Great Dissenter" for his frequent, often eloquent, **didactic** dissents. Holmes retired from the Supreme Court in 1932 and passed away in 1935. Many of his landmark opinions, including *Lochner v. New York* about labor unions and *Schenck v. United States* about free speech, still survive as his legacy.

---

1. What is the meaning of **baubles** as it is used in paragraph 1?

a. expensive treasures
b. family heirlooms
c. strange occurrences
d. showy ornaments

2. In paragraph 1, what does **faux pas** mean?

a. social blunder
b. moral instruction
c. verbal attack
d. debate

3. What is the meaning of **burgeoned** in the context of the passage?

a. moved slowly
b. developed rapidly
c. began suddenly
d. escalated senselessly

4. In paragraph 1, what does the word **curmudgeon** suggest about Holmes?

a. He was irascible.
b. He was realistic.
c. He was intelligent.
d. He was diplomatic.

5. What characteristic is suggested by **ascetic** in paragraph 2?

a. arrogance
b. extravagance
c. self-denial
d. ambition

6. What does **didactic** most likely mean as it is used in paragraph 3?

a. clearly researched
b. carefully worded
c. unnecessarily verbose
d. morally instructive

Vocabulary for Comprehension

Part 1

Read this passage, which contains words in ***boldface*** *that appear in Units 13–15. Then choose the best answer to each question based on what is stated or implied in the passage. You may refer to the passage as often as necessary.*

Questions 1–10 are based on the following passage.

From the French painter Nicolas Poussin to the Italian composer Antonio Vivaldi to the contemporary American artist Jasper Johns, the seasons have inspired memorable works of art in western culture. It is thus not especially surprising that in ancient Greek mythology the seasons were regarded as the **apotheosis** of nature and personified as the goddesses known as the Horae, from which our word *hours* is derived. In the *Iliad,* Homer refers to the Horae as guarding the gates of Olympus, the home of the gods. Around the same time, the seasons are described by Hesiod, the early Greek poet, as the daughters of Themis, goddess of justice and righteousness. Hesiod regards the Horae as the **apogee** of civic and political virtue, naming them Eunomia (Good Government), Dike (Justice), and Eirene (Peace).

In most other early references, however, the seasons are associated with the rhythms of nature rather than with political or ethical concepts. The Horae are the **resplendent,** benevolent deities who ensure the flowering and growth of all creatures. Curiously from our modern perspective, the goddesses form a triad rather than a quartet, as if there had been a **sub rosa** agreement to omit winter. Thus, in Athens of the classical period (fifth century BCE) the Horae were known as Thallo, Auxo, and Carpo. Associated with spring, Thallo presided over **burgeoning** buds and blooms; somewhat later, in ancient Rome, she was known by the name Flora. Auxo, from a Greek verb meaning "increase," was the personification of summer, **meting** out growth and fertility. Carpo, whose name denoted one who brings food, was the goddess of autumn, presiding over ripening and the harvest.

As pleasant and **unimpeachable** benefactors of humanity, the Horae were welcome and **beguiling** guests in mythological accounts of notable weddings and births. In fact, the earliest known appearance of the Seasons in ancient Greek art is on the François vase (c. 570 BCE) in connection with the fabled wedding of Peleus and Thetis, the parents of the hero Achilles. Somewhat later in a **disparate** context, Greek philosophers such as Plato used the recurrent rhythms of the Seasons as an argument for the existence of a divine order. In the late Roman period, the Horae metamorphosed into a set of four, personified as the daughters of the Sun and the Moon and awarded **accolades** as the handmaidens of Hera, the wife of Zeus.

Even as minor goddesses, the Seasons were in good mythological company. The ancient Greeks also personified a triad of divinities known as the Charites, or Graces. These deities were incarnations of grace, charm, and beauty. Daughters of Zeus, their benefactions overlapped with those of the Horae to some extent: for example, various texts refer to the Charites as making roses grow and protecting springtime flowers.

The Horae may also be compared to the most celebrated group of minor goddesses in Greek mythology: the nine Muses. The daughters of Zeus and the goddess Mnemosyne (Memory), the Muses were patrons of poetry, music, drama, dance, and intellectual pursuits such as history, philosophy, and astronomy. Like the Seasons, the Muses sang and danced at festive occasions, and like the Seasons they inspired artists and works of art.

1. The primary purpose of the passage is to
A) provide a brief overview of the seasons personified in Greek mythology.
B) compare and contrast the political and natural personifications of the seasons.
C) describe the transition between the depiction of the seasons as a trio and their visualization as a quartet.
D) explain some differences between the depiction of the seasons in ancient Greece and their personification in Rome.

2. According to the first paragraph, the name associated with the seasons as paragons of civic and political virtue is
A) Homer.
B) Hesiod.
C) Poussin.
D) Vivaldi.

3. In the second paragraph (lines 21–42), the author suggests a characterization of the Seasons that is
A) intriguingly ambiguous.
B) ominously menacing.
C) predictably repetitive.
D) overwhelmingly favorable.

4. Which choice provides the best evidence for the answer to the previous question?
A) Lines 24–27 ("The Horae . . . creatures")
B) Lines 27–30 ("Curiously . . . winter")
C) Lines 30–33 ("Thus, in Athens . . . Carpo")
D) Lines 33–37 ("Associated . . . Flora")

5. As it is used in line 30, "sub rosa" most nearly means
A) flowery.
B) reddish.
C) secret.
D) conspiratorial.

6. According to the author, the Horae were often invited as guests at celebrations because of their
A) benevolence to humanity.
B) divine parentage.
C) breathtaking beauty.
D) lavish costumes.

7. As it is used in line 43, "unimpeachable" most nearly means
A) certifiable.
B) unquestionable.
C) renowned.
D) documented.

8. As it is used in line 60, "accolades" most nearly means
A) portraits.
B) nicknames.
C) kudos.
D) premiums.

9. The author's main purpose in the final two paragraphs (lines 62–84) is to
A) compare the Horae with the Graces and the Muses.
B) explain the origins of various minor goddesses.
C) describe the arts favored by the Muses.
D) discuss how Greek philosophers explained the phenomenon of the Seasons.

10. The author's tone in the passage might best be described as
A) impartial and restrained.
B) urgent and emotional.
C) dry and scholarly.
D) wry and satirical.

Vocabulary for Comprehension Part 2

*Read this passage, which contains words in **boldface** that appear in Units 13–15. Then choose the best answer to each question based on what is stated or implied in the passage. You may refer to the passage as often as necessary.*

Questions 1–10 are based on the following passage.

In 1799, the English nobleman Thomas Bruce, seventh Earl of Elgin, was appointed ambassador of His Majesty's Government to the Ottoman Empire, which then ruled Greece. A lover of art and antiquities, Elgin deplored the dilapidated state of the Parthenon, the renowned ancient temple of Athena constructed on the Athenian acropolis around 440 BCE. He sought permission of the authorities to remove many of the masterful marble sculptures that had been carved to decorate the building. Although the precise terms of the original authorizing document remain unclear, Elgin was granted a sufficient writ to enable him to detach and transport about half the surviving sculptures, as well as a number of ornamental architectural elements.

The sculptures' removal and transport to England took the better part of a decade. The collection remained private at first, but soon the outcry suggested that Elgin was guilty of more than just a **contretemps**. Lord Byron, newly acclaimed as a poet, **fulminated** against Elgin as an **unconscionable** vandal. Many other critics concurred, accusing Elgin **dogmatically** of theft. While Elgin's detractors **bickered**, Parliament deliberated on acquiring the marbles for the nation. In 1816, a purchase price was agreed upon, amounting to about half of Elgin's costs. The following year, the marbles were displayed at the British Museum. In contrast to Byron's **fustian**, poet John Keats praised the "wonders . . . of Grecian grandeur."

The British Museum has housed the Parthenon sculptures for two centuries, despite consistent demands from Greece for their return. The resulting "repatriation" debate has important implications for art works and museums worldwide. On the one hand, retentionist nations such as Greece argue that the Parthenon sculptures are integral to their national heritage and are to be considered cultural symbols. This argument has **stigmatized** figures such as Elgin as imperialist exploiters who despoiled indigenous cultures for profit or **vainglory**. Far from being shrugged off as a mere **faux pas**, Elgin's actions should be reversed through full restitution, as well as an official apology. Thus far, the British Museum has declined to meet these demands.

The British museum's position on the issue serves as a representative summary of the other, "internationalist" side of the repatriation debate. According to this view, nationalism has been misleadingly superimposed on the true provenance of most antiquities. As a later development, Greek nationalism cannot fairly claim to embrace the cultural value of the Parthenon sculptures, executed more than two millennia before the existence of a Greek nation-state. Indeed, the sculptures have been in the British Museum longer than the Greek nation has existed. Britons, too, are heirs to the classical tradition. There is every reason to believe that conservation and preservation of the marbles were carried out in Britain more effectively than they would have been in Greece, at least during most of the nineteenth and twentieth centuries.

Perhaps most important, according to the internationalist view, artifacts such as the Parthenon sculptures form part of a universal, common heritage, and there is no more fitting venue for their display than an "encyclopedic" institution such as the British Museum.

1. The main purpose in the first paragraph is
A) to refute a thesis.
B) to provide background.
C) to consider solutions for a problem.
D) to frame the terms of a debate.

2. In the first paragraph, the author suggests that some doubt still persists about
A) the date of Elgin's arrival in Athens.
B) Elgin's love for ancient artifacts.
C) the terms and conditions of the permission secured by Elgin.
D) the individual items removed by Elgin from the Parthenon.

3. Which choice provides the best evidence for the answer to the previous question?
A) Lines 1–5 ("In 1799 . . . Greece")
B) Lines 5–9 ("A lover . . . 440 BCE")
C) Lines 9–13 ("He sought . . . building")
D) Lines 13–19 ("Although . . . elements")

4. As it is used in line 25, "contretemps" most nearly means
A) opportunity.
B) blunder.
C) catastrophe.
D) pitfall.

5. It can reasonably be inferred from the second paragraph (lines 20–38), that
A) Parliament was lamentably stingy in its offer of a purchase price to Elgin.
B) Elgin did not really have to sell the marbles but did so out of patriotism.
C) the Greek government should have objected to the sale then and there.
D) the reactions of Byron and Keats to the situation were strikingly different.

6. As it is used in line 30, "bickered" most nearly means
A) wrangled.
B) acquiesced.
C) complained.
D) expostulated.

7. The third paragraph (lines 39–57) indicates that all of the following can be reasonably associated with the "retentionist" side of the debate EXCEPT
A) national pride.
B) cultural symbolism.
C) anti-imperialist feelings.
D) precise determination of provenance.

8. As it is used in line 52, "vainglory" most nearly means
A) diffidence.
B) achievement.
C) pride.
D) poise.

9. In the fourth paragraph (lines 58–85), the writer accords special emphasis to which of the following?
A) the exceptional conservation efforts of the British Museum
B) the concept of a universal, common heritage
C) the unselfish motives of Lord Elgin
D) the recent history of Greece as a nation-state

10. The main purpose of the passage is to
A) investigate Lord Elgin's motives for taking the marble sculptures.
B) describe and praise the restoration and preservation of the marble sculptures by the British museum.
C) inform the reader of the Elgin marbles and the wider debate about repatriation of art.
D) argue in favor of the repatriation of the Elgin marbles to Greece.

Synonyms

*From the word bank below, choose the word that has the same or nearly the same meaning as the **boldface** word in each sentence and write it on the line. You will not use all of the words.*

accolade	**beguile**	**disingenuous**	**mete**
accoutrements	**chronic**	**disparate**	**populous**
apropos	**coalesce**	**expound**	**protocol**
bauble	**cull**	**faux pas**	**sub rosa**

1. Some deep-sea fish use body parts that glow to **lure** smaller fish to come close; then they snatch their prey in their teeth. __________

2. The campsite was equipped with all kinds of modern **gear**, including electricity and a reliable Wi-Fi signal. __________

3. The art gallery will **choose** the most significant and striking pieces it has acquired and put them on display in its upcoming show. __________

4. I hated being **two-faced**, but I did not want to give away the surprise and reveal that we were buying a computer for her. __________

5. Is there a **code of conduct** that must be followed when receiving an award from the scholarship committee? __________

6. In the short story titled "The Necklace," the main character is devastated to learn that what she thought was a valuable piece of jewelry is in fact no more than a common **bagatelle**. __________

7. The protesters met to **combine** their messages in order to present a united front when meeting the dean. __________

8. The team that wins the world championship will be greeted with many forms of **acclaim** upon its return home. __________

9. Both Manhattan and Hong Kong are small, **crowded** islands. __________

10. The play is set in the 1950s, so we must choose background music that will be **relevant** to the era. __________

11. The fable called "The Boy Who Cried Wolf" shows that people who are **habitual** complainers risk not being taken seriously if they report a problem. __________

12. After seeing a natural wonder such as the Great Barrier Reef, it is understandable that you would want to **elucidate** its beauty. __________

Select the pair of words that best completes the meaning of each of the following sentences.

1. The last ____________ of the previous century's iron ore mining industry are apparent in that tiny Michigan ghost town that today is one attraction, among many, in the state's ____________ tourism industry.

a. jeremiads … hauteur
b. factionalisms … stigmatizing
c. probities … supervening
d. vestiges … burgeoning

2. Even the young preschool children were unimpressed by the new teacher's ____________ and clichéd advice—and they were utterly exasperated by his ____________ and inflexible approach to instruction.

a. polemics … truncated
b. bromides … dogmatic
c. resplendent … noxious
d. immaculate … mercurial

3. Years ago, all art had two ____________ purposes: to point out a moral or adorn a tale. Accordingly, no work was judged to be really complete if either the ____________ or the decorative element was not in evidence.

a. ineluctable … licentious
b. complementary … didactic
c. unimpeachable … chauvinistic
d. vestigial … dogmatic

4. Without conscious ____________, after years of living in abundance and in an overpopulated city, she finally pursued a simple and ____________ life in a tiny cabin with a small patch of farmland.

a. repartee … ineluctable
b. convolution … licentious
c. imprecation … acerbic
d. volition … ascetic

5. During the Civil War, Robert E. Lee's freedom of choice was seriously ____________ by the fact that the South could never replace the losses it sustained through normal battlefield ____________.

a. adumbrated … imprecation
b. truncated … convolution
c. inhibited … attrition
d. palliated … volition

6. During the election of 1860, the Democrats could not present a united front because the party was torn asunder by ____________ strife and petty regional ____________.

a. contumacious … attrition
b. factional … bickering
c. unconscionable … vainglory
d. dogmatic … repartee

7. "The man is not a disinterested observer of the passing scene," I said. "He is essentially a(n) ____________ who uses his column in the newspaper as a kind of soapbox from which to ____________ against the iniquities of those around him."

a. polemicist … fulminate
b. opportunist … truncate
c. chauvinist … palliate
d. curmudgeon … exculpate

WORD STUDY

In the passage "A Gap Year Makes Sense" (see pages 200–201), the writer points out that today's high school students are "burning the candle at both ends." The meaning of this phrase may not be obvious, as it means something different from the literal meanings of the individual words within it.

In fact, this phrase is an **idiom**. In the unit opener passage, it means staying up late and getting up early in order to get a lot of work done, requiring artificial light at both "ends" of the day.

Choosing the Right Idiom

*Read each sentence. Use context clues to figure out the meaning of each idiom in **boldface** print. Then write the letter of the definition for the idiom in the sentence.*

1. The leaders were worried that the poor trade deal would make them **lose face** and thus anger the citizens. ______
2. This is, **hands down**, the greatest lasagna I've ever eaten. What is the secret ingredient? ______
3. Our financial team acted unquestionably **above board** and so our records are spotless. ______
4. Let's **get this straight**. You have the flu and a very high fever. You are not going to work today. ______
5. She refuses to **lie low**; the punitive action, in fact, has made her even more outspoken. ______
6. We need to get this **in black and white** so that you can get started hiring your staff. ______
7. It is clear you didn't want to see this movie. **Give it a rest** and now just try to enjoy yourself. ______
8. This is his last month on the job—our manager wants to **phone it in** and doesn't care who's affected. ______
9. Sure, I would **toe the line** for this corporation if someone would assure me a livable wage. ______
10. My best advice to you is to **mind your ps and qs**. Your grandparents are from a different generation. ______

a. do a task with little effort or enthusiasm

b. make something clear and reach an understanding

c. behave yourself and don't offend anyone

d. open and honest; without fraud

e. in writing or in print; make official

f. accept the rules and authority of a group

g. be humiliated

h. easily; without question

i. avoid attention and notice

j. stop talking about, or doing, something annoying

Classical Roots

temp—time

This Latin root appears in **contretemps** (page 206), which means "an inopportune or embarrassing mishap." Some other words based on the same root are listed below.

contemplative	**extempore**	**temperance**	**tempest**
contemporaneous	**temperamentally**	**temperature**	**tempestuous**

From the list of words above, choose the one that corresponds to each of the brief definitions below. Write the word in the blank space in the illustrative sentence below the definition.

1. in an impromptu, unrehearsed manner; on the spur of the moment
After hearing the mayor's disturbing statement, an irate citizen delivered a rebuttal ____________________.

2. stormy; violent; turbulent
Their ____________________ relationship ended when the stress became too much to bear.

3. moderation, self-restraint; total abstinence from alcohol
My brother, a cautious person, follows the path of ____________________ in all areas of life.

4. a violent storm; a tumult, uproar
The small fishing boat foundered in the raging ____________________.

5. inclined to consider intently, thoughtful; meditative; pensive
Rodin's famed sculpture *The Thinker* shows a man sitting in a(n) ____________________ pose.

6. existing or occurring at the same period of time
The lives of writers Christopher Marlowe and Sir Walter Raleigh were ____________________ with that of William Shakespeare.

7. by nature, disposition; moodily; impulsively
Although she had always dreamed of being an investigative journalist, she soon realized that she was ____________________ unsuited for the job.

8. the degree of hotness or coldness in a body or an environment; the specific degree of hotness or coldness as measured on a scale
The parents worried when the baby continued to run a high ____________________ for three days.

FINAL MASTERY TEST

Synonyms

Select the two words or expressions that are most nearly the same in meaning.

	a.	b.	c.	d.
1.	**a.** cozen	**b.** complete	**c.** complement	**d.** nullify
2.	**a.** delay	**b.** solecism	**c.** lucubration	**d.** thought
3.	**a.** collection	**b.** morass	**c.** syndrome	**d.** swamp
4.	**a.** banter	**b.** satire	**c.** claque	**d.** persiflage
5.	**a.** harbinger	**b.** debauch	**c.** herald	**d.** memory
6.	**a.** lugubrious	**b.** mournful	**c.** ambivalent	**d.** determined
7.	**a.** emolument	**b.** schism	**c.** confusion	**d.** split
8.	**a.** strength	**b.** acerbity	**c.** forte	**d.** interest
9.	**a.** uncooperative	**b.** picaresque	**c.** passive	**d.** supine
10.	**a.** time frame	**b.** lexicon	**c.** vocabulary	**d.** divination
11.	**a.** sagacious	**b.** immaculate	**c.** salubrious	**d.** spotless
12.	**a.** outline	**b.** adumbrate	**c.** ponder	**d.** beleaguer
13.	**a.** foresight	**b.** determination	**c.** panache	**d.** prescience
14.	**a.** melee	**b.** crisis	**c.** fight	**d.** peccadillo
15.	**a.** apogee	**b.** expression	**c.** contretemps	**d.** faux pas

Antonyms

Select the two words that are most nearly opposite in meaning.

	a.	b.	c.	d.
16.	**a.** malleable	**b.** noxious	**c.** foreign	**d.** inflexible
17.	**a.** volition	**b.** affinity	**c.** obloquy	**d.** acclaim
18.	**a.** clarify	**b.** obfuscate	**c.** pander	**d.** coalesce
19.	**a.** quixotic	**b.** ancillary	**c.** practicable	**d.** intellectual
20.	**a.** effete	**b.** identical	**c.** oblique	**d.** disparate
21.	**a.** liturgy	**b.** criticism	**c.** paean	**d.** pastiche
22.	**a.** plebeian	**b.** patrician	**c.** youthful	**d.** inchoate
23.	**a.** contumelious	**b.** trained	**c.** gargantuan	**d.** minuscule
24.	**a.** dexterous	**b.** parlous	**c.** considerate	**d.** maladroit
25.	**a.** macrocosm	**b.** metamorphosis	**c.** microcosm	**d.** embezzlement

Select the pair of words that best completes the meaning of each of the following sentences.

26. Far from solving the problem, all we've done is offer a(n) ________________ of ________________ attempts at a solution.

a. cognate … iconoclastic
b. plethora … abortive
c. charisma … execrable
d. didactic … de facto

27. The ________________ of the leadership of this organization will seemingly never change; people seem to have a(n) ________________ attitude toward new candidates for office.

a. pundit … systemic
b. purview … insouciant
c. hierarchy … hidebound
d. empathy … contumacious

28. The disaster was such a(n) ________________ that I couldn't help but let out a(n) ________________ of despair.

a. liaison … remand
b. enclave … cull
c. interstice … icon
d. cataclysm … caterwaul

29. I don't mean to ________________ you, but your constant annoying behavior has made you the ________________ of my existence!

a. bode … curmudgeon
b. browbeat … bane
c. impinge … bromide
d. auger … bellwether

30. While I realized that forgetting the words to the song would keep my solo from being the ________________ of the school musical, I saved a ________________ of self-respect by carrying on with words I made up myself.

a. quid pro quo … quagmire
b. pìece de résistance … vestige
c. hoi polloi … matrix
d. in media res … euphoria

31. People with a tendency towards ________________ often expect ________________ praise for even the smallest achievement.

a. éclat … ecumenical
b. rapacity … insouciant
c. nemesis … waggish
d. narcissism … effusive

32. Irish author, playwright, and man-about-town Oscar Wilde was famous for his witty ________________ and his ability to find the ________________ for any situation.

a. repartee … mot juste
b. mystique … volition
c. sycophant … zealot
d. xenophobia … protocol

FINAL MASTERY TEST

Supplying Words in Context

To complete each sentence, select the best word from among the choices given. Not all words in the word bank will be used. You may modify the word form as necessary.

abeyance	**fait accompli**	**gothic**	**philippic**
aegis	**flamboyant**	**imbue**	**resplendent**
bruit	**folderol**	**internecine**	**touchstone**
deracinate	**foray**	**nihilism**	**viable**

33. The conflict is ____________________: All parties involved will suffer.

34. He criticism of the social order was indicative of the ____________________ of her philosophy.

35. His bitter disapproval led him to deliver a ____________________ during the trial.

36. You should seek to ____________________ your bad habits as you would pull a bad tooth.

37. The dark and gloomy plot marked the reading selection as part of the ____________________ school of literature.

38. The performer was so ____________________ that he brought to mind a showy peacock.

bilious	**elixir**	**homily**	**philistine**
bowdlerize	**ensconce**	**labyrinth**	**polarize**
carte blanche	**fetid**	**nepotism**	**sacrosanct**
disparity	**gambol**	**opt**	**tendentious**

39. The ____________________ was so circuitous that I feared we wouldn't find our way out.

40. His ____________________ reaction made plain his disgust.

41. Grandpa offered a short ____________________ explaining his attitude toward life.

42. In the fairy tale, the magic ____________________ made the princess sleep for a hundred years.

43. He appointed his nephew to the new position; it was a clear case of ____________________.

44. I was given ____________________ to choose whatever method I wanted.

*Select the word or expression that best completes the meaning of the sentence or answers the question, with particular reference to the meaning of the word in **boldface** type.*

45. If you refer to someone's reactions as **maudlin**, you are
a. showing utter indifference
b. expressing sympathy
c. charging deliberate misrepresentation
d. complaining of excessive sentimentality

46. People who are affected by **xenophobia** are
a. unlucky in love
b. suspicious of foreigners
c. afraid of heights
d. fond of rich food

47. Your situation might well be described as **precarious** if you were
a. lolling in a hammock
b. attending the Senior Prom
c. hanging from the edge of a cliff
d. playing tennis with a weak opponent

48. From a renowned **raconteur** you would expect
a. an entertaining story
b. a superb dinner
c. the perfect crime
d. expert legal advice

49. An **empirical** analysis of a problem is based primarily on
a. wishful thinking
b. experience
c. the laws of chance
d. preconceived ideas

50. A person who has just received a **lagniappe** would most likely
a. mend his or her ways
b. take some medication
c. say, "Thanks!"
d. seek revenge

51. The expression "**vicissitudes** of life" refers to life's
a. ups and downs
b. side issues
c. beginning and end
d. pleasures

52. People who indulge in **casuistry** are most likely
a. spreading rumors
b. overeating
c. feeling sorry for themselves
d. splitting hairs

53. We would expect **aficionados** of the opera to
a. attend opera performances often
b. picket the local opera house
c. never go to an opera
d. sing the lead role in *Carmen*

54. Deeds of **derring-do** are associated particularly with
a. suburban commuters
b. knights-errant
c. scholars and intellectuals
d. politicians

55. Which of the following indicates **kudos**?
a. "What have I done to deserve this?"
b. "Get out of my life!"
c. "You're the greatest!"
d. "Do what I say, not what I do."

56. What advice might you give to a person who is guilty of a **tautology**?
a. "Stop that abusive language."
b. "Speak more slowly and distinctly."
c. "See your doctor immediately."
d. "Don't repeat yourself."

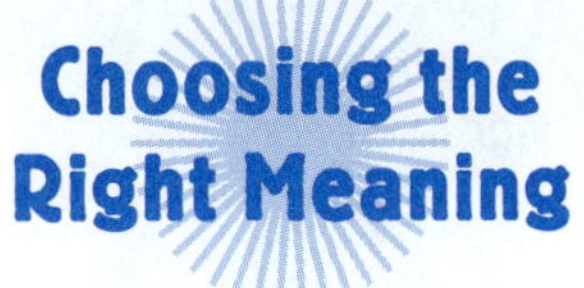

Read each sentence carefully. Then select the item that best completes the statement below the sentence.

57. The soft light of dawn filtered through the **diaphanous** curtains.

The word **diaphanous** is best defined as

a. oblivious **b.** pragmatic **c.** lamentable **d.** translucent

58. Perhaps you can use a **mnemonic** to help you remember the events.

The word **mnemonic** most nearly means

a. tempest **b.** cue **c.** persona **d.** vassal

59. It was only a brief **vignette**, but nonetheless it was revealing of the character's strong sense of right and wrong.

The word **vignette** most nearly means

a. anecdote **b.** matrix **c.** poltroon **d.** respite

60. I think that such a menial job is not **commensurate** with my abilities and education.

The word **commensurate** most nearly means

a. adjunct **b.** victorious **c.** corresponding **d.** appositive

61. As a welcoming gesture, the restaurant offers an appetizer **gratis**.

The word **gratis** is best defined as

a. free **b.** tasty **c.** prurient **d.** pleasant

62. The idea that we would fall for such an obvious ruse was **risible**.

The word **risible** is best defined as

a. ineffable **b.** expensive **c.** equal **d.** laughable

63. They demand quiet in the museum so please ask members of your group to **modulate** their voices.

The word **modulate** most nearly means

a. soften **b.** truckle **c.** inveigle **d.** refer

64. The emotions expressed in the poem run the **gamut** from sheer exhilaration to unimaginable despair.

The word **gamut** most nearly means

a. beatitude **b.** corollary **c.** range **d.** analogy

65. The terrible storm was a **traumatic** event for the entire community.

The word **traumatic** most nearly means

a. naughty **b.** jolting **c.** ribald **d.** waggish

WORD LIST

The following is a list of all the words taught in the Units of this book. The number after each entry indicates the page on which the word is defined.

WORD LIST